The Homeowner's Survival Manual

A BEGINNER'S GUIDE TO HOME MAINTENANCE AND REPAIR

CONSULTING EDITOR: ALEX MARKOVICH

CONTRIBUTING AUTHORS: GARY BRANSON, NANCY COOPER, RICHARD DAY, LEE GREEN, RICHARD GREENHAUS, AND MORT SCHULTZ

ILLUSTRATORS: ALAN ANDRESON AND RON CARBONI

Friedman Group

A FRIEDMAN GROUP BOOK

ISBN   0-517-06522-3

THE HOMEOWNER'S SURVIVAL MANUAL:
A Beginner's Guide to Home Maintenance and Repair
was prepared and produced by
Michael Friedman Publishing Group, Inc.
15 West 26th Street
New York, New York 10010

Editor: Elizabeth Viscott Sullivan
Art Director: Jeff Batzli
Designer: Beverly Bergman
Illustrators: Alan Andreson
           and Ron Carboni
Chapter Opener Illustrations:
Arturo Palombo Architecture
Morristown, NJ

Typeset by Classic Type, Inc.
Color separation by United South Sea Graphic Art Co., Ltd.
Printed and bound in Hong Kong by Leefung-Asco Printers Ltd.

Contents

Chapter 4

ELECTRICITY AND WIRING   64

Chapter 5

ATTICS AND BASEMENTS   76

Chapter 6

HEATING AND COOLING SYSTEMS   90

About This Book and How to Use It

Before an airliner takes off, standard practice requires the crew to review a checklist of safety procedures. The purpose of the checklist, of course, is to ensure that the crew will not overlook a step that could prove critical to the safe operation of the plane.

For similar reasons, we've chosen the idea of the checklist as the guiding structure for this book. Your home, while not as intricate as an airliner, is still made up of a complex of systems that require regular maintenance if they're to operate safely and efficiently.

Therefore, each chapter in this book includes a maintenance checklist appropriate to the system or area of the home discussed. In addition, the book provides a maintenance calendar with a checklist for each month on pages 184–187.

Most chapters also include Tools and Materials sections relevant to the project—except where the tools are too basic to require discussion.

Following the Tools and Materials section are maintenance and repair projects that are critical to maintaining the condition of the structure and the comfort of the family that lives there. To use this book effectively, review the Tools and Materials list at the beginning of each project, and then read the instructions carefully to see what you'll actually need to complete the project. Most projects in this book require only basic, inexpensive hand tools. A few projects require power tools or expensive specialized tools, but they can be rented. When you buy tools, don't scrimp on quality; you usually get what you pay for.

Before starting a maintenance or repair project, also consult the "Safety First" and "Avoid These Pitfalls" boxes included with most sections. The "Safety First" box contains critical information that can help protect you from making a mistake with unpleasant or even fatal consequences. The "Avoid These Pitfalls" box can keep you from making the kinds of mistakes that turn what should be an easy project into a major frustration.

Finally, two guides—to lumber and fasteners—are included at the back of this book. They can familiarize you with the availability of those products before you visit your local hardware store or lumberyard.

The Homeowner's Survival Manual was written by five do-it-yourself writers—Mort Schultz, Gary Branson, Richard Greenhaus, Richard Day, and Lee Green—who have decades of experience in advising homeowners on how to cope with the everyday problems that come with home ownership. In an age when handymen are hard to find and specialists such as plumbers and electricians are reluctant to make calls for small jobs, knowing how to do those tasks yourself often is less a question of saving money on labor than it is a matter of getting the job done at all.

Even if you don't intend to do a maintenance or repair job yourself, knowing the basics about your home's systems will help you communicate with contractors and evaluate what they suggest should be done.

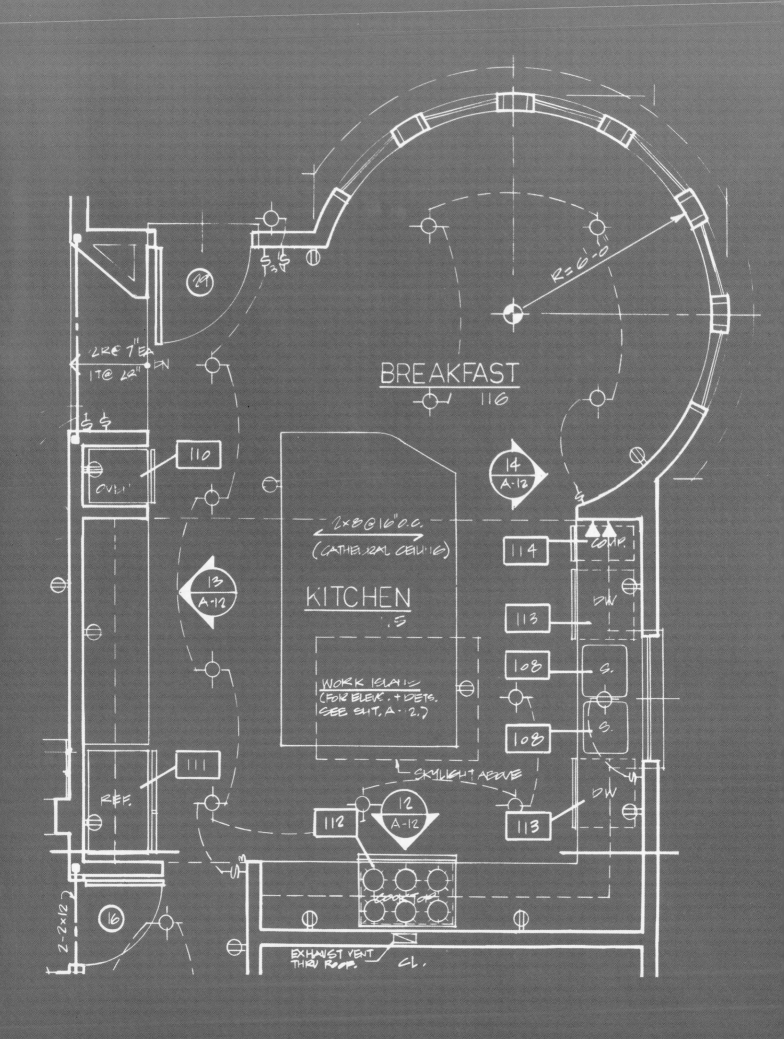

KITCHENS

Today's kitchen appliances have taken the drudgery out of cooking and cleaning. You no longer have to wash the dishes by hand, defrost the refrigerator, or even clean the oven. But you pay a price for that convenience: When one of those sophisticated appliances malfunctions, the cost of repair may rival the original purchase price. That's why rigorous maintenance is essential to extending the life of your appliances.

Though this chapter discusses the maintenance of appliances in some detail, you should nevertheless rely upon the manufacturer's manual for maintenance procedures specific to your appliance.

While maintenance is important, most of this chapter is devoted to repair and troubleshooting. The included guides should help you diagnose problems and may save you a costly service call.

TOUCHING UP A DAMAGED APPLIANCE

Dealers who sell appliance repair parts generally stock paint that matches the appliance colors. Paint for touching up nicks and scratches usually comes in small bottles with a brush attached to the cap. Paint for spraying entire panels comes in larger, pressurized cans.

Follow these steps when you touch up or spray:

1. Before painting, unplug the appliance (or unscrew the fuse or switch off the circuit breaker).

2. Remove dirt and wax from the damaged area with warm water and a mild dishwashing detergent. Rinse with clear water and dry with a clean soft cloth.

3. If the damaged area is rusted, clean it with extra-fine sandpaper. Before spraying, cover nearby chrome strips and panel surfaces to protect them from overspray.

4. Whether you touch up a spot or spray an entire panel, remember that two or more light coats are better than a single heavy coat. Let the paint dry between coats to prevent runs and sags.

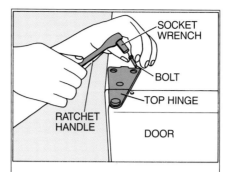

Figure 1. A socket on a ratchet handle makes quick work of removing the hinge of a refrigerator door.

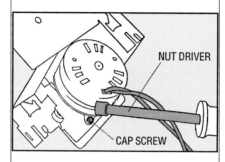

Figure 2. Removing tiny cap bolts with a nutdriver is much easier than turning them with pliers.

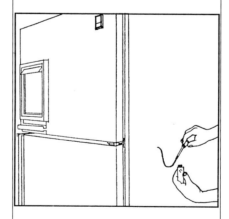

Figure 3. Small bottles of enamel touch-up paint in various colors are available from dealers of appliance parts.

Checklist

☐ Clean refrigerator condenser coils every three months. At the same time, remove and wash drain pan.

☐ Inspect refrigerator door gasket once a year to make sure it is airtight.

☐ Inspect the door seal on a microwave oven once a year.

☐ To save energy, check the temperature of hot water in the kitchen. Turn on the hot-water faucet and hold a thermometer in the water stream for several minutes. If the reading is higher than 160°F (71°C), adjust the water heater.

☐ Spin the spray arm in the dishwater periodically to make sure it rotates freely. If it binds, check for caked detergent and food.

☐ Periodically clean the ports in a dishwasher's spray tube.

☐ Clean an electric range frequently to remove grease from surface elements, bowls, and terminals.

☐ If you have a gas range, periodically lift out the burners and use toothpicks to remove grease from the ports. Then wash and dry the burners. Also remove dust and debris from air vents and from around the pilot light.

USING AN OHMMETER

You need an ohmmeter to test electrical parts when troubleshooting. This instrument is often combined with a voltmeter in a single unit called a multitester, multimeter, or volt-ohmmeter. The ohmmeter is the only tester you'll need for the repairs discussed in this chapter, but you may not be able to find one without the voltmeter.

An ohmmeter measures resistance to the flow of current, while a voltmeter measures voltage flowing through a circuit. Usually, an ohmmeter alone can establish whether a part is defective. Occasionally, a diagnosis may require use of a voltmeter—but we don't recommend voltage testing for do-it-yourselfers. Such testing is dangerous because it's done with the power to the appliance turned on.

The ohmmeter is a safe test instrument because it's used with power to the appliance turned off and wires to the suspect part disconnected. (Trying to use an ohmmeter with the power on is not only dangerous; it can damage the ohmmeter.)

Ohmmeter tests establish whether the circuit through a part is intact. The term used to describe a complete electrical circuit is "continuity." If the needle of the meter deflects toward "0" when the ohmmeter probes are attached to the terminals of the part you're testing, it indicates that continuity exists and the part is sound. If the needle hits the infinity (∞) mark, the circuit is incomplete, or open, and the part must be replaced.

Note: When you buy an ohmmeter, look for one with a detailed instruction manual. Read the manual carefully.

TROUBLE-SHOOTING AND REPAIRING RANGE HOOD AND EXHAUST FANS

Tools and Materials:
Phillips or flat-blade screwdriver; Allen wrench; open-end or adjustable wrench; needle-nose pliers; self-adhesive labels; crayons; light machine oil.

While range hood and exhaust fans look different, they do a similar job: Both draw away cooking odors and smoke.

A range hood—essentially a housing containing an exhaust fan—is normally mounted 21 to 30 inches ($\frac{1}{2}$ to $\frac{3}{4}$ meter) above the range. An ordinary exhaust fan, however, is installed in a wall or ceiling, where it draws odor and smoke to the outside.

Some range hoods are vented. They draw smoke and odors through a duct to the outside. Most have a mesh filter to trap grease particles in the smoke.

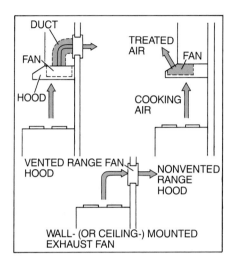

Fig. 4. The items illustrated above are, clockwise from upper left: a vented range hood, which draws smoke and odor outside; a nonvented range hood, which filters out smoke and odor and recirculates the air; an exhaust fan mounted in a wall (some fans are mounted in the ceiling).

A nonvented range hood draws smoke- and odor-laden air through a charcoal filter and then recirculates the cleansed air into the kitchen. A separate filter may be built in to trap grease particles.

Range hoods use two types of fan assemblies. One type is the motor-driven three- or four-blade fan **(Figure 5)**. The other is a "squirrel cage" **(Figure 7)** made up of a pair of motor-driven wheels. One wheel is attached to each end of the motor.

Kitchen exhaust fans are powered by the same conventional three- or four-blade fan found in some range hoods. In the discussion that follows, information that applies to the fan of a range hood also applies to a wall- or ceiling-mounted exhaust fan, except where noted.

SAFETY FIRST

- ❏ Keep flammables away from a range hood.
- ❏ Keep the filter and hood surface clean. Grease is flammable.
- ❏ Never make any electrical repairs without first switching off the circuit breaker or removing the fuse to shut off current.

Replacing a Switch

If a wall- or ceiling-mounted exhaust fan doesn't go on when you flip the wall switch, and the circuit breaker hasn't tripped or the fuse hasn't blown, the switch may be faulty. One indication of that is a loose toggle (the part your finger flips to turn on the fan). Another is the absence of an audible click as you turn the switch on or off (unless it's a silent switch).

Replacing the wall switch of a wall- or ceiling-mounted exhaust fan is done the same way as replacing any other wall switch; see Chapter 4, Electricity and Wiring, page 67.

The switch (or switches) controlling the fan or squirrel cage and the light of a kitchen range hood is usually in the hood itself. If a switch in a range hood has gone bad, proceed as follows:

Note: This information does not apply to hoods with solid-state, or electronic, touch controls.

Troubleshooting Guide

Problem	Causes	What to Do
Range hood light doesn't go on	Burned-out bulb	Replace bulb
	Faulty switch	Replace switch (see "Replacing a Switch," this page)
	Break in wiring	Repair (call technician)
Fan or squirrel-cage motor doesn't go on	Tripped circuit breaker or blown fuse	Restore power (if trouble recurs, call technician)
	Faulty switch	Replace (see "Replacing a Switch," this page)
	Burned-out motor	Replace (see "Replacing a Burned-Out Fan Motor," page 14)
Range hood fan or squirrel cage doesn't draw all smoke/odor from kitchen	Dirty filter	Wash in hot, soapy water and let dry; replace filter if extremely clogged
Noisy fan motor	Motor needs lubricant	Remove and oil motor (see "Silencing a Noisy Fan," page 14)
	Loose fan blades	Retighten (see "Silencing a Noisy Fan," page 14)

---

1. Switch off the circuit breaker or remove the fuse to turn off the electricity.
2. Remove the filter and its cover from beneath the hood. The cover is usually held by screws.
3. Remove the switch knob. If you can't simply pull it off, it's probably secured by a small Allen screw in a hole in the knob. Loosen the screw with an Allen wrench.
4. Look under the hood to see whether the switch is held by a clip or screws. Use needle-nose pliers to pull off the clip, or remove the screws with a screwdriver. Let the switch drop.
5. Disconnect the wires from the switch. Bring the old switch to the hardware store to make sure you get the correct replacement switch.
6. Reverse the disassembly procedure to install the new switch.

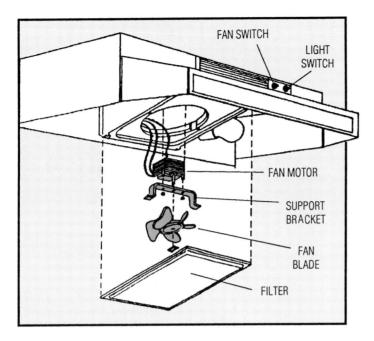

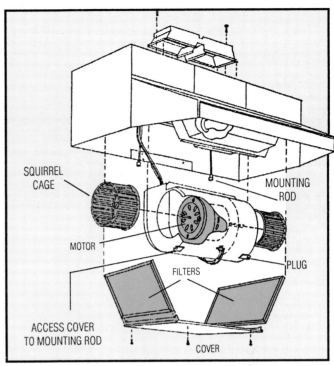

Fig. 5. This range hood with a conventional fan shows the key parts that you'll need to recognize when making repairs.

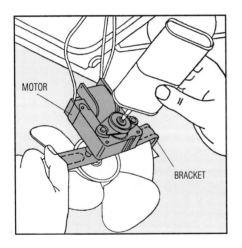

AVOID THESE PITFALLS

- ❏ Don't let the grease on the range hood get on your hands; wear latex gloves.
- ❏ When removing wires from a bad switch, don't assume you'll remember which wire goes where; use adhesive labels and crayons to color-code each wire and the terminal to which it attaches so you can reconnect the wires correctly.

Fig. 7. This illustration of a range hood with a squirrel-cage assembly shows the key parts you'll need to recognize when making repairs.

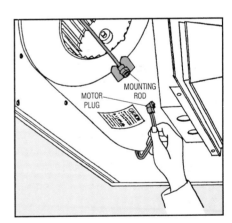

Fig. 6. In most wall- and ceiling-mounted exhaust fans and range hoods, the fan motor is attached to a bracket. To service the motor, release the bracket and remove the fan and bracket together. A few drops of light machine oil on the shaft should help silence the motor.

Fig. 8. To remove an assembly, pull apart the quick-release plug connecting the motor to the house current and release the assembly from the mounting rods.

Replacing a Burned-Out Fan or Squirrel-Cage Motor

1. Switch off the circuit breaker or remove the fuse to turn off the electricity.
2. Remove the grille over a wall- or ceiling-mounted exhaust fan, or the filter or filters and cover from a range hood.
3. If the wire supplying electricity to the fan motor has a quick-disconnect plug, pull the two halves of the plug apart and unscrew the fan from the wall, ceiling, or hood. Bring the assembly to a hardware or appliance parts store to make sure you get the right replacement motor. You may also be able to replace a burned-out squirrel-cage motor by pulling the plug and releasing the motor from its mounting rods, as described in "Silencing a Noisy Squirrel Cage," later on this page. (If the wire disappears into the fan motor and there's no plug, let a technician replace the fan.)

Silencing a Noisy Fan

Rumbling or grinding noises from a wall- or ceiling-mounted exhaust fan or range hood fan may mean the motor needs lubrication. That's an easy job. (Note that the motor of a squirrel-cage unit is permanently lubricated and sealed, so lubrication isn't possible.)

1. Switch off the circuit breaker or remove the fuse to turn off the electricity.

2. Remove the filter or filters and cover of a range hood. Unscrew the grille over a wall- or ceiling-mounted exhaust fan.
3. Unscrew the bracket holding the motor and draw the assembly out of position. Don't let the motor hang by its wires.
4. Turn the motor so its back faces you, and squirt two or three drops of light machine oil on the motor shaft **(Figure 6)**.
5. Turn the blades to spread the oil.
6. Reassemble the unit.

   A wall- or ceiling-mounted exhaust fan or range hood fan that makes a scraping noise may indicate loose blades. Follow steps 1 and 2 above. Then, with the blades exposed, grasp one blade to hold the assembly steady while you use a wrench or screwdriver to tighten the fastener that holds the assembly to the motor.

Silencing a Noisy Squirrel Cage

1. Switch off the circuit breaker or remove the fuse to turn off the electricity.
2. Remove the filter and cover from the range hood.
3. Unplug the wire that supplies electricity to the motor.
4. While supporting the motor, slightly loosen the nuts of the mounting rods on the sides of the housing and let the motor drop far enough so you can reach inside the squirrel cage. (If you're replacing the motor, loosen the assembly until it's free of the range hood.)
5. Use an Allen wrench to tighten the screws that secure the squirrel cages to the motor shaft.
6. Reassemble the unit.

TROUBLE-SHOOTING AND REPAIRING ELECTRIC RANGES

Tools and Materials:
Ohmmeter; screwdriver; self-adhering labels; crayons.

Electric ranges come in three types: freestanding, set-in, and cook-top. Freestanding and set-in ranges have the surface elements and oven combined in one cabinet. Cook-tops have surface elements set into a countertop, with the oven located elsewhere in the kitchen. (Technically, referring to elements of an electric range as "burners" is incorrect. The term applies only to gas ranges.) Most electric ranges have coil-type surface elements, but newer models may have solid elements.

Ovens are either self-cleaning, continuous-cleaning, or noncleaning. Despite those variations, troubleshooting and repair procedures are similar for all three types.

Of the dozen or so problems that can afflict an electric range, the most common is an element that fails to get hot. (In freestanding and set-in models, both oven and surface elements may be affected.) If testing indicates that an element is burned out, the element must be replaced.

If all of the elements fail to get hot, you may need the help of a professional. But before calling a technician, see whether the failure is simply the result of a tripped circuit breaker or a blown fuse.

SAFETY FIRST

☐ Before you start to work on an electric range, turn off the power at the circuit breaker or fuse panel. If you're not sure which circuit breaker or fuse monitors the range, turn on an element that's working and let it get hot. Then turn off each circuit breaker or remove each fuse in turn. To find the proper circuit, hold your hand about 1 foot (⅓ meter) above the hot element for a few minutes. If the element gets cold, you've identified the proper circuit breaker or fuse.

☐ When turned on, surface elements become red-hot. Be sure to keep your hands clear. Don't wear loose clothing that can ignite upon touching a glowing element.

☐ Be careful when removing elements. Some edges of the range cabinet may be sharp.

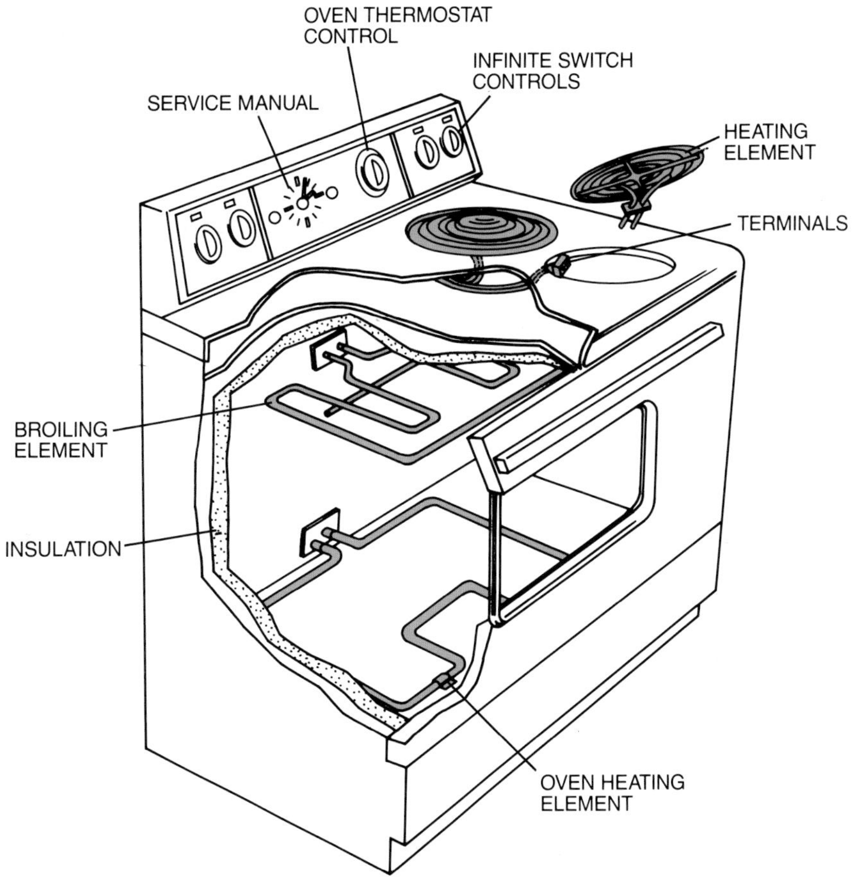

Fig. 9. An exploded view of a typical electric range.

Testing a Surface Element

Most ranges have two 4-inch (100mm) elements and two 8-inch (200mm) elements that are either plugged into or screwed to their receptacles. Those elements can weaken and fail from use. You don't have to turn off the electricity to test a plug-in element. You do have to turn off the electricity before testing an element that is screwed to its receptacle.

Troubleshooting Guide

Problem	Causes	What to Do
Element doesn't heat	Element has burned out	Replace element (see below)
	Receptacle or wire to which the element connects has failed	Have technician replace failed component
	Bad switch	Test and replace (only advanced do-it-yourselfers who have the proper repair manual should attempt this repair)

Testing a Plug-In Element

1. Pull the nonworking element **(Figure 10)** and the other element of the same size from their receptacles.
2. Insert the nonworking element into the receptacle that held the working element.
3. Turn the control knob to High. If the element then gets hot, it's not defective; the fault is in the other receptacle or its control switch. However, if the element doesn't heat up, then it's burned out.
4. Before installing a new element, try to determine why the old one failed by examining its terminals. Careless handling, indicated by bent terminals, can cause premature failure. So can grease on the terminals, which makes them burn. The telltale clue is a blue cast on the terminals.
5. When you install the new element, hold the terminals as straight as possible as you insert them into the receptacle.

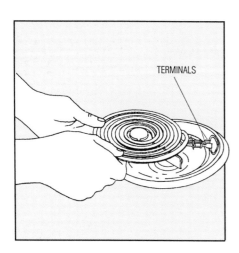

Fig. 10. Most electric ranges have plug-in elements. When removing or installing an element, hold it as straight as you can to avoid damage.

Testing an Element That Is Screwed On

1. Turn off the power.
2. Draw the element from its position, but be careful not to strain the wires.
3. Undo the screws holding the terminals to the receptacle and free the element.
4. Test the element with an ohmmeter by holding one probe to one terminal and the other probe to the other terminal **(Figure 11)**.

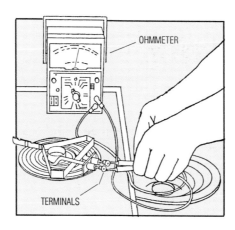

Fig. 11. If you can't switch two surface elements easily, use an ohmmeter to test the one that isn't working.

An element that works properly usually shows an ohmmeter resistance reading of 10 to 70 ohms. If you get a reading above or below that range, check with the manufacturer or a dealer before you replace the element; specifications vary from one manufacturer to another. A reading of infinity (∞) definitely means that the element should be replaced.

Testing an Oven Element

The broil and bake elements of most ranges are secured to the rear wall of the oven by screws. If an element doesn't get hot, test it as follows:

1. Turn off the electricity.
2. Remove the screws and draw the element gently toward you until the terminal screws are accessible.
3. Color-code each terminal and its wire with adhesive labels and crayons.
4. Using a screwdriver, unscrew the wires from the element.
5. Test the element with an ohmmeter the same way you would a surface element **(Figure 12)**. Most broil and bake elements are designed for a resistance of 10 to 40 ohms, but you should check with the manufacturer or a dealer for the correct specification. Again, if the ohmmeter shows an infinity (∞) reading, the element should definitely be replaced.
6. If the element passes the test, the problem is in the switch or wiring. Call a technician.

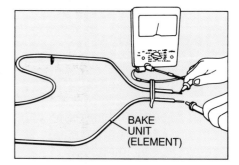

Fig. 12. If the ohmmeter fails to record the resistance specified by the manufacturer, or if it shows an infinity (∞) reading, replace the element.

AVOID THESE PITFALLS

❏ Don't let grease get on the terminals of surface elements or the receptacles to which the elements connect; it can burn out the elements. Follow the recommendations for cleaning your range in the use-and-care guide provided by the manufacturer.

❏ If the broil or bake element of your oven fails to work, don't call a technician or perform tests until you check the clock timer to make sure it's in the manual position. If someone accidentally moved the timer to the automatic position, the element won't glow until the clock reaches the time set on the timer.

❏ If your range has a top that lifts so you can reach underneath for cleaning, don't swing the top all the way up. Straining the wires can pull them apart and cut off current to the elements. Before closing the top, make sure no wires will be pinched and cut between the top and body of the range.

❏ If oven elements are working properly but you're having problems with uneven browning, see the recommendations in the use-and-care manual provided by the manufacturer. You may simply be using the wrong pan or failing to preheat the oven. If you've misplaced the manual, write the customer service department of the manufacturer for another copy.

Fig. 13. This illustration shows the components of a typical gas range.

TROUBLE-SHOOTING AND REPAIRING GAS RANGES

Tools and Materials:
Pliers; screwdriver; nut driver; scissors; string.

Gas ranges, like electric ranges, come in freestanding, set-in, and cook-top versions. And ovens come in self-cleaning, continuous-cleaning, and noncleaning models. Gas ranges are less complicated to service than electric ranges. But don't be careless. If not handled with care, a gas range can be explosive—literally.

The most common problems in a gas range are gas leaks and burners that won't light or stay lit when on a low flame.

Usually, burners won't light or stay lit on a low flame because of a problem in a pilot light—a term that is sometimes used incorrectly. In some gas ranges, pilots fueled by gas ignite the burners. In other ranges, the parts that ignite the burners use electricity and are called spark igniters.

Servicing Spark Igniters

A typical gas range that uses spark igniters has two igniters **(Figure 14)**; each serves two burners.

Three basic parts enable a spark igniter to do its job: the electrode (the part that sparks); the control you turn to activate the electrode and supply the gas to the burner; and the relay,

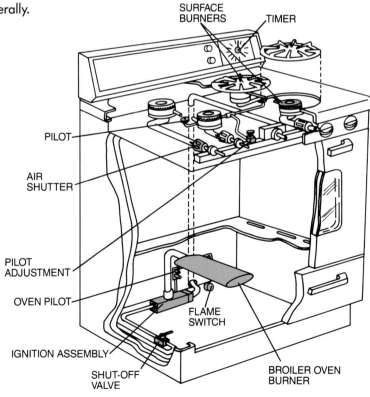

SURFACE BURNERS — TIMER

PILOT

AIR SHUTTER

PILOT ADJUSTMENT

OVEN PILOT

IGNITION ASSEMBLY

SHUT-OFF VALVE

FLAME SWITCH

BROILER OVEN BURNER

which ties both spark igniters to the house current. There is only one relay, and both spark igniters are wired to it.

Unless you are an advanced do-it-yourselfer, replacing those parts is best left to a technician. Still, you can determine whether the control or the electrode-and-relay combination is causing burner failure. Here's how:

1. Don't turn off the gas or electricity. Turn on the control of the nonworking burner. If you hear a series of clicks, the spark igniter isn't to blame for the failure of the burner to light. Turn off the burner control, and check the flash tube and burner parts for obstructions.

2. If you don't hear clicking, turn on the control of the other burner served by the same spark igniter. If the spark igniter then clicks, it's the control serving the nonworking burner that has failed. An advanced do-it-yourselfer with a repair manual may be able to install a new control. Others should leave the repair to a technician.

3. If the spark igniter doesn't click when either control is turned on, the electrode, the relay, or the spark igniter itself is the culprit. Take the following steps if you're experienced, or call a technician.

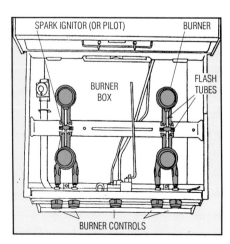

Fig. 14. Overview of a gas range.

Troubleshooting Guide

Problem	Causes	What to Do
Gas odor	Burner control not fully turned off	Turn off control and ventilate house
	Pilot light out	When odor has dissipated, relight and adjust pilot (see "Adjusting Gas Range Pilot Lights and Burners," page 21)
	Unexplained gas leak	If odor is mild, turn off main gas valve, ventilate house, and call the gas company. If odor is overbearing, ventilate and leave the house immediately. Call both the gas company and the fire department. In either case, do not create a spark or light a flame
Surface burner doesn't light, or lights but goes out on a low flame	Pilot light or spark lighter has failed	Relight and adjust pilot light (see "Adjusting Gas Range Pilot Lights and Burners," page 21); test spark igniter (see below)
	Burner and/or flash tube out of line	Seat properly (see below)
	Clogged lighter and/or burner ports	Remove and clean (see below)
	Misadjusted air shutter	Readjust (see "Adjusting Gas Range Pilot Lights and Burners," page 21)
Oven burner doesn't go on	Clock timer set on automatic	Move timer to manual control
	Pilot light out	Relight and adjust pilot light (see "Adjusting Gas Range Pilot Lights and Burners," page 21)
	Sensing tube has failed	Replace tube or call technician

Replacing a Spark Igniter

Buy a new spark igniter from a dealer who sells your make of range. A spark igniter consists of an electrode with an attached wire. Note the model number of your range to make sure you get the correct part. Proceed as follows:

1. Turn off the electricity and switch the relay wires back the way they were before you did your initial test.
2. Use scissors to snip the wire just below the old, faulty electrode **(Figure 15)**. Unscrew and discard the old electrode.

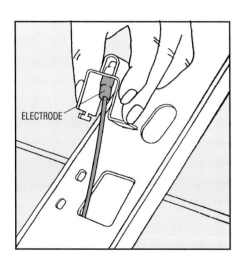

Fig. 15. Unscrew the burned-out electrode, cut it from its wire, and discard it.

3. Tape or tie the end of the new spark igniter wire securely to the old wire **(Figure 16)**.
4. Disconnect the old wire from the relay and pull the wire from the range. Fish the new spark electrode wire through to the relay. Then untape or untie the two wires and discard the old wire.
5. Connect the end of the new wire to the relay and install the cover.
6. Place the electrode in its bracket. Make sure the electrode is mid-

way between the burners and secure it with the screw.

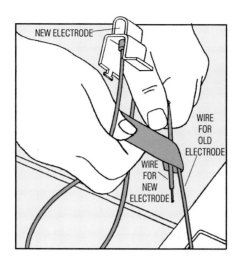

Fig. 16. Tape or tie the old electrode wire to the wire of the new electrode. When you reach the relay, fish the old wire out of the range as you install the new electrode and its wire.

Replacing a Relay

1. Turn off the electricity by disconnecting the power plug or by turning off the power to the range at the circuit breaker or fuse panel.
2. At the rear of the range, remove the cover over the relay with a nutdriver. Some ranges have a removable cover cut into the back panel that you must remove to reach the relay. In other ranges, you have to remove the entire back panel. You can identify the relay by following the wires that extend to it from the spark igniters.
3. Transpose the wires attached to the relay **(Figure 17)**.
4. Restore the electricity and try the controls of the burners that weren't working. If you then hear a clicking noise and the

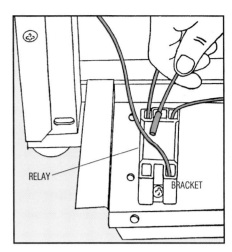

Fig. 17. To determine whether a spark igniter or the relay is faulty, transpose the wires at the relay and see whether the spark igniter works.

spark igniter lights the burners, the relay is defective. (Usually a relay does not fail completely and render both spark igniters useless.)

5. To replace the relay, first turn off the electricity. Then disconnect all wires, unscrew the relay, install a new relay, and reattach the wires.
6. If there is still no clicking sound after you transpose the wires at the relay (step 3), the spark igniter is faulty.

Servicing Burners and Flash Tubes

Gas ranges have tubes, called flash tubes, that extend between the pilot lights (or spark igniters) and the burners. When you turn on a burner, gas flows through the tube, ignites, and causes a flashback that ignites the burner.

If a burner fails to ignite, make sure the burner and flash tube are seated properly. One end of the burner should be inserted into the jet that feeds it the gas. The flash tube should intersect with the burner-lighter port. If that setup seems in order, the burner ports or the burner-lighter port are probably clogged. Remove the burner and use toothpicks to remove grease from the ports. Wash and dry the burner and reinstall it.

If a burner ignites but fails to stay lit on a low flame, the burner air supply may not be adequate. See "Adjusting Gas Range Pilot Lights and Burners," page 21.

AVOID THESE PITFALLS

❏ Don't let grease clog the burner ports. When a burner fails to light, or when it lights but won't stay lit on a low flame, the cause is usually an interruption in the flow of gas caused by grease. Check the manufacturer's use-and-care manual for recommendations about cleaning. If you've misplaced the manual, write to the customer service department of the manufacturer for another copy.

❏ If your range has spark igniters and a lift top, don't swing the top all the way up if that strains the wires. Also, make sure you don't pinch any wires between the top and body of the range when you close the top.

SAFETY FIRST

❏ If you smell gas, don't turn on a surface or oven burner! Call the gas company.

❏ In case of a gas leak, you should know where the main gas valve is located so you can shut it off quickly. Look for it on the pipe that supplies gas to the range. Turn it 90 degrees to shut off the gas supply. (You may need a pair of pliers to turn the valve.) If the main gas valve is not near the range, it's on the gas supply pipe in your basement, crawl space, or utility room.

❏ If the gas supply pipe is a solid rather than flexible pipe, do not move the range for any reason. You may rupture the pipe and cause a gas leak. If the range has to be moved, the solid gas supply pipe must first be disconnected—a job for a technician.

❏ If you replace a faulty spark igniter yourself, first turn off the electricity, as follows. Raise the top of the range and look for an electric power cord that plugs into a receptacle. Unplug the power cord from the electrical outlet. If you can't find the plug, turn off the power at the circuit breaker or fuse panel.

Troubleshooting Guide

Except as noted, the procedures in the chart below apply to a range that uses either natural gas or LPG.

Problem	Causes	What to Do
Pilot light out	Location of range is too drafty (near window, for example)	Relight; reduce draft (keep window closed or move range)
Pilot light won't stay lit	Pilot flame not adjusted to correct height	Adjust (see below)
Burner fails to light	Burner or flash tube not positioned correctly	Reposition (see "Servicing Burners and Flash Tubes," page 19).
	Air supply to burner not adequate	Adjust air shutter (see below)
Burner flame lifts off burner ports **(Figure 18)**.	Too much air	Close air shutter (see below)
Flame flashes back toward burner **(Figure 19)**.	Too little air	Open air shutter (see below)
Burner flame is yellow (natural gas only)	Too little air	Open air shutter (see below)
Soot forms on bottoms of pans	Too little air	Open air shutter (see below)
Only part of burner ignites	Clogged ports	Clean (see below)

ADJUSTING GAS RANGE PILOT LIGHTS AND BURNERS

Tools and Materials:
Screwdriver; matches; baking soda; plastic scouring pad.

Most gas ranges can be adapted to run on either natural gas or liquid petroleum gas (also known as LPG or propane). LPG is usually used where natural gas distribution pipes aren't available, particularly in rural areas.

This section explains how to relight and adjust the pilot lights and surface burners of cooking ranges, whether they use natural gas or propane. Adjustments and repairs not covered here should be left to a technician. If your home uses natural gas, call your gas company for technical assistance. If your home uses LPG, call the company that supplies your propane.

Adjusting a Burner

A properly adjusted flame—one combining the proper amounts of gas and air—forms a blue cone, with the tip of the flame a lighter blue than the rest. When the burner control is set on High, flames should measure about 3/4 inch (19 mm) from base to tip. To adjust the flame, proceed as follows:

1. Turn off the burner.

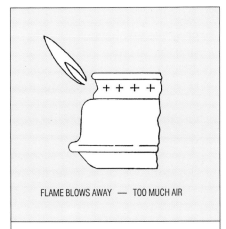

Fig. 18. If the flame of a burner blows away from (lifts off) the ports, close the shutter to decrease the amount of air in the gas mixture.

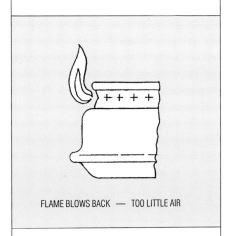

Fig. 19. If the flame of a burner flashes back toward the ports, open the shutter to increase the amount of air in the gas mixture.

2. Remove the burner grates and lift the top of the range.

3. Find the air shutter of the burner you're working on. The air shutter is part of the venturi that extends from the control to the burner.

4. Loosen the screw holding the adjustment slide over the air shutter **(Figure 20)**. Move the slide a little at a time to close off the opening (decrease air) or extend the opening (increase

SAFETY FIRST

❏ Don't smoke while making repairs.

❏ If the light is too dim, use a flashlight. Don't strike a match or bring a lamp close to the range.

❏ Some of the procedures described in this section require that the burners be turned on. Keep your hands away from the flame. Don't wear loose or flammable clothing that can ignite.

❏ When using matches to relight a pilot, be careful where you lay the box or book. If placed too close to a lighted burner, the matches can ignite.

❏ Check whether the flames of the surface burners lap over the edge of a pot you place on them. If they do, have a technician adjust the height of the flame.

air), as necessary. The air shutters of most models rotate, but on some models they move vertically.

5. Tighten the adjustment slide screw, lower the range top, and put the grates back in place.

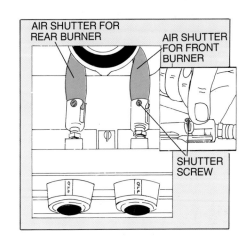

Fig. 20. Adjusting the burner flame.

6. Turn on the burner. If your adjustment doesn't produce the desired result, call a technician. The amount of gas delivered to the burner may have to be adjusted.

Relighting and Adjusting Pilot Lights

1. Before relighting, turn off the burner controls, open the window to dispel gas that may have leaked, and wait 60 seconds.

2. To reach the pilot of a surface burner, remove the grates over all the burners and lift the top of the range. To reach the pilot of an oven burner, remove whatever is necessary—in most ranges, the oven racks and a cover.

3. Hold a match to the pilot. (If an oven pilot has been out for a while, it probably won't relight for about 30 seconds.) If the pilot won't relight after several tries, call a technician.

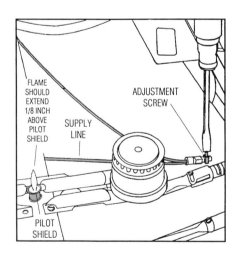

Fig. 21. Adjusting the pilot light.

4. Adjust the flame to a height of about 1/8 inch (3mm), as in **Figure 21**. To make the adjustment, trace along the gas supply line until you find a small adjusting screw. With a screwdriver, turn the screw a little at a time (usually counterclockwise to increase the height of the flame, clockwise to reduce the flame).

Cleaning a Burner That Lights Partially

Follow the instructions for cleaning burners that are outlined in your range's use-and-care guide. Generally, those instructions call for soaking the burners in warm, soapy water.

If the dirt is stubborn, clean the burner with a plastic nonabrasive scouring pad and a paste made of baking soda and water. Then clean congealed grease from the burner ports with a straight pin or a toothpick. Probe gently so you don't enlarge the ports.

To dry a wet burner quickly, place it in the oven and set the oven temperature at 140°F (60°C) for a few minutes.

AVOID THESE PITFALLS

❏ To avoid damaging the finish, never clean the burners with steel wool, scouring powder, dishwasher detergent, or metal polish. And never wash burners in a dishwasher.

TROUBLE-SHOOTING AND REPAIRING REFRIGERATOR/ FREEZERS

Tools and Materials:
Thermometer; screwdriver; nut driver; flashlight; wire hanger and/or turkey baster; two pieces of lumber (see "Avoid These Pitfalls," page 25).

Most refrigerator/freezer combinations are self-defrosting; as frost forms on the evaporator, it melts automatically. The runoff seeps through a drain in the floor of the refrigerator to a pan underneath, where it dissipates.

The evaporator is the part of the refrigerating system through which refrigerant flows. As the refrigerant circulates through the evaporator, it cools the air in the refrigerator and freezer when it's warmer than the setting on the thermostat.

If the self-defrosting system fails, frost builds up on the evaporator, making it harder for the refrigerant to cool the air in the cabinet. The compressor, which pumps the refrigerant through the system, runs for longer periods of time in an unsuccessful attempt to get the refrigerator and freezer compartments cold enough.

The self-defrosting system includes a heating element placed near the evaporator. Other parts of the defrost system are a timer, a small fan, and a temperature sensor. When one of those parts fails, determining which one is faulty is a job for a trained professional. But before you call a technician, you can check and eliminate several less complex causes of compressor run-on and warmer-than-normal compartment temperatures.

Another common problem in self-defrosting models is water collecting on the floor of the refrigerator compartment. Usually the cause is an obstruction in the drain. A solution to this problem is also offered below.

SAFETY FIRST

☐ Unless instructed otherwise, don't begin any repair until you unplug the refrigerator/freezer or switch off the proper circuit breaker or unscrew the fuse.

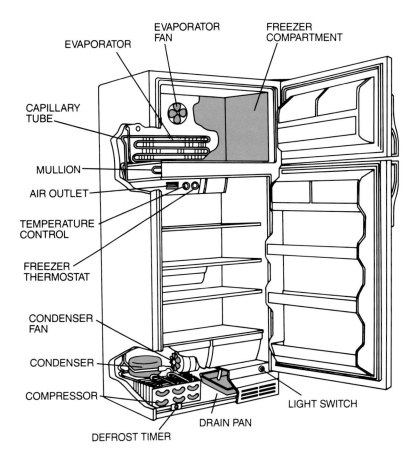

Fig. 22. This illustration identifies the parts of a refrigerator discussed in the text.

Refrigerator/ Freezer That's Too Warm or a Compressor That Runs On

Don't just guess that the temperature is too warm. Place a thermometer well back on the top shelf of the refrigerator and leave it there for 24 hours. Try not to open the door too often during this period. After 24 hours, open the door and read the thermometer immediately.

The proper temperature for a refrigerator is 32° to 40°F (0° to 4°C), although on hot days it can climb as high as 50°F (10°C) if you

Troubleshooting Guide

Problem	Causes	What to Do
Temperature in cabinet too warm, or compressor runs on	Overloading or poor food distribution	Remove excess or redistribute items
	Leaking door gasket	Replace faulty gasket
	Dirty condenser	Vacuum (see below)
	Door switch doesn't shut off when door is closed, and bulb generates heat.	Open door after it's been closed for a while and feel bulb; if bulb is hot, have a technician replace the door switch. Until then, unscrew the bulb
	Defective defrost system	Test fan motor, timer, defrost heater, and temperature sensor; have technician replace faulty parts

open the door often. In hot weather, the compressor will normally run for longer periods than in cool weather. Taking that variation into account, adjust the temperature control if the temperature reading is outside the normal range.

Test the freezer compartment in the same way. The temperature of a properly operating freezer should range from 0° to 5°F (minus 18° to minus 24°C).

Checking Door Gaskets

Standing at the sides of the refrigerator, check the gasket all around the door. If you see a gap, buy a new gasket from a dealer who sells your make of refrigerator, and install the gasket as follows:

1. Disconnect the electric power.
2. Open the door and roll open the gasket; the gasket is probably held by a metal retainer.
3. Loosen but don't remove the screws holding the retainer. Then slide the gasket from behind the retainer **(Figure 23)**.

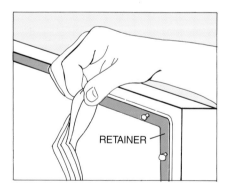

Fig. 23. After loosening the retainer screws, pull the worn gasket from its seat behind the retainer.

4. Starting at a corner and working toward one side, press the lip of the new gasket under the retainer. Tighten the retainer screws until the retainer just grips the gasket. Overtightening can warp the door.

Cleaning a Condenser

The job of the condenser is to transfer heat from the refrigerant to the atmosphere. If the condenser is covered with dust, the refrigerant retains heat. That makes the temperatures in the compartment too warm, and it makes the compressor run on. Cleaning the condenser is easy:

1. Disconnect the electric power and move the refrigerator away from the wall.
2. Pull or pry off the grille at the lower front of the refrigerator.
3. Remove the lower access cover on the rear of the unit **(Figure 24)**, using a screwdriver or a nut driver to undo the screws.

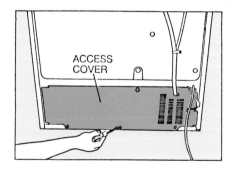

ACCESS COVER

Fig. 24. To reach the condenser, remove the screws holding the lower access cover to the rear panel.

4. Use the wand attachment of your vacuum cleaner to clean under the front and rear of the cabinet. A flashlight will let you see where to point the wand. Be sure to clean the coils of the condenser.
5. While the front grille is off, remove the drain pan and wash it in cool, sudsy water. (The pan is often the source of odors; clean it about every three months.)
6. Reinstall the pan, making sure it's supported on both sides by its rails; otherwise, the pan will tip.
7. Reinstall the front grille and rear access panel.

Clearing the Drain Line

If you find water on the floor of the refrigerator compartment, food or ice may be blocking the drain line so that melted frost can't run down to the drain pan. Both the refrigerator and freezer compartments have drains; usually they're in the refrigerator compartment, where they're relatively easy to reach. (If you find only one drain in the refrigerator, you can assume the drain for the freezer is under the evaporator. Clearing the freezer drain is probably a job for a service technician, since part of the liner must be disassembled.)

Here's how to clear a clogged drain:

1. Turn off the electric power.
2. Remove food, shelves, and bins from the refrigerator.
3. Look for the drain hole on the floor of the refrigerator compartment. Also check for a drain

trough, high in the compartment, that allows melted frost from the freezer to run down the back side of the refrigerator to the drain in the floor and on into the drain pan **(Figure 25)**.

4. Straighten the end of a wire hanger and use it to clear debris from the drain hole in the floor. If the wire hanger is too thick to fit into the hole without force, try thinner gauge wire.

5. To clear ice, fill a turkey baster with warm water and squirt it into the drain hole. You may need three or four applications.

6. If your unit has a blocked freezer drain trough in the refrigerator compartment, the blockage is probably caused by ice. Pour a glass or two of warm water into the trough to clear the line to the drain pan.

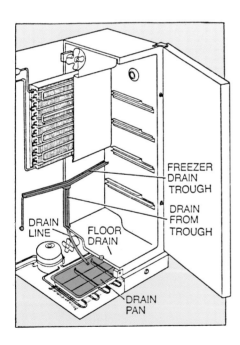

Fig. 25. Look for a drain trough high in the refrigerator cabinet. Melted frost from the freezer flows into it and then down to the drain pan.

AVOID THESE PITFALLS

❑ Don't try to move a refrigerator/freezer unless you use two fairly long, narrow pieces of thin lumber to protect your flooring. Standing on one side, tip the cabinet while a helper slides one of the boards underneath. Then tip the cabinet from the other side, for the second board. You can slide the appliance away from the wall without damaging the flooring.

TROUBLE-SHOOTING AND REPAIRING MICROWAVE OVENS

Tools and Materials:
None.

This section doesn't tell you how to take a microwave oven apart to make repairs. That's a job for a technician. Removing screws and panels from a microwave oven, even with the electric power turned off, may compromise safety and void the warranty.

In many instances, however, problems are external and easily solved. If the suggestions in the Troubleshooting

Guide on the next page don't help, read the warranty that came with your appliance. Some components may still be covered. If so, check the phone book or the owner's manual for a listing of repair shops authorized by the manufacturer of your unit. Some manufacturers provide a toll-free telephone number to help you find an authorized repair shop.

SAFETY FIRST

❑ Don't let a plugged-in power cord hang; rest it on a shelf or on the floor, or keep it taut.

❑ Keep the power cord away from heating system duct, baseboard, range, toaster, and other sources of heat.

❑ Whether radiation from microwave ovens is harmful is still in dispute. To be safe, keep away from the oven when it's operating. (Pregnant women and those who have heart pacemakers should leave the room.)

❑ If food or a covering such as a paper towel catches fire inside the microwave oven, push the shutoff (cancel) control to turn off the oven. Keep the door closed until the fire burns itself out.

❑ If the fuse or circuit breaker that monitors the microwave oven blows or flips off, change the fuse or reset the circuit breaker. Should the problem recur, call a technician who services microwave ovens.

❑ During an electrical storm don't leave the oven on unless you have a surge protector. A power surge caused by lightning can damage the oven. A surge protector acts like a fuse. You can buy one in an appliance or hardware store.

Troubleshooting Guide

Problem	Causes	What to Do
Arcing (electrical flashes) during operation	Temperature probe is not inserted in food	Remove the probe from the oven when it's not being used
	Aluminum foil	Keep foil at least 1 inch (25mm) from the oven's sides and floor
	Other metallic objects	Do not use metal twist ties, metal-trimmed dishes, or metal utensils
	Metal cooking rack isn't secure	Hook rack in place securely or remove it
Control panel does not accept a program	Door is open	Close door
	Improper program entered	Check the owner's manual for programming information
	Temperature probe is plugged in, so oven accepts only a temperature probe entry	Remove the probe
	Oven is plugged into a nongrounded electric outlet	Move the microwave oven within reach of a grounded outlet, or have a grounded outlet installed
Oven seems to operate after cooking is completed	Oven fan is heard after timer turns off	That's normal for some ovens; check your owner's manual
	Oven is operating on "keep warm" cycle	Open door or turn off oven by hitting shutoff (cancel) control; reprogram
Popping noises	Spattering by food with heavy fat content	To minimize spatter, cover food
	Buildup of pressure in foods having skins or foods encased in membranes	Pierce skin of foods such as potatoes and squash; use a toothpick to pierce egg yolks; cut a small slit in cooking pouches

AVOID THESE PITFALLS

- ❏ Don't neglect to provide an air space of at least 2 inches (50 mm) on all sides of a microwave oven. Covered or blocked heat vents will overheat oven and activate an internal shutoff device.
- ❏ Never operate programming controls while the microwave oven is on, or you might blow an internal fuse. Replacing the fuse is a job for a technician. Push the shutoff (cancel) control before you reprogram.
- ❏ During an electrical storm, don't leave the oven on unless you have a surge protector. A power surge caused by lightning can damage the oven. A surge protector acts like a fuse. You can buy one in an appliance or hardware store.

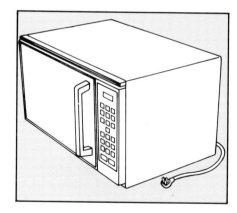

Fig. 26. A typical microwave.

TROUBLE-SHOOTING AND REPAIRING DISHWASHERS

Tools and Materials:

Thermometer; work gloves; pencil eraser; grease pencil; adjustable pliers; screwdriver; nut driver; putty knife; flashlight; ohmmeter; self-adhering labels; crayons.

Dishwasher problems are often caused by operator error. Consult the owner's manual before calling a technician.

Dishwasher manufacturers list three problems as the most common: (1) The dishes don't come clean; (2) The dishwasher leaks water; (3) The dishwasher fails to fill with water.

This chapter covers all three problems.

Other common problems: The dishwasher doesn't run at all, or it fails to pump out water. In either case, probably the motor or pump has failed. But if the machine doesn't run, check for a blown fuse or a tripped circuit breaker before calling a technician.

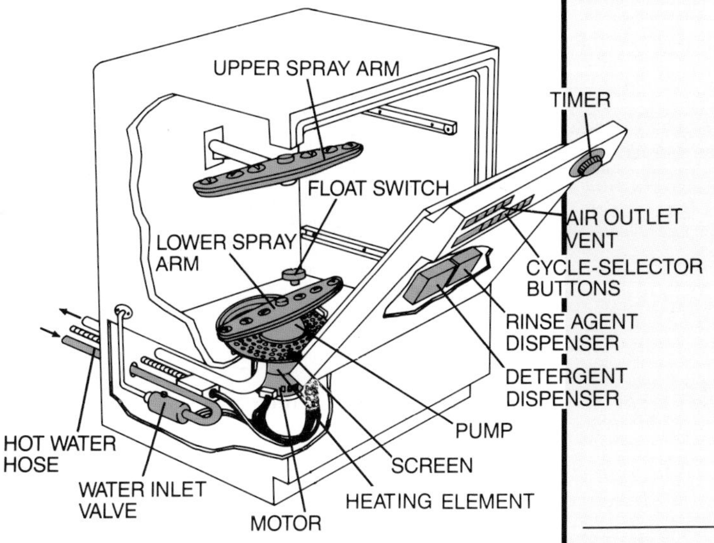

Fig. 27. This illustration identifies the parts of a dishwasher discussed in the text.

Labels: UPPER SPRAY ARM; TIMER; FLOAT SWITCH; AIR OUTLET VENT; LOWER SPRAY ARM; CYCLE-SELECTOR BUTTONS; RINSE AGENT DISPENSER; DETERGENT DISPENSER; HOT WATER HOSE; PUMP; WATER INLET VALVE; SCREEN; MOTOR; HEATING ELEMENT

Troubleshooting Guide

Important: Perform tests and repairs in the order in which they're presented. The most likely causes and easiest tests are listed first.

Problem	Causes	What to Do
Dishes don't come clean	Water temperature is too low	Raise temperature
	Old detergent or incorrect amount	Evaluate
	Dishes not loaded properly	Redistribute dishes (see below)
	Inoperative spray arm	Repair
	Inadequate amount of water-fill	Repair
Water leaks from dishwasher	Improper detergent	Use only dishwasher detergent; others create excessive suds that can cause leakage
	Dishes not loaded properly	Redistribute dishes (see below)
	Water temperature too low, causes excessive suds	Raise temperature
	Spray-arm damage	Replace spray arm
	Loose water intake or drain hose, or split hose	Tighten couplings or replace hose
	Bad pump seal	Have technician overhaul pump
Dishwasher runs but doesn't fill	Faulty water-inlet valve	Replace valve (see below)

SAFETY FIRST

❑ Turn off electricity to the dishwasher if you're making any repair where that caution is stressed. With a portable dishwasher, simply unplug the power cord. With a built-in, you'll have to unscrew the fuse or flip the circuit breaker.

❑ If glass shatters inside a dishwasher, wear heavy work gloves to retrieve the pieces.

Testing Water Temperature

1. Turn on the hot-water faucet and let the water run for at least a minute to allow it to reach maximum temperature.
2. Hold a thermometer under the running water for 30 seconds.
3. The thermometer should register between 140° and 160°F (60° to 71°C). If it doesn't, readjust the water heater in your house.
   Note: Setting the temperature above 160°F (71°C) wastes energy and may etch glassware.

Overcoming Problems Caused by Detergent

If your dishes don't come clean, check the following:

❑ Be sure the detergent is fresh. An open container of detergent that's more than three months old is suspect if dishes aren't coming clean.

❑ Use a detergent specifically designated for dishwashers. Laundry detergent or dishwashing detergent causes excessive suds and may damage the dishwasher.

❑ Use the proper amount of detergent, as specified in the owner's guide.

❑ Keep detergent in a dry cupboard. Even fresh detergent can cake if you store it in a damp area such as under the sink. Caked detergent is ineffective.

Load Correctly

An improperly loaded dishwasher can shatter glassware during the washing cycle. Consult the owner's guide.

Testing Spray-Arm Operation

Some dishwashers have one, two, or three spray arms; some have a spray arm for the lower rack and a spray tube for the upper rack.

1. Examine each spray arm for an open seam **(Figure 28)**. If a spray arm is split, replace it.
2. Spin the spray arm by hand. A spray arm that binds can cause leakage and prevent dishes from coming clean.

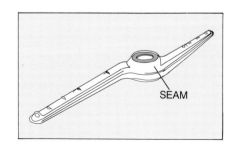

Fig. 28. Replace a spray arm with a damaged seam.

3. If a spray arm binds, remove it and wash it **(Figure 29)** and the tower to which it attaches, to remove caked detergent and food.
4. If the spray arm continues to bind, replace it. Note: A lower spray arm may bind because of a problem with the pump. If the replacement spray arm doesn't turn freely after cleaning, call a technician.
5. If your dishwasher has a spray tube, clean the ports in the tube by inserting a pencil eraser through them. Then remove the cap from the end of the tube and run the dishwasher through a cycle, without detergent, to flush particles from the tube.

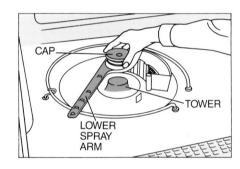

Fig. 29. Remove a spray arm by unscrewing its fastener. (This spray arm uses a cap fastener.) Pull the arm off the tower.

Testing the Water Level

1. If your machine is a portable, pour 7 quarts (7 liters) of water into the tub; if it's an under-the-counter unit, pour in 9 quarts (9 liters). Using a grease pencil, mark the inside of the tub at the waterline.

2. Pour in 2 more quarts (2 liters) of water. Make another mark at the waterline.

3. Latch the door and set the timer past the Wash cycle, so the water is pumped out of the tub.

4. After allowing 30 seconds for the water to pump out, open the door before Dry cycle begins.

5. Close the door and latch it, then turn the timer to Start. Let the dishwasher fill in the normal manner.

6. When you hear the water-inlet valve shut off (indicating that the Fill cycle has finished), open the door and check the water level.

If the level isn't between the two lines you've drawn, the problem is inadequate water intake.

Poor water pressure in the house is one reason for inadequate water-fill. You can compensate for that by not running the water in other parts of the house when the dishwasher is operating.

A kinked water-supply hose can also cause that problem. Remove the lower access panel and check that the water-supply hoses running from the hot-water pipe at the sink to the water-inlet valve and from the water-inlet valve to the tub aren't bent.

A clogged water-inlet valve screen is yet another possible reason for inadequate water-fill. If a screen is present, it's usually inside the water-supply hose coupler, where it connects to the water-inlet valve. To get at it, turn off the electricity and the valve on the hot-water pipe, and remove the lower access panel. Undo the hose coupling at the water-inlet valve **(Figure 30)**. Pry the filter screen out of the coupling. Wash it or buy a new one in a hardware store, and install it in the hose coupling.

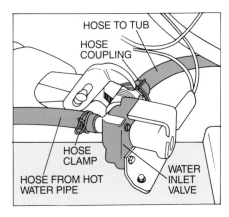

Fig. 30. The water-inlet valve has two hoses: one from the hot-water pipe to the water-inlet valve, and one from the water-inlet valve to the tub. Remove the hose with the coupler to find the filter screen.

Tightening or Replacing Hoses

Besides the two water-supply hoses mentioned above, a dishwasher has a drain hose running from the pump of the dishwasher to the drain.

If water leaks from the machine, proceed as follows:

1. Turn off the electricity and water.

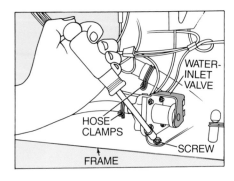

Fig. 31. A wire hose clamp such as this one generally secures drain hoses. To remove a damaged hose, use a screwdriver to loosen the clamp and slide it off the hose.

2. Remove the lower access panel.

3. Using a flashlight to illuminate the area under the appliance, check for loose and damaged hoses.

4. Use a screwdriver or adjustable pliers to tighten hose couplings where possible.

5. If a hose is split, replace it.

If the Dishwasher Won't Fill

Failure of the water-inlet valve is the most common reason for water not entering a dishwasher. However, other components, including a faulty timer and a bad overflow switch, can be to blame. So don't simply replace a water-inlet valve without first testing it with an ohmmeter.

Note: Be sure the valve on the pipe supplying hot water to the dishwasher is open. A valve that was shut off to make a repair, such as replacing a washer in the hot-water faucet, may be preventing water from getting to the dishwasher.

Test the water-inlet valve as described in the repair manual for your machine, or as follows:

1. Turn off the electricity and the valve on the hot-water pipe serving the dishwasher.

2. Remove the lower access panel.

3. Using a flashlight to illuminate the area, find the water-inlet valve. It's the part to which the hose from the hot-water pipe connects. If it's necessary to turn the valve to reach its terminals, use a nut driver to remove the screws holding the valve to the frame of the dishwasher.

4. Remove one wire at a time from the water-inlet valve, color-coding each wire and its terminal with self-adhering labels and crayons to assure proper reassembly.

5. Hold the probes of an ohmmeter across the terminals of the water-inlet valve. If the ohmmeter doesn't read from 500 to 2,000 ohms, the water-inlet valve is faulty. Take the old valve with you to an appliance parts dealer to make sure you buy the right replacement.

6. Install the new valve, and turn on the hot water and electricity.

TROUBLE-SHOOTING AND REPAIRING GARBAGE DISPOSERS

Tools and Materials:
Piece of handle cut from an old broom, or a wooden spoon; long-handled tongs.

Whether you call it a garbage disposer or a waste-disposal unit, the chopper connected to the drain of a kitchen sink is easy to troubleshoot, and easy to repair—that is, unless the motor has failed. If that is the case, it may not pay to fix the old appliance. To decide, compare the cost of having the motor replaced by a technician with the cost of buying and installing a new unit.

Troubleshooting Guide

Problem	Causes	What to Do
Motor doesn't start	Blown fuse; tripped circuit breaker	Check main service panel and install new fuse or turn circuit breaker back on; if problem recurs, call a technician.
	Overload protector has tripped	Activate overload-protector switch
	Wall switch is bad (continuous-feed model only)	Replace the switch as described in ''Replacing Wall Switches'' (see chapter on electric repairs, page 67)
	Frozen turntable	Free up turntable (see below)
	Defective motor	Have technician replace motor or buy a new disposer
Motor hums, but turntable doesn't turn	Frozen turntable	Free up turntable (see below)
	Defective motor	Have technician replace motor or buy a new disposer
Disposer is unusually noisy	Utensil has dropped onto turntable	Turn off power and fish object from disposer with long-handled tongs
	Broken turntable grinder	Have technician replace grinder

Two types of garbage disposers are available: batch-feed and continuous-feed. A batch-feed model is turned on by a switch in the neck of the unit that's activated when you insert and turn the stopper. Thus, you can't add waste to the disposer while it's running—a safety feature.

A continuous-feed model is turned on by flipping a wall switch. You can continue sweeping scraps into the unit while it's running, but be careful not to get your fingers too close to the drain.

The instructions that follow apply to both types of units.

SAFETY FIRST

❑ Even if the wall switch controlling a continuous-feed disposer is off, or the stopper of a batch-feed disposer isn't in the neck, never put your hand into a disposer.

❑ If debris is jamming the disposer, turn off the appliance and clear the blockage with long-handled tongs.

Activating an Overload Protector

Most garbage disposers have an overload protector that turns the motor off if the unit jams. Once you relieve the jam by pulling waste from the disposer, you must push a button to release the protector.

To see whether your unit has an overload protector release, check the face and bottom of the unit for an activation switch. It's usually a small

red button, often marked "overload protector" or "overload switch" **(Figure 32)**. Proceed as follows:

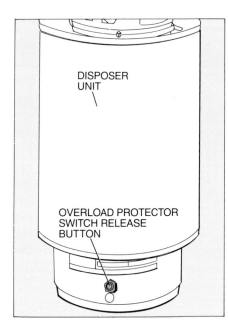

Fig. 32. Look for the overload protector button on the face of the unit or under the base.

AVOID THESE PITFALLS

❑ Don't pack the disposer with waste; shred a little at a time.

❑ Don't try to shred metal, glass, pottery, china, rubber, cloth, or leather. Check the owner's manual for other materials you shouldn't put into the disposer.

❑ Don't shred anything with the disposer dry. Make sure the sink faucet provides a flow of cold water into the disposer.

❑ Don't pour any chemical, including a chemical drain cleaner, into a disposer.

1. Turn off the power to the disposer if the disposer was running when the overload protector shut it off.

2. Remove whatever is jamming the unit; use long-handled tongs.

3. Turn on the power and press the button marked "overload protector." (If the disposer was running when the overload protector shut it off, wait at least 15 minutes before turning on the power.)

4. If the unit starts and shuts off again, and there is no waste in the disposer, the turntable may be frozen (see below). If not, the problem is in the motor; call a technician or buy a new unit.

Garbage disposers that don't have an overload protector button reactivate themselves automatically. Turn off the unit, wait 15 minutes, and try running the disposer again. If it doesn't run after a couple of tries, the motor is probably defective; call a technician or buy a new unit.

Unfreezing a Stuck Turntable

1. With the power off, insert a handle you've cut from an old broom or a wooden spoon into the disposer and rest it against one of the turntable grinders **(Figure 33)**.

2. Give the turntable a shove, first in one direction and then in the other.

3. Remove the wooden stick, turn on power, and press the overload protector switch release button.

4. If the turntable doesn't respond, repeat the procedure two or three times, at 15-minute intervals, before calling a technician.

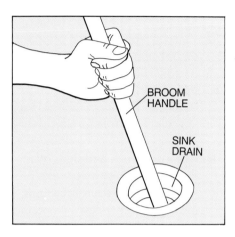

BROOM HANDLE

SINK DRAIN

Fig. 33. With the power off, shove a broom handle or wooden spoon handle against a jammed turntable.

REPAIRING PLASTIC-LAMINATE COUNTERTOPS

Tools and Materials:

Small paintbrush; acrylic latex caulk for countertops; chisel; laminate adhesive; auto paste wax; cloth; hammer; wood block; silicone spray; measuring tape; pencil; saber saw with fine blade; router with laminate-trimmer bit; spray lubricant; tempered-glass insert or butcher block; goggles.

Plastic laminates are durable and easy to clean, but they can be damaged by accident or abuse. Be careful with knives, hot pans, and inked food wrappers that might damage or stain countertops.

Even superficial scratches in laminates can't be repaired permanently. However, lemon oil will recolor the crystals in the laminate and help conceal minor scratches. Washing the laminate removes the lemon oil, so you must reapply the oil after each washing.

Holes and scratches deep enough to accept patching material can be filled and repaired. Use an acrylic latex caulk made specifically for countertops; it's available in most laminate colors to provide a good match.

Excessive heat can damage plastic laminate. Keep a chopping block or breadboard handy, or install a butcher block or a tempered-glass insert into the countertop. Protective inserts are available in many colors and even with decorative art. They are available from kitchen-cabinet dealers.

SAFETY FIRST

❑ Trim plastic laminates with a router and a laminate-trimmer bit. Spray the bit guide with lubricant so the bit won't pick up laminate adhesive and damage the edge of the laminate.
❑ Always wear goggles when using power tools.

AVOID THESE PITFALLS

❑ Tiny pores left in laminate surfaces during the forming process can hold stains from the ink or dye on packaging. Apply paste wax to plastic laminates to protect them from stains.
❑ In older plastic laminates, the basic material was black; colors and patterns were only skin-deep, and nicks in the surface color let the black show through. Consider replacing such surfaces with a solid-color laminate so scratches won't be conspicuous.

Repairing Loose Edging Around the Countertop

1. Prop loose laminate away from the edge of the countertop, using a stick or a pencil **(Figure 34)**.
2. Clean off old laminate cement with a chisel, or apply lacquer thinner for solvent cement.
3. Replace the stick prop with a nail so you have access to the entire surface of the edge **(Figure 35)**.
4. Apply laminate cement with a small brush.
5. Hold a wood block over the area being repaired, and tap the block with a hammer to assure a good bond.

You can use an insert to cover a countertop that is already damaged:

1. Place a cutting template over the damaged area and mark around the edges.
2. Use a saber saw to cut a hole in the countertop.
3. Drop in the insert, and secure it with retaining clips supplied by the manufacturer.

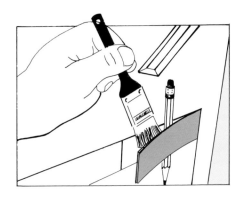

Fig. 34. A stick or pencil is handy for holding loose laminate away from the countertop edge, giving you room to work. Chisel away old laminate cement, or use lacquer thinner for solvent cement.

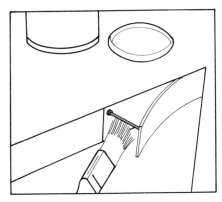

Fig. 35. A nail in place of the stick prop gives you access to the entire edge. Brush on the laminate cement and tap the repair with a wood block and a hammer for a good bond.

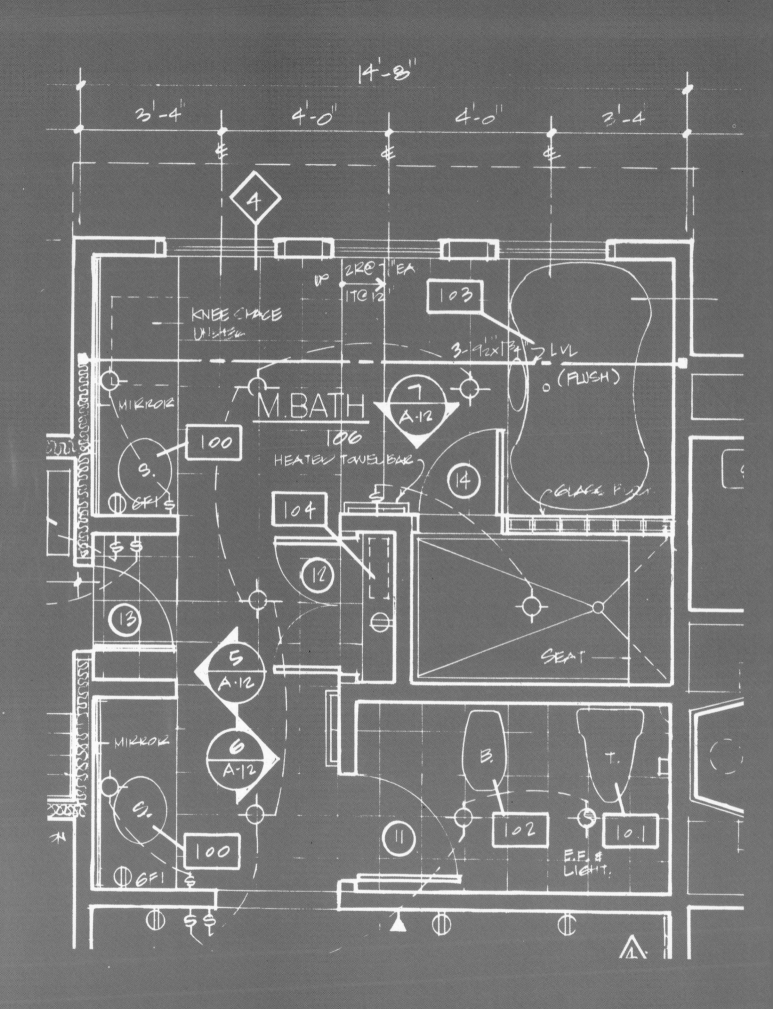

BATHROOMS

Bathrooms are probably the most persistent maintenance headache. Plugging the leaks that form because of loose or missing caulk around the tub edge or because of cracked and crumbling grout between the tiles is an ongoing battle. New, more flexible caulk formulations have helped slow the separation of the caulk from the tub, but none ever prove to be a permanent cure. Nor has anyone developed a grout that can withstand the moisture that seeps into the wall behind the tile. The most permanent remedy is a fiberglass or acrylic tub surround—but that's an expensive option and one that may not please your tastes.

At least the following steps can make those inevitable maintenance and repair jobs easier and less frequent.

REPAIRING BATHROOM TILES AND ACCESSORIES

Tools and Materials:

Scraper; toothpicks; masking tape; ready-mixed tile cement; ready-mixed grouting compound; sponge; grease pencil; drill with carbide bit; metal punch; ball-peen hammer; goggles; anchors appropriate to wall surface; glass cutter; straightedge; nippers or pliers.

Ceramic bathroom or kitchen tiles are durable. But even they can scratch or crack, or even work loose and fall out. Water leaks, vibration, settling of the house, or simply poor installation can cause tiles to loosen. Plumbing repairs that require opening a wall may also necessitate retiling.

SAFETY FIRST

- ❏ Ceramic tile can shatter and chips can fly. Wear goggles.
- ❏ Use the right tools. Claw hammers shouldn't be used with cold chisels or punches.
- ❏ Broken tile may have sharp edges: Beware.
- ❏ Wear waterproof gloves when working with acids or wet grout.
- ❏ Don't mix bleach with other cleaning materials. Some combinations, such as bleach and ammonia, produce toxic fumes.

AVOID THESE PITFALLS

- ❏ Don't drop tools on ceramic surfaces; you may crack the tile or fixture and turn a small job into a large one.
- ❏ When replacing tile, don't take shortcuts; remove old cement thoroughly.
- ❏ Remove excess grout and cement promptly. Cleaning up is much more difficult after they've set.
- ❏ Don't use outdoor caulking compounds in bathrooms. Many of them aren't flexible enough for bathroom caulking.

Repairing Loose Tiles

Whenever possible, reuse the old tiles. That way, you needn't try to match existing tile with replacement tile. And you needn't cut any tiles to the proper size and shape.

1. Scrape the old cement from the back of the tile and from the exposed wall surface; it pays to scrape thoroughly.
2. Coat the back of the tile liberally with ready-mixed tile cement.
3. Press the tile firmly into place.
4. Use toothpicks as spacers on each side to center the tile in the space, and fasten the tile with masking tape. Let the cement harden (usually overnight) before removing the tape and toothpicks.
5. Apply grouting compound to the joint spaces around the tile to finish the job. Ready-mixed grouting compound, available from hardware outlets and tile dealers, is convenient to use.

Press in the compound with your fingertip until all voids are filled, then remove any excess from the tile with a damp cloth or sponge.

Checklist

- ❏ Replace any cracked or loose ceramic tiles.
- ❏ Inspect the caulking at the joints between walls and fixtures and replace if loose or cracked. Pay special and frequent attention to the joint between the top of the tub and the wall tiles and replace the caulking if you see any separation.
- ❏ Replace worn decals in the tub or shower area.
- ❏ When painting the bathroom, use a satin- or gloss-finish paint. On new wallboard, first apply a sealer.
- ❏ Periodically remove and clean pop-up drains.
- ❏ Clean debris from floor drain strainers frequently.

Removing Damaged Tiles

Tiles that are cracked or damaged but not loose are best removed with a cold chisel and a ball-peen hammer **(Figure 1)**.

1. Smash the center of the damaged tile. Wear safety goggles. Do *not* use a regular claw hammer for that job; claw hammers have a hardened face that can chip the tile and send pieces flying.
2. When you've broken open the center of the tile, pry out the remaining pieces with a putty knife and clean any loose or uneven cement from the cavity **(Figure 2)**.

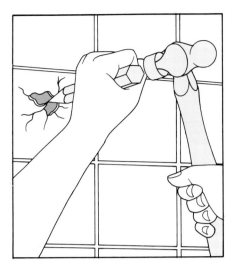

Fig. 1. If a ceramic tile is loose, simply pry it out without damaging adjoining tiles. To remove a damaged tile that is firmly mounted, smash its center with a cold chisel and ball-peen hammer. Goggles are a must. Working from the center out, pry out the pieces.

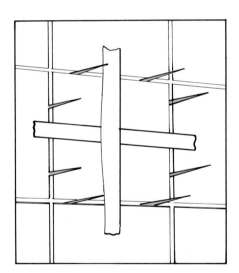

Fig. 2. Once you've removed the old tile, clear away any broken shards or pieces of old cement. Apply tile adhesive to the back of the replacement tile and set the tile in place, using toothpicks for uniform spacing. Masking tape holds the new tile in place for about 16 hours or until the cement hardens. Apply grout to finish the job.

Cutting Replacement Tiles

Unless you're very lucky, you'll have to cut and shape the replacement tiles to make them fit **(Figure 3)**.

1. Measure the opening carefully and mark the cutting line on the new tile with a grease pencil. A useful trick is to fit the replacement tile against one edge of the opening and use the grout lines of the adjoining tiles above and below to indicate where the ends of the cut should be.

2. With a glass cutter, score the glazed surface of the tile along the marked line. Use a straight-edge to ensure a straight cut.

3. Place a pencil on the floor and position the tile, glazed side up, so the scored line is directly on top of the pencil. Press down on both sides of the tile **(Figure 4)**, and it should snap cleanly along the scored line.

4. Mark a curved cut on the tile with a grease pencil **(Figure 5)**. Then use a glass cutter to score a square grid, about 1/2 inch (13mm) to the square, on the area of the tile you wish to

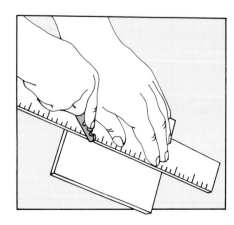

Fig. 3. Score the glazed side of the tile with a glass or tile cutter. Make a single, firm score.

remove. Use tile nippers or pliers to chip away the area of the grid, square by square. File the rough edges smooth.

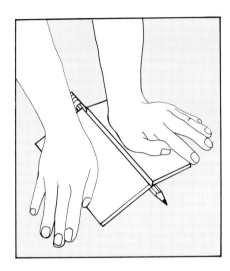

Fig. 4. To break the tile, place it over a pencil and use both hands to press down evenly on both sides of the scored line. The tile should snap, leaving a smooth edge.

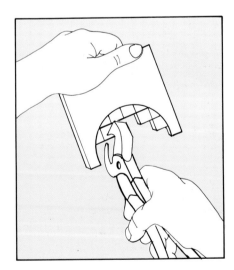

Fig. 5. Cutting a curve requires making a series of short, straight cuts to approximate the curve. Mark the curve with a grease pencil and score a checkerboard pattern on the portion to be removed. With pliers or tile nippers, break away one square at a time. File the edge of the cut smooth, and finish with emery paper.

Replacing Broken Ceramic Bathroom Accessories

You can generally remove a broken ceramic soap dish or towel rack the same way you'd remove a broken tile.

The original accessories were probably installed with the original tile and fastened with mortar. Using mortar to mount a replacement is difficult, as it's not easy to obtain a strong enough bond to the wall. You're generally better off with a replacement that attaches to the wall with screws **(Figure 6)**.

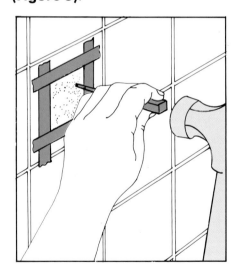

Fig. 6. If a built-in towel rack or grab bar breaks, you're usually better off using a replacement that attaches to the wall with screws. Protect the undamaged portion of the tile with masking tape. With a ball-peen hammer and cold chisel, chip off as much of the broken fixture as you can (wear goggles). Then use a sanding attachment on an electric drill to grind the broken tile as flush and smooth as you can.

While some replacements are designed to be glued on (they usually come with adhesive), you'll probably have better luck with one that has a base that screws to the wall through the tile.

1. Fill the opening behind the old fixture with a new flat tile.
2. When the cement has set, mark the position of the screw hole on the tile with a grease pencil. Protect the surrounding area with masking tape.
3. Put on goggles and use a metal punch and ball-peen hammer to knock small chips off the surface of the tile so the drill bit won't skid.
4. Drill through the tile with a carbide-tipped masonry bit, using the bit size specified in the accessory manufacturer's instructions.
5. Insert suitable lead or plastic wall anchors if you have a plas-

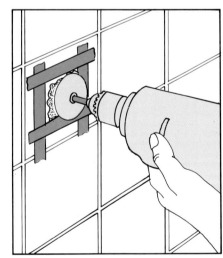

Fig. 7. To salvage the base of an old accessory, grind the surface smooth with a drill equipped with a sanding disc. This procedure is practical only if the base of the replacement accessory is large enough to cover the ground-down area.

ter wall—or hollow-wall anchors or toggle bolts if you have a dry wall.

Instead of filling the opening behind the old towel rack or soap dish with a replacement tile, you may be able to salvage the base of the old accessory. Chip off any protruding pieces with a ball-peen hammer and cold chisel, and sand the surface smooth with a sanding disc mounted in an electric drill **(Figure 7)**. Wear goggles for both of those steps. If you follow that route, make sure the replacement fixture you buy has a large enough base to cover the damaged area of the base you've salvaged.

CLEANING AND REPLACING CAULKING AND GROUT

Tools and Materials:
Old toothbrush; scouring cleanser; punch-type can opener; ready-mixed grouting compound; rubber or plastic gloves; sponge; single-edge razor blade; scraper; silicone caulking.

Grout—the material between tiles—is porous and readily attracts soil. At least twice a year, clean lightly soiled grout with an old toothbrush and a scouring cleanser to keep soil from making a permanent home there.

Replacing Grout

Eventually, scrubbing will no longer be enough to restore the grout to respectability. You'll have to replace the grout. It's not a difficult job, but it's time-consuming:

1. Scrape out the old grout, using a punch-type can opener. Drag the point forcefully between the tiles until all dry or cracked grout is removed.

2. Wear rubber or plastic gloves when you fill the cleared groove with grouting compound. Ready-mixed compound is available at hardware stores or from tile distributors; it's easier to work with than cement-based grouting materials, which require mixing with water. Force the grout into the groove with your finger **(Figure 8)**. If the grout is too thick to spread easily, thin it with a bit of water before applying.

Fig. 8. Force the grout into the joint with a finger; wear a rubber or plastic glove. Wipe off excess compound with a damp sponge, leaving the level slightly below the surface of the tile.

3. Wipe off any excess compound immediately with a damp sponge; the level of the grout should be slightly below the surface of the tile.

Caulking Tub and Shower Joints

Bathroom caulking compounds are made to remain flexible after they have set. That permits slight movement, without cracking, between the caulked surfaces. Use caulk to seal the joints between walls (or floors) and fixtures such as bathtubs or shower stalls.

Caulking compounds come in tubes with applicator tips for small jobs, or in cartridges for use in caulking guns. In either case, cut off the tapered applicator tip so the opening is slightly larger than the width of the joint to be filled.

If the old caulk is loose, cracked, or discolored, replacing it is usually a simple job:

1. To separate flexible caulk, use a thin knife or single-edge razor blade and peel the caulk off. Rigid caulk or grout calls for a chisel or putty knife. Scrape both surfaces with a putty knife before applying new caulking compound.

2. Apply a bead of flexible caulk such as silicone to the joint, pushing the nozzle of the tube away from you to force the compound into the joint.

3. Draw a wet finger along the bead to smooth it.

The most troublesome joint to fill is the one between the top of the bathtub and the wall tiles. To keep cracks from forming in this joint, first fill the bathtub so the weight of the water opens the joint as wide as possible **(Figure 9)**. Fill the gap with a flexible caulk such as silicone, and don't drain the tub until the caulk cures.

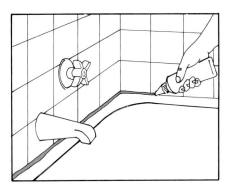

Fig. 9. Before caulking the gap between the tub and the wall tiles, fill the tub. The weight of the water will open the joint, preventing separation later on.

BATHROOM CLEANING

Tools and Materials:

Glass cleaner; all-purpose cleaner; nonabrasive powdered cleanser; phosphoric acid cleaner; glass cleaner; citrus solvent; household chlorine bleach; plastic trigger-spray bottles; rust remover or oxalic-acid powder; vinegar or lime remover; rubber or plastic gloves; goggles; nylon scrub pad; sponge; synthetic-bristle brush; toilet brush; old toothbrush; razor-blade tool; lots of cleaning cloths; wrench for removing the shower head.

An everyday bathroom spruce-up begins with a mild cleaner; save the more powerful ones for heavy soil and specialized cleaning jobs. Dilute cleaners according to label recommendations. (If your usual supplier lacks the cleaner or tool you need, try a janitorial-supplies dealer.)

General Cleaning

Instruct family members to rinse the wall with warm water after each shower to keep soap scum from building up. About once a week, clean ceramic tile walls and the insides of tub/shower doors with an all-purpose cleaner and a cloth. For stubborn soil and deposits, use a hard-surface, non-abrasive cleanser or a phosphoric acid cleanser. Apply it with a nylon brush or nylon scrub pad.

To avoid mildew, keep the bathroom well ventilated. If the bathroom has no window, leave the shower doors or curtains open when the area is not in use. If mildew does develop, apply a 50-50 solution of household bleach and water with a sponge or damp cloth and rinse thoroughly. Twice a year, scour the grouting between the tiles with an old toothbrush and a scouring cleanser.

Clean and polish glass and plastic with a glass cleaner. Wipe chromed hardware with a damp cloth; if it's very dirty, use an all-purpose cleaner. Buff dry with a soft cloth.

Use powdered cleanser on the inside surfaces of porcelain or enamel tubs, shower basins, and washbasins; on fiberglass fixtures, use a nonabrasive powdered cleanser. Turn on the shower head to rinse the tub or shower clean. Clean the outside of these fixtures with an all-purpose cleaner and a damp, soft cloth.

Clean the inside of the toilet bowl with powdered cleanser or toilet-bowl cleaner and a toilet brush. Flush to rinse.

Specialized Cleaning Jobs

Problem surfaces and stains call for special treatment. The simplest cure for a dirty or stained plastic shower curtain often is replacement. Otherwise, scrub mildewed areas with a paste made from baking soda and water and wash the curtain in a clothes washer, along with some clothes. Hang the curtain to dry.

To remove hardened soap and mineral deposits from ceramic tile and fixtures, soften the deposits with an all-purpose cleaner, and then scrape them off with a razor-blade tool.

Use lemon juice to get rid of light rust stains on ceramic fixtures. For heavier stains, use a solution of 4 ounces (about 100 grams) of oxalic acid dissolved in 1 quart (1 liter) of hot water **(Figure 10)**. Wear rubber gloves and apply the solution with a brush. Let the solution dry, then brush away the crystals and rinse thoroughly with water. This treatment also works on the green copper stains that form on sinks and tubs.

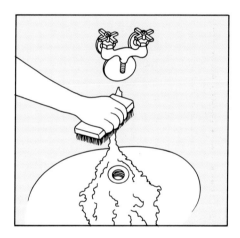

Fig. 10. Remove rust stains on ceramic fixtures with a commercial rust remover or with 4 ounces (about 100 grams) of oxalic acid dissolved in 1 quart (1 liter) of hot water. Wear rubber gloves and apply the solution with a brush. Let the solution dry, then brush away the crystals. Repeat if necessary. Caution: The acid is poisonous and can damage skin and eyes. If you get any on your skin, flush immediately with lots of water.

AVOID THESE PITFALLS

- ❏ To avoid corrosion, don't use a cleaner with ammonia on aluminum.
- ❏ To avoid scratching the surface, don't use an abrasive cleanser on fiberglass or acrylic fixtures or enclosures.

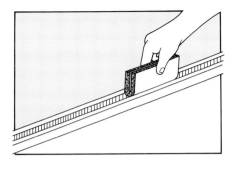

Fig. 12. Clean bathtub door tracks with an all-purpose cleaner and a nylon scrub pad or brush.

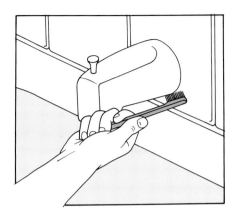

Fig. 14. Clean hard-to-reach crevices such as those around faucets with an old toothbrush.

Fig. 11. Remove hard-water mineral scale from tile with a phosphoric acid cleaner and scour with a nylon scrub pad. Wear rubber gloves.

Fig. 13. Scrape off unwanted decals with a razor-blade tool. Then soak the remaining adhesive with a full-strength citrus solvent and scrub with a nylon scrub pad. Take care not to scratch the ceramic surface beneath.

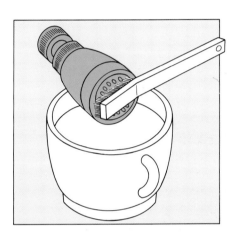

Fig. 15. Remove a scale-encrusted shower head with a wrench and soak it in vinegar or lime remover to soften the buildup. Then scour it with a small brush.

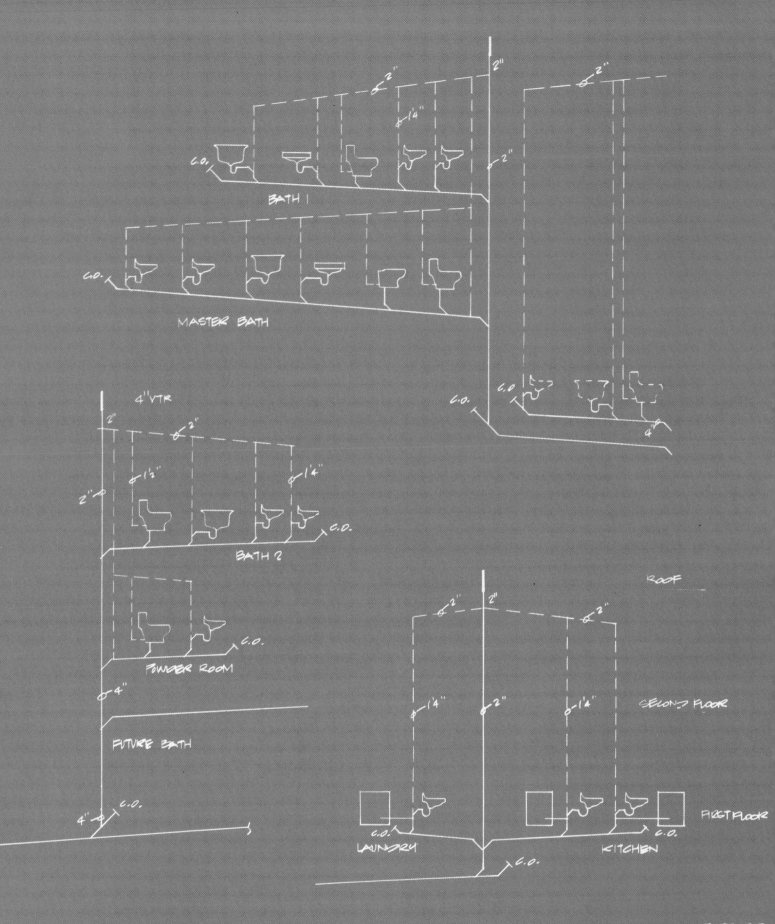

BATH 1

MASTER BATH

4" VTR

BATH 2

POWDER ROOM

FUTURE BATH

LAUNDRY

KITCHEN

ROOF

SECOND FLOOR

FIRST FLOOR

BASEMENT

Chapter Three

PLUMBING MAINTENANCE AND REPAIRS

It's the little nuisance problems—dripping faucets, clogged drains —that account for most house calls by plumbers. And those are the very problems this chapter deals with.

Your home's plumbing consists of two separate systems: water supply and waste disposal. Both systems include many feet of pipe joined by fittings.

The repairs described here generally don't require a permit or review by an inspector. However, if you intend to install new plumbing, check first whether your project conforms with local codes and whether a permit is required.

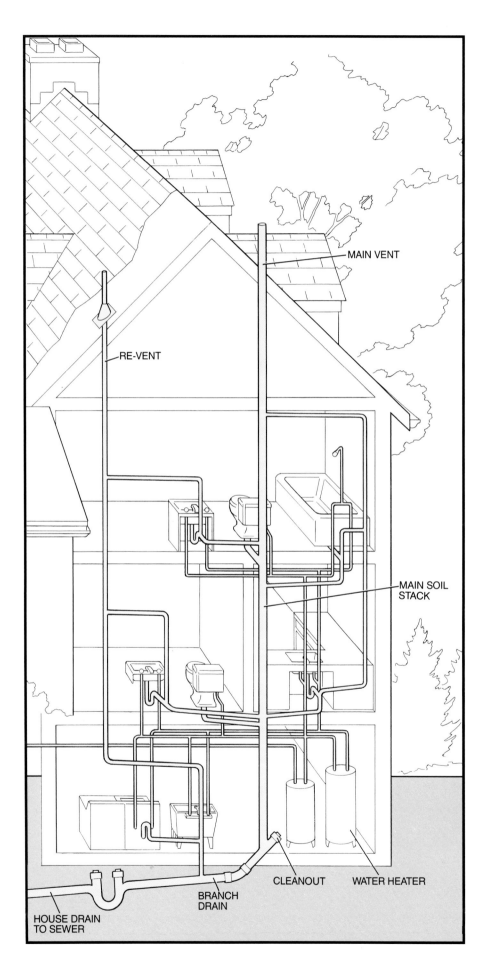

MAIN VENT

RE-VENT

MAIN SOIL
STACK

HOUSE DRAIN
TO SEWER

BRANCH
DRAIN

CLEANOUT   WATER HEATER

Fig. 1. This illustration shows the layout of a plumbing system in a standard two-story home.

Fig. 2. These are the tools you may need to perform the various repairs listed in this chapter.

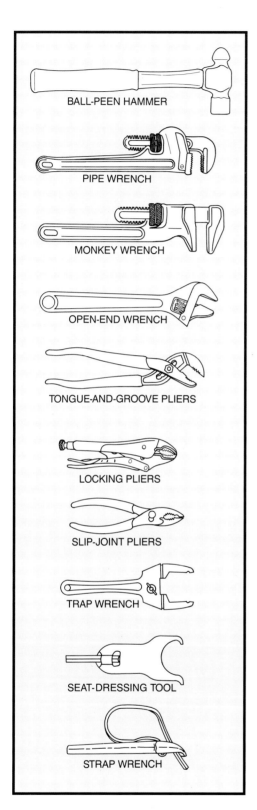

BALL-PEEN HAMMER

PIPE WRENCH

MONKEY WRENCH

OPEN-END WRENCH

TONGUE-AND-GROOVE PLIERS

LOCKING PLIERS

SLIP-JOINT PLIERS

TRAP WRENCH

SEAT-DRESSING TOOL

STRAP WRENCH

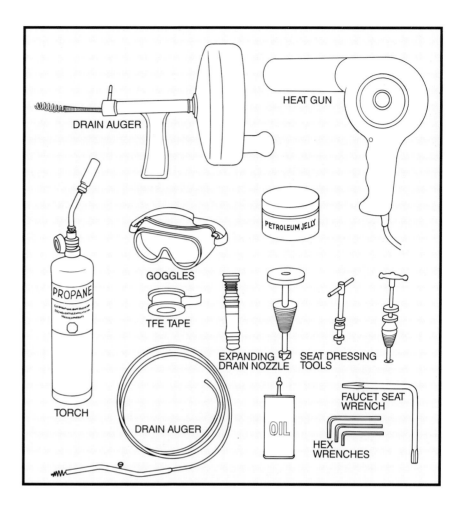

DRAIN AUGER

HEAT GUN

PROPANE

GOGGLES

PETROLEUM JELLY

TFE TAPE

EXPANDING DRAIN NOZZLE

SEAT DRESSING TOOLS

TORCH

DRAIN AUGER

OIL

FAUCET SEAT WRENCH

HEX WRENCHES

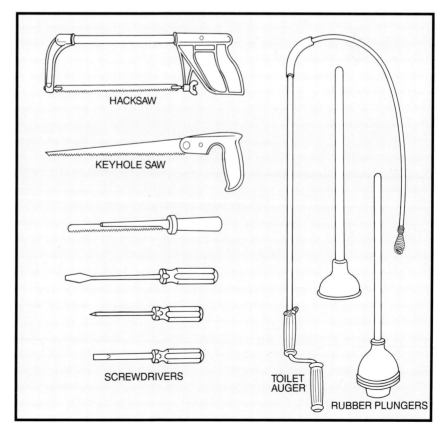

HACKSAW

KEYHOLE SAW

SCREWDRIVERS

TOILET AUGER

RUBBER PLUNGERS

THE RUNNING TOILET

Tools and Materials:

Flat-tipped screwdriver; pliers; adjustable open-end wrench; locking pliers; sponge; plumber's putty or silicone rubber sealant; fine steel wool.

A toilet that runs is a major water waster. Normally the sound of running water alerts you to the problem, but not always.

If the test with food coloring described in the Checklist on this page indicates a leak, the problem is probably in the refill valve or the flush valve.

The refill valve refills the flush tank with water after each flush and then shuts the water off. The flush valve discharges the water in the tank into the bowl each time the trip lever is depressed.

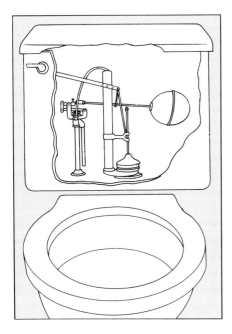

Fig. 3. A cutaway view of a toilet.

When a toilet runs, look for one of the following causes:

❑ The refill valve doesn't close tightly.
❑ The flush valve doesn't close tightly.
❑ The water level in the tank is so high that water runs out through the overflow pipe.
❑ The lift chain is too short.
❑ The trip lever doesn't return fully after being depressed and released.
❑ The bowl-refill tube is inserted below the water level in the overflow pipe, causing toilet tank water to be siphoned off.
❑ The float is waterlogged, causing the water to run out the overflow pipe. To check, remove the float and shake it. If you hear water inside, replace the float.

AVOID THESE PITFALLS

❑ Though most flush valves use a flush ball or a rubber flapper, some toilets have different valve designs, such as a tilting bucket or plastic flapper. Be sure you buy the right parts.
❑ When tightening the hold-down nut on the refill valve of a new toilet tank, avoid overtightening, or the threads may strip or the tank may crack. About half a turn beyond hand-tight is sufficient.
❑ If you need to tighten or loosen the nut holding the trip-arm mechanism, remember that it uses left-hand threads.

Checklist for Toilets

❑ To make sure the toilet isn't running and wasting water, put red food coloring into the flush tank. If after several hours the water in the toilet bowl has a reddish cast, there is a leak. Make the appropriate repair, as described below.
❑ Check the trip lever and trip arm on the toilet to make sure they return fully to their original position after a flush; adjust the lift mechanism, if necessary.
❑ Check the condition of the flush ball; replace it, if necessary, with a flapper mechanism, which is more reliable.
❑ Inspect washer-type and washerless faucets for leaks from the spout and around the handle; repair, if necessary, as described below.
❑ Periodically pour a kettle of boiling water down sink and tub drains to dissolve grease, and remove and clean debris from drain strainers or pop-up drains.

SAFETY FIRST

❑ Be sure that the replacement refill valve you use is the anti-siphon type. It will prevent contaminated toilet-tank water from backing up into your home's potable water system.
❑ If you need to see down into the toilet tank, use a flashlight rather than a droplight. In plumbing work, plug-in electrical appliances pose a lethal shock hazard.

Servicing the Refill Valve

Check the water level in the flush tank. If the level is too high, bend the float arm down; if the level is too low, bend the float arm up **(Figure 4)**. In a toilet equipped with a float-cup refill valve, slide the float's pinch-clip down to lower the water level and up to raise it. To lower the water level in a tank with a submerged diaphragm-type inlet valve, turn the adjustment screw 180 degrees counterclockwise. After you make the adjustment, flush the toilet and check the level again.

If the water level in the tank is properly adjusted and the inlet valve still leaks, replace the entire inlet-valve assembly as follows:

1. Turn off the water and flush the tank completely.

2. Soak up any water remaining in the tank with a sponge and transfer it to the toilet bowl.

3. Disconnect the water supply tube below the tank, and remove the hold-down nut at the lower end of the inlet valve. To keep the inlet valve assembly from turning, grip it with locking pliers from inside the tank.

4. When the nut is removed, lift out the valve assembly.

5. Safeguard against future leaks by placing a ring of plumber's putty or silicone rubber sealant around the inside of the tank opening before positioning the inlet valve.

6. Install the new inlet valve, using one of the antisiphon types that reach above the tank water level **(Figure 5)**. Make sure you install the rubber washer on the inside of the tank and the hard washer on the outside.

7. Thread on and tighten the hold-down nut. Make sure that the bowl-refill tube is installed correctly into the overflow pipe **(Figure 6)**, and that the float is free-moving inside the tank.

8. Connect the water supply tube, turn on the water, and let the tank fill.

9. Make any necessary float adjustments to get the proper water level.

Servicing the Flush Valve

Check that the trip lever and trip arm come back fully after a flush, leaving a bit of slack in the lift rods or chain. You can straighten or rebend the lift rods to lengthen or shorten the stroke of the flush ball. The rods should lift straight and high enough for a complete flush, but they shouldn't hold up the weight of the trip lever. On the other hand, the lift mechanism has too much slack if you have to hold the lever down to get a complete flush.

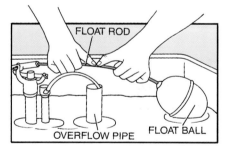

Fig. 4. To lower the flush tank's water level, bend the float arm down; to raise the level, bend up. The water level should be about 3/4 inch (19mm) below the top of the overflow pipe.

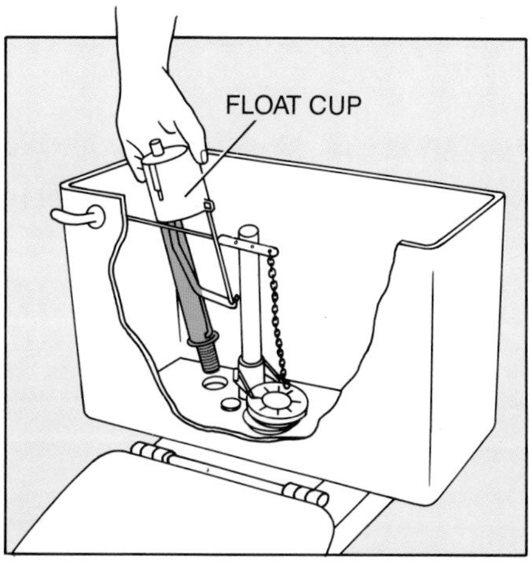

Fig. 5. The simplest, surest cure for a leaking refill valve is to replace it with a new antisiphon model. Lower the new valve through the opening in the bottom of the tank and install the hold-down nut from below, tightening it with a wrench.

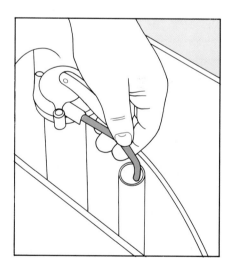

Fig. 6. The end of the bowl-refill tube should enter the top of the overflow pipe but not extend below water level. Normally, a clip holds the tube in position.

Servicing Flush Balls and Flappers

If the toilet uses a flush ball instead of a flapper, make sure the flush ball can close fully on its seat. If the guide arm is too high, loosen the clamping screw and slide the guide arm down **(Figure 7)**. Make sure the arm is centered over the seat before you retighten the screw. If the guide arm is too low, you'll have to hold down the trip handle to complete the flush; if the guide arm is too high, the ball may drop back off-center and rest on the valve's rim, causing a leak.

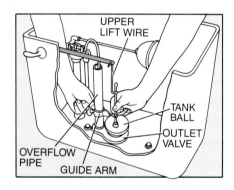

Fig. 7. Adjust the guide arm up or down, keeping it centered over the seat, so the flush ball stays up while flushing and closes squarely and tightly on its seat afterward.

Replace a flush ball or flapper that is slimy, out-of-round, soft and squishy, or hard and cracked. Clean away deposits on the seat of the flush valve, using fine steel wool **(Figure 8)**. If you can hear the water leak, try

pushing down on the flush ball or flapper for a tighter seal. If the sound of the leak stops momentarily and then returns when you lift your hand, the flush ball or flapper is defective.

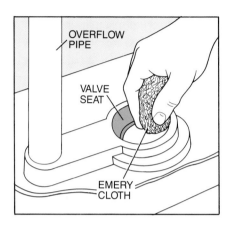

Fig. 8. If the seat of the flush valve has accumulated deposits, remove the flush ball or flapper and clean the seat with fine steel wool or emery cloth.

To install a new flush ball, unscrew the old one from its lower lift rod and thread on a new one in its place. To install a flapper, slide the old one up and off the overflow pipe, and slide on the replacement until it rests squarely on its seat **(Figure 9)**. Adjust the lift chain or cord to leave some slack.

Because a flapper is more reliable than a flush ball, you should replace a leaking flush ball with a flapper. To do so, remove the lift rods and guide arm, along with the old flush ball. Slide the new flapper onto the overflow pipe until it sits squarely on the seat. Connect the lift chain to the trip arm, leaving a little slack.

Replacing the entire flush-valve assembly is seldom necessary. Since

you must remove the tank from the toilet bowl to do so, it makes more sense to repair the old assembly.

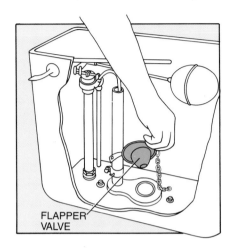

Fig. 9. To install a flapper, slide it down over the overflow pipe until it rests squarely on its seat. Adjust the lift chain or cord to leave slack.

FIXING LEAKY WASHER-TYPE FAUCETS

Tools and Materials:

Knife; screwdriver; adjustable open-end wrench; locking pliers; faucet washer; faucet-seat wrench; new seat or seat-dressing tool; spindle O-ring or packing.

Faucets in most older homes have washers. They're known as compression faucets because closing the faucet compresses a rubber or composition washer at the bottom of the spindle against the seat, shutting off the water.

You can often tell whether a faucet is a washer-type by its handles. It has two—one for cold water and one for hot. When you turn them off, they come to a soft, cushioned stop. When a washer-type faucet leaks from the spout, turning the handles tighter reduces the drip.

AVOID THESE PITFALLS

❏ Don't forget to turn off the shut-off valves immediately beneath the fixture or turn off the main house shutoff valve before you work on a faucet.

❏ Pliers can mar a chrome-plated spindle nut. Protect the nut by wrapping the jaws of the pliers with tape.

❏ Some faucet washers have two flat faces; others have one flat and one tapered face. In the latter case, the flat face should face the spindle.

❏ When dressing a faucet seat, remove the grindings before reassembling the faucet. Otherwise, they may make the faucet leak.

Spout Leaks

Y ou can usually cure a spout leak in a washer-type faucet by replacing the washer, which is at the end of the spindle **(Figure10)**. Sometimes, the faucet seat is scored,

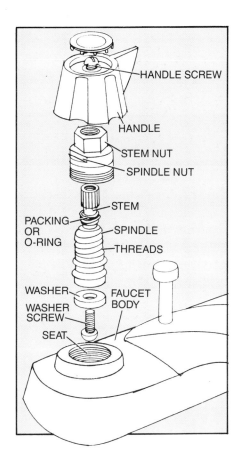

Fig. 10. Exploded view of compression faucet.

SAFETY FIRST

❏ When removing and tightening the faucet washer, you may find the screw hard to turn. To protect your hand in case the screwdriver slips, hold the spindle with locking pliers; tape the jaws first.

and you may have to smooth or replace it to fix a spout leak **(Figures 12** and **13)**. New washers, seats, and spindles are widely available in hardware and plumbing-supply stores.

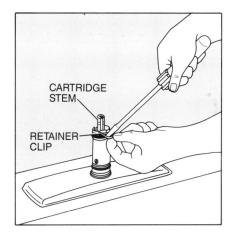

Fig. 11. Removal of old packing is shown above.

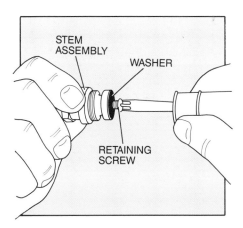

Fig. 12. Remove the brass washer screw and replace the washer on the spindle with one of the same size.

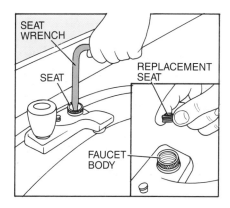

Fig. 13. If the seat has a square or hexagonal opening, use a faucet-seat wrench to unscrew it, turning counterclockwise. Screw in a matching replacement seat.

Leaks Around the Handle

I f a washer-type faucet leaks around the handle, replacing the stem packing (found on older washer-type faucets) or installing a new stem O-ring (found on newer faucets) should stop the leak **(Figure 15)**.

In either case, remove the handle and spindle assembly from the faucet body as follows:

1. Take off the handle.
2. Unthread the spindle nut.
3. Unscrew the spindle by turning it in the On direction. (You can reinstall the handle loosely and use it to turn the spindle.)

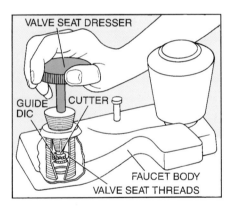

Fig. 14. If the seat won't come out, install a seat-dressing tool according to the directions that come with it and rotate the handle clockwise to smooth the old faucet seat.

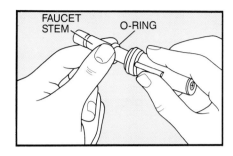

Fig. 15. Coat a new O-ring with petroleum jelly and roll it onto the spindle. If the faucet requires packing instead of an O-ring, wrap new packing around the stem just below the spindle nut.

FIXING LEAKY WASHERLESS FAUCETS

Tools and Materials:

Knife or flat-tipped screwdriver; No. 2 Phillips screwdriver; tongue-and-groove pliers; tape; needle-nose pliers; hex wrench; old table knife or ball-type faucet combination tool; petroleum jelly.

T he new washerless faucets are much less likely to leak than washer-type faucets.

Four kinds of washerless faucets are common: diaphragm, disc, ball, and cartridge. You can often identify a washerless faucet by the single handle that controls both the flow and the temperature of the water. However, some washerless faucets—diaphragm and disc—have two handles. A double-handle diaphragm-type faucet closes gently and with less rotation than a washer-type faucet. When you turn off a disc faucet, the handle comes to a hard, abrupt stop. Moreover, closing a disc faucet's handle more tightly has no effect on a spout leak.

AVOID THESE PITFALLS

- ❏ Unless you have the owner's sheet for the faucet you are working on, avoid buying parts until you disassemble the faucet. Take the old parts to the store to make sure you get the right replacements.
- ❏ Before you replace parts in a ball-type faucet, try a simple collar adjustment to cure a leak at the faucet handle or spout.
- ❏ You don't need to replumb the hot- and cold-water pipes if a cartridge-faucet repair has reversed the hot and cold water. Simply remove the handle, turn the cartridge stem 180 degrees, and reinstall the handle.
- ❏ When working with small parts such as retainer clips, springs, and seals, cover the sink drain so the parts don't fall in.

SAFETY FIRST

❏ When pulling hard to remove a tight cartridge from the faucet body, keep your head back from the line of force so you don't hit your face if the cartridge suddenly releases.

Curing Spout and Handle Leaks

Washerless faucets may leak from the spout or from beneath the handle. Those with swiveling spouts may also leak at the joint where the spout attaches to the faucet. To fix a leak, begin by turning off the water shutoff valves; then remove the handle. Proceed with the repair steps appropriate to the type of faucet you're fixing.

Diaphragm faucet.

1. Remove the faucet handle to expose the locknut.
2. Unscrew the nut with an adjustable open-end wrench and lift out the stem.
3. Replace the O-ring and diaphragm **(Figure 17)**.

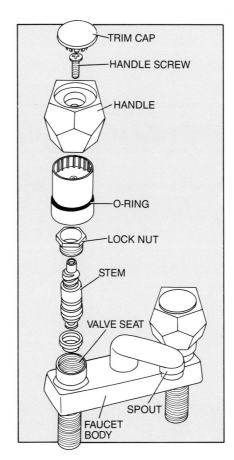

Fig. 16. Exploded view of diaphragm faucet.

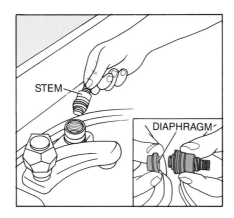

Fig. 17. With stem of diaphragm faucet removed, replace the O-ring and diaphragm.

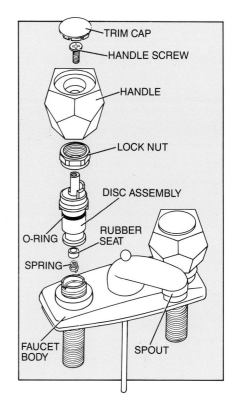

Fig. 18. Exploded view of disc faucet.

Disc faucet.

1. Unthread the bonnet nut.
2. Grasp the stem with pliers, and pull the stem straight up and out of the faucet **(Figure 19)**. Tape the jaws so you don't mar the stem.

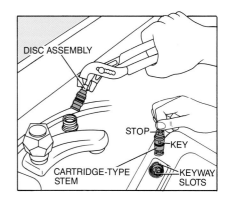

Fig. 19. Before you pull the stem from a disc faucet, tape the jaws of the pliers.

To stop a handle leak, replace the O-ring if it's worn, or the stem assembly if it's cracked or pitted.

To cure a dripping spout, use needle-nose pliers to pick out the spring and the ceramic or rubber seat from the recess in the bottom of the faucet body **(Figure 20)**. Replace them with new parts from a repair kit.

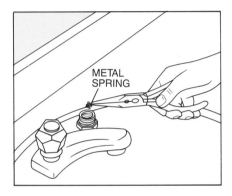

Fig. 20. Needle-nose pliers are handy for removing spring and seat from bottom of faucet body.

Rotating-ball faucet.

1. Tighten the collar **(Figure 22)** just enough so you can still move the ball's stem without installing the handle.

2. If the faucet still leaks, unscrew the chromed cap with taped tongue-and-groove pliers **(Figure 23)** and lift out the cam, cam washer, and rotating ball. (The adjusting collar comes off with the cap.)

3. Replace the seats and springs **(Figure 24)**.

4. Adjust the collar so the rotating ball moves readily.

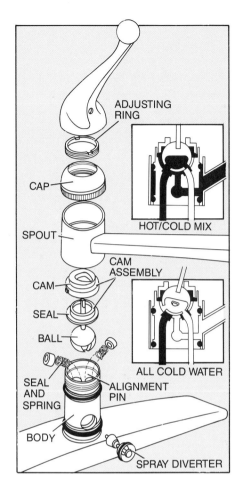

Fig. 21. Exploded view of ball faucet.

5. Turn on the water and check for leaks.

6. Tighten the collar adjustment until leaking stops.

7. To ease a hard-to-turn handle, loosen the adjusting collar with a combination tool or the back of an old table knife; turn the collar counterclockwise.

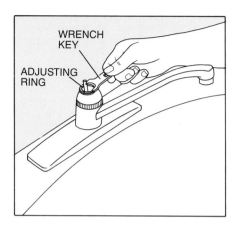

Fig. 22. Tightening the collar on a rotating-ball faucet may stop a leak —but don't overdo it. If you can't move the ball's stem without installing the handle, the collar is too tight.

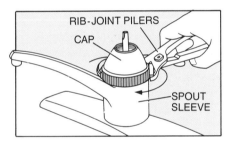

Fig. 23. Apply tape to tongue-and-groove pliers to keep from marring the chromed cap.

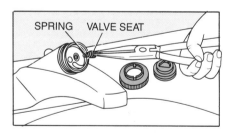

Fig. 24. Replacing the seats and springs should cure a leaky rotating-ball faucet.

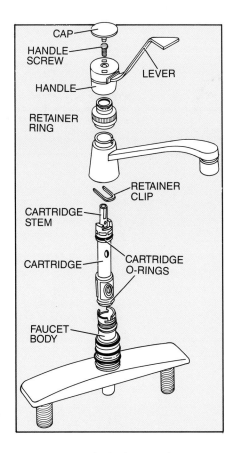

Fig. 25. Exploded view of cartridge faucet.

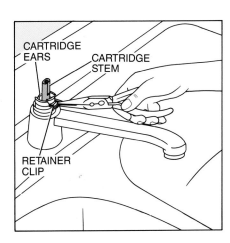

Fig. 26. To disassemble a cartridge faucet, unthread the spindle nut and remove the spindle retainer clip. Then replace the cartridge.

Cartridge faucet.
1. Remove the handle screw and handle by unhooking it from the end of the spindle.
2. Unthread the spindle nut with tape-jaw pliers and take off the spindle retainer clip (**Figure 26**).
3. Pull out the cartridge with pliers and install a new cartridge.

Ceramic-disc single-lever cartridge faucet. Cleaning the three seals at the bottom of the cartridge (**Figure 28**) may be sufficient. Or replace the cartridge as follows:
1. Remove the handle and cap to expose the cartridge.
2. Remove the three hold-down screws.
3. Lift out the cartridge body.
4. Reinstall the new cartridge so its three ports align with their openings in the bottom of the faucet.

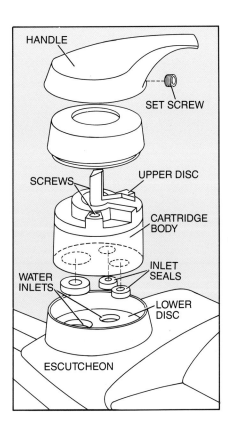

Fig. 27. Exploded view of ceramic-disc single-lever cartridge faucet.

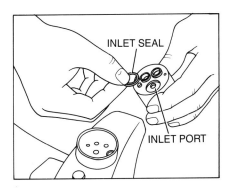

Fig. 28. Cleaning the three seals at the bottom of the cartridge may cure a leaky ceramic-disc single-lever cartridge faucet.

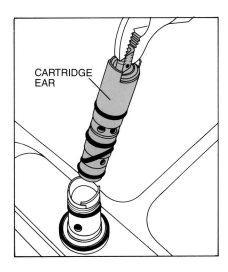

Fig. 29. If the leak persists, replace the cartridge, making sure its three ports align with the openings in the bottom of the faucet.

OPENING CLOGGED DRAINS

Tools and Materials:

Rubber plunger; drain auger; toilet auger; penetrating oil; trap wrench; strap wrench; hacksaw; adjustable open-end wrench; coat-hanger wire; pail; trap O-rings; toilet-bowl gasket; safety goggles; rubber gloves.

All draining fixtures—sinks, bathtubs, showers, and washing-machine standpipes—have a J-shaped section of pipe underneath called a trap. The curved section ensures that some water always remains in the trap to block sewer gas from backing up through the drain into the house. In addition, the curve in the trap catches any items such as jewelry that accidentally fall down the drain. Unfortunately, that same curve also catches human hair, oil, and other debris, making the trap a common spot for clogging.

Before removing the trap to clear a clogged drain, make sure the blockage is in the trap and not beyond it in the house drain. The way water flows down the drain provides a reliable clue to where the blockage is located. If water backs up into the fixture immediately, you can assume the blockage is in the trap.

SAFETY FIRST

❑ Avoid using drain-cleaning chemicals. If they fail, other trap-unclogging procedures will expose you to the caustic chemicals.
❑ When working on a backed-up fixture or trap into which a chemical drain-cleaner has been poured, wear safety goggles, rubber gloves, and an old long-sleeved shirt.
❑ Wear safety goggles and rubber gloves while using a drain auger.

AVOID THESE PITFALLS

❑ Turn off the water to a fixture before removing the trap. That can prevent a minor flood should someone inadvertently use the fixture while the trap is off. Likewise, don't flush a toilet until you're sure the blockage is cleared. Instead, pour a pail of water into the bowl to check whether the drain is working.
❑ Turn a drain auger clockwise, even when you back it out. Cranking it counterclockwise may uncoil the cable and ruin it.
❑ When an item such as a ring falls down a drain, don't run the water until you remove the trap and empty its contents.

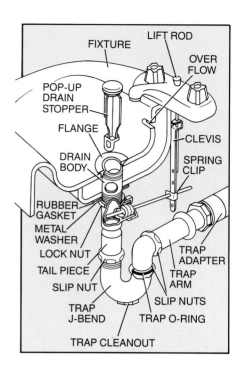

Fig. 30. This illustration shows a typical bathroom sink drain.

Unclogging the Trap

To help you avoid unnecessary work, we have listed the remedies in order of increasing difficulty.

1. Pour a kettle of boiling water down the drain to dissolve grease.

2. Remove the pop-up drain or strainer and use a plunger (**Figure 31**). A plunger is effective on the upward stroke as well as on the downward stroke, so pull up sharply. In a bathtub, washbasin, or double sink, seal off the overflow or other drains with wet rags, or have an assistant seal the opening with the palm of a hand.

3. Attach an expanding drain nozzle to a garden hose and insert it into the drain.

4. Push a drain auger down the drain and through the trap (**Figure 32**).

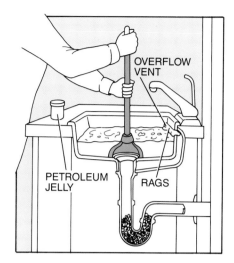

Fig. 31. When using a plunger on a sink drain, first remove the stopper. Then spread a thin coat of petroleum jelly on the plunger's face and lower it into several inches of standing water in the fixture. Plunge forcefully 10 times. On the last cycle, snap the plunger upward sharply to create strong back-pressure. Repeat several times.

5. Remove the cleanout plug on the trap and pull out the debris with coat-hanger wire. Put a pail under the trap to catch the drainings. If the trap has no cleanout plug, remove the trap **(Figure 33)**. While you loosen the slip nuts with a trap wrench, place the handle of another wrench through the curved section of the trap to keep the trap from twisting.

If you can't loosen the slip nuts with a trap wrench, squirt penetrating oil on the threads and wait for it to penetrate. If you still can't budge the slip nuts, saw through their flats with a hacksaw to loosen their grip.

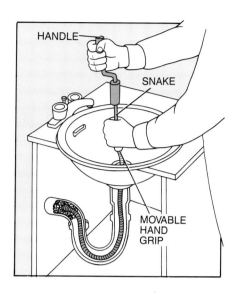

Fig. 32. Rotate the drain auger clockwise as you feed it through the drain passage, feeling for the blockage.

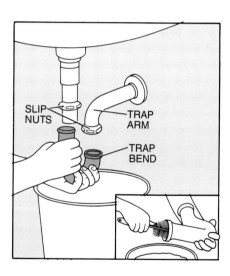

Fig. 33. If a trap has no cleanout plug, loosen its slip nuts and remove the trap. Clean out the blockage with a long wire or bottle brush. Any lost valuable caught in the trap should turn up during cleaning.

Unclogging Toilet, Bath, and Shower Traps

While most fixtures have separate traps, a toilet trap is built into the bowl. To reach it, disconnect the bowl from the toilet tank and from the flange at the floor. Then clear the blockage with a toilet auger **(Figure 34)**.

Some bathtub and most shower traps can't be removed. You must clear them either through the open fixture drain or through a removable trap cover. If you can't work through the drain opening in a bathtub, remove the overflow cover and auger down through the overflow opening.

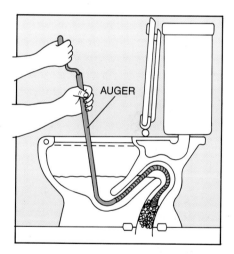

Fig. 34. Start a toilet auger with the auger coiled all the way up in its housing. Position the end of the housing with the cable aimed up into the bowl's trap and crank clockwise, advancing the cable slightly with each turn. Keep cranking until the auger is in all the way. Try to hook the obstruction and pull it out, still turning clockwise.

OPENING CLOGGED HOUSE DRAINS

Tools and Materials:

Pipe wrench; penetrating oil; monkey wrench or trap wrench; old rags; garden hose; expanding drain nozzle; 1/4-inch drain auger; rented 5/16-inch powered drain auger; rented 1/2-inch or larger power auger; pail; safety goggles; heavy rubber gloves; toilet-bowl gasket; rented 1/2-inch or 1-inch sewer tape; TFE tape.

Sometimes the blockage that causes a sluggish or clogged drain is beyond the trap, in one of the drain lines. To unclog it, first determine where the blockage is. If only one fixture is affected, the problem nearly always is in that fixture's drain, or waste pipe. A waste pipe usually runs 3 to 5 feet (1 to 1 1/2 meters) horizontally to a vertical vent stack. (Vertical drains hardly ever clog.) If two or more fixtures drain sluggishly, the blockage is probably in a common drain that serves both fixtures. The common drain can be any length. If water backs up in a first-floor bathtub whenever a second-floor toilet is flushed, you can bet the house drain or sewer is blocked.

Most fixtures have 1 1/2-inch (38mm) waste pipes; showers usually have 2-inch (50mm) wastes; toilets, 3- or 4-inch (75 or 100mm) wastes. Common drains are often larger.

SAFETY FIRST

❏ Electricity can kill. Never use power tools in damp or wet areas. Plug the power cord into a receptacle protected by a ground fault circuit interrupter (GFCI) or into a portable GFCI; wear dry protective gloves; and do not hold the tool or cable with one hand and touch anything metallic with another part of your body. Make sure tools with three-prong grounding plugs are used in three-slot grounding receptacles and with three-wire grounding extension cords.

❏ A plugged-in droplight is a shock hazard when you do plumbing work. Use a flashlight instead.

❏ Drain water is likely to be contaminated. Protect yourself with safety goggles and heavy rubber gloves. Wash up after finishing the job.

❏ If you run a garden hose into a drain to unclog it, don't leave the hose unattended in the pipe. The contaminated drain water can back up through the hose into your house water supply.

How to Proceed

To avoid unnecessary work, take drain clearing step-by-step.

1. Start with the fixture's waste pipe, located in the wall behind the fixture. To reach it, remove the fixture's trap. Bathtub and shower waste lines, if not fitted with accessible and removable traps, should be cleared through the fixture's drain opening. To reach a toilet's waste line, auger through the bowl with a toilet auger or remove the bowl from

AVOID THESE PITFALLS

❏ When using a power auger on plastic drain piping, keep the tool moving; a cutter can carve through the wall of a plastic pipe or fitting. If the cutter has trouble getting past a bend in the pipe, replace the cutter with a bulb-type tool.

❏ Clean and oil a drain auger after each use and store it in a dry place to prevent rusting. Give rented tools the same care before returning them.

❏ To avoid damaging the cable of a drain auger, always crank it clockwise, even when backing it out of a drain.

❏ Be careful when removing a main cleanout plug; a blockage can have quite a bit of water backed up behind it. If water seeps from around the threads when you loosen the plug, undo the plug gradually, letting the water drain into a pail. Remove the plug only when no more water is seeping from around the threads.

❏ Whenever you use a garden hose and an expanding drain nozzle on a blockage, make sure the water doesn't back up into the fixture and overflow onto the floor.

the floor. If you remove the bowl, use a new toilet-bowl gasket when you replace it.

2. All horizontal sections of a drain run have cleanout openings at the upper end. Look for such openings in the basement or crawl space or, in a slab house, low on the outer wall or on the floor in the area of the affected fixtures. The main cleanout is usually 3 or 4 inches (75 or 100mm) in diameter and is located at the bottom of the main vent stack.

Once you've gotten to the opening, apply pressure to the blockage with a garden hose **(Figure 35)**. Insert the hose as far as possible through the cleanout, and seal around the opening with wet rags. Have someone turn on the water full force.

3. Fit an expanding drain nozzle that matches the size of the drain pipe to the end of the hose **(Figure 36)**. Insert the hose into the drain and turn on the water.

4. Try augering next **(Figure 37)**. When you use an auger, a bend in the piping feels like a hard obstruction, and a blockage usually feels soft. Try to snag the blockage with the auger and pull it back out. Then test the drain for free flow.

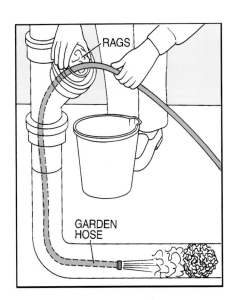

Fig. 35. Insert a garden hose into the end of a fixture waste pipe, seal around the opening with tightly held wet rags, then have someone turn on the water full force. Most blockages will blow out.

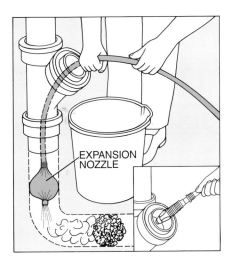

Fig. 36. An expanding drain nozzle of the right size and a garden hose inside the drain can clear a blockage by pulsing water pressure on and off.

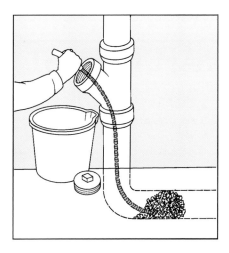

Fig. 37. Use a drain auger through the fixture's waste pipe, rotating clockwise as you feed about 10 inches (25 cm) of cable at a time. Keep going until about 5 feet (1½ meters) of cable has entered the waste pipe, then back out the auger and test the flow.

Fig. 38. To remove a cleanout plug, apply penetrating oil, wait 30 minutes or longer, and turn the plug counterclockwise with a pipe wrench. When you replace the plug, wrap TFE tape around its threads.

Augering the Main Drain

An ordinary drain auger may not suffice for a large main drain. If that's the case, rent a powered drain auger with a cable 5/16 inch (8mm) or larger in diameter and an assortment of tools. Run the auger through the cleanout or open drain a little at a time, then stop and release more cable before proceeding **(Figures 39** and **40)**. Test by running water from a garden hose into the drain. The cable needn't be removed during the test. If the drain accepts the water, it's clear. A rented sewer tape is also effective against a house sewer blockage.

If all of these measures fail, call a technician, who can auger the drains through the roof vent stacks and house trap.

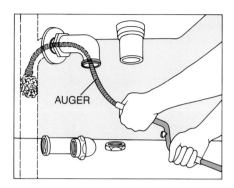

Fig. 39. Insert a rented drain auger or sewer tape through the main cleanout to clear a main drain or house sewer. Test with water from a garden hose to see whether the blockage has been cleared.

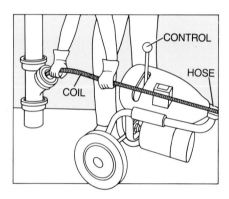

Fig. 40. A large rented power auger lets you do an industrial-type drain-cleaning job. If roots in a sewer line are the problem, use a root-cutting tool on the end of the auger.

WASHING MACHINE AND DISHWASHER OVERFLOWS

Tools and Materials:

Pail; bath towels; mop; plastic bailing can; siphon hose; dry board; rubber gloves; rubber boots; wet-dry shop vacuum; receptacle equipped with a ground fault circuit interrupter (GFCI) or portable GFCI.

SAFETY FIRST

❑ Electricity and water make a deadly combination. Don't step into a wet area or touch a damp or wet electrical appliance or its power cord until the electricity has been turned off.

❑ When turning off the electricity at the service panel, stand on a dry board and wear rubber gloves. If you can't get to the panel without stepping into a wet area, call the utility company to shut off all power at the meter.

❑ When the electricity is shut off, unplug the overflowing washer and nearby dryer. A dishwasher is usually wired in, so you must turn off its branch electrical circuit at the service panel. Once power to the appliance is off, you can restore power to the dry parts of the house.

AVOID THESE PITFALLS

❑ Don't wait for an emergency. Locate and label the main water shutoff valve in your house now. Instruct other family members on how to use the valve.

❑ Locate and label the fuse panel or circuit-breaker panel and the main-disconnect switch. Also label the specific fuses or circuit breakers serving the washer and dishwasher.

Fixing a washing machine or a dishwasher that overflows is a job for an expert. Before calling a technician, do the following:

1. Shut off the water. To avoid shock, use the main water-supply shutoff valve **(Figure 41)**, not the shutoff valve on the appliance itself.

2. Cut off the electricity to the overflowing appliance and any nearby appliances. Don't touch any of those appliances until the electricity is off.

3. With the electricity off, it's safe to close the appliance's shutoff valves. The hot- and cold-water shutoff valves for an automatic washer are usually in back; a dishwasher's single shutoff valve is often under the kitchen sink.

4. Turn on the main valve to restore water to the rest of the house.

5. To clean up the overflow, lay rags or bath towels in the water **(Figure 42)** and wring them out in a nearby basin, or use a floor mop and a wringer. A wet-dry shop vacuum is also useful if the outlet is protected by a GFCI. Unplug the vacuum each time before emptying its canister.

6. Bail out the water from the tub of the appliance **(Figure 43)**, or siphon it out **(Figure 44)**. Open the windows to ventilate the room, and call a technician to fix the appliance.

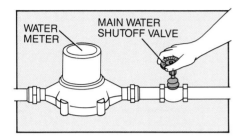

Fig. 41. Turn off the water at the main shutoff valve—usually located in the basement. Then cut all electricity to the appliance at the circuit breaker or the fuse box.

Fig. 42. Build a dam of rags or bath towels to contain the overflow, and begin mopping up.

Fig. 43. Once the water has cooled, bail it from the tub with a plastic cup. Place bath towels in front of the dishwasher to soak up any water that spills out when you open the door.

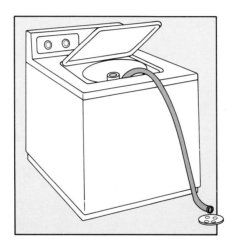

Fig. 44. The easiest way to remove water from the tub of a clothes washer is to siphon it out with a hose. Lead the hose to a convenient draining spot or into a pail.

MAINTAINING WATER HEATERS AND WATER SOFTENERS

Tools and Materials:
Pail; rubber garden hose; adjustable open-end wrench; screwdriver.

Water heaters and softeners require little service; just a bit of maintenance keeps them working at peak efficiency.

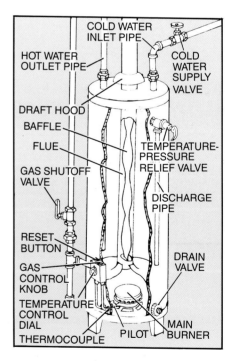

Fig. 45. This illustration shows the inner workings of a water heater.

Preventing Sediment Buildup in Water Heaters

Whether your water heater is powered by gas or electricity, sediment will gradually build up in the bottom of the heater tank, reducing performance and wasting energy. A clue to such buildup is a rumble when the heater fires. To prevent buildup, flush out the sediment twice a year (or every other month if the water heater is new).

1. Turn off the gas **(Figure 46)** or electricity.
2. Close the heater's cold-water supply valve **(Figure 47)** and open its drain valve fully **(Figure 48)**.
3. Open the hot-water faucet to let air into the top of the tank. Continue flushing until the drain water runs clear (usually after about five gallons [19 liters] have drained). Water that

remains rusty may indicate a badly corroded heater tank that will soon leak.
4. After you've flushed the heater, close the drain valve and open

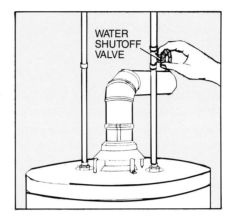

Fig. 47. To shut off the water to a water heater, turn the cold-water inlet valve clockwise as far as it goes.

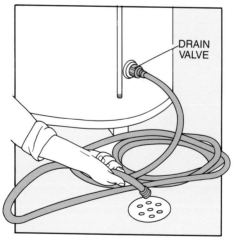

Fig. 48. Flush sediment from the heater tank by opening the drain valve. Thread a garden hose onto the drain valve and lead it to a nearby drain.

the cold-water inlet valve. Watch the open hot-water faucet until all trapped air has escaped, then close the faucet.
5. Turn on the gas and relight the pilot, following instructions on the heater, or turn on the electricity.

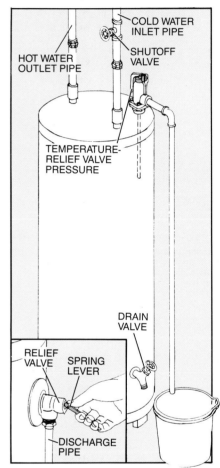

Fig. 49. Every six months or so, drain off 1 quart (1 liter) of water by lifting the lever of the temperature-and-pressure relief valve.

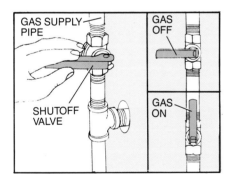

Fig. 46. Shut off the gas to a water heater by turning the handle or flat knob of the valve crosswise to the pipe.

Checklist for Water Heaters

❑ A water heater accumulates sediment, which should be flushed out twice a year—or every other month if the unit is new. Watch for signs of rust in the water that does not clear. The heater tank may be corroding and may need replacement.

❑ Test the temperature-and-pressure valve twice a year and replace it if necessary.

❑ Check the draft diverter on gas-fired water heaters to make sure it is aligned squarely over the heater's vent outlet and the vent pipe is squarely on top of the draft diverter.

❑ Periodically check the color of the burner flame and pilot light in gas-fired units. If the flame is yellow or orange, or if it's blue, and noisy, have a technician adjust the burner.

❑ Listen to an electric water heater as it heats. A boiling sound indicates either that the temperature setting is too high or that hard-water scale has built up around one or both heating elements. In either case, call a technician.

❑ If you see signs of water around the heater tank or notice any dripping from the tank, turn off the gas or electricity and the water supply and call a technician.

Other Water Heater Checks

1. Every water heater—gas or electric—should have a temperature-and-pressure relief valve on top or high on the side. That safety device prevents excessive temperature and pressure from making the heater explode. Twice a year, lift the lever to open the valve and let off a little hot water through the relief line **(Figure 49)**. If no water comes out, or if the flow continues after you release the lever, the temperature-and-pressure valve may need replacing. That's a job for a technician.

2. If water continually drips from the relief line, a lower temperature setting may cure the drip.

3. If water drips from the heater tank, turn off its gas or electricity and water supply and call a technician.

4. If the water temperature of a gas heater runs too hot or too cold, reset the temperature-control dial. The ideal water temperature is the lowest one that provides all the hot water you need. Setting halfway between Warm and Normal—about 130°F (55°C)—is often best. But if you have a dishwasher, the Normal setting may be better. Rarely is the Hot setting needed.

5. On a gas-fired water heater, check that the draft diverter is aligned squarely over the heater's vent outlet and that the vent pipe is squarely on top of the draft diverter. Realign both, if necessary. Don't neglect that check; if the vent pipe is askew, it could allow deadly carbon monoxide to back up into the house.

6. Look behind the burner cover plate at the main-burner flame and the pilot flame of a gas heater. If either is yellow or orange, or blue and noisy, call a technician to make an air adjustment. Generally, an air adjustment is needed every other year.

7. Listen while an electric water heater heats. A cooking or boiling sound may mean the temperature setting is too high. Or it may mean that hard-water scale has built up around one or both heating elements—if so, removing the buildup is a job for a technician.

CURING WATER-SOFTENER WOES

Checklist for Water Softeners

❑ Add salt or recharge, as indicated.

❑ If you're not getting sufficient soft water between regenerations, make timer adjustments, following the manufacturer's instructions. If you are experiencing this problem and your unit uses a hardness sensor instead of a timer, call a technician.

SAFETY FIRST

❏ Water coming from a water heater's drain valve or temperature-and-pressure valve can scald. Keep your face and hands clear.

❏ The temperature-and-pressure valve can keep a runaway water heater from exploding. If your unit doesn't have such a valve, turn off the heater's gas or electricity and have a plumber install a valve and a pressure-relief line.

❏ If steam or boiling-hot water comes out of the temperature-and-pressure valve, the water heater is probably running too hot. Shut down the heater and call a technician.

❏ Careless relighting of the pilot can be dangerous. Follow the instructions on the water heater or in the owner's manual.

❏ If you smell gas, leave the house immediately. Don't use the telephone or any electrical equipment, and don't light a flame. If the main gas-supply valve is outdoors, turn it off. Call the gas company or fire department from a neighbor's telephone.

❏ Adjusting the temperature of an electric water heater requires opening the heater's access panel, which exposes 240-volt wires and uninsulated terminals. Leave the job to a technician.

❏ If you ever get a shock from an electric water heater or from any plumbing connected to it, turn off all electricity at the main service panel and call an electrician.

❏ Unplug the timer control before working on any part of a water softener.

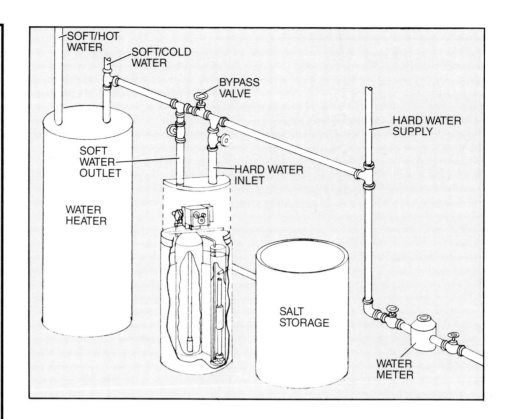

Fig. 50. This illustration shows a typical hot-water system.

1. Sometimes the hardness of the incoming water varies throughout the year. Should the water "break hard" on an automatic water softener that is controlled by a timer, adjust the timer to increase the frequency of regenerations **(Figure 52)**. Decrease the frequency of regenerations if the heater uses excessive amounts of salt and supplies too little soft water between regenerations. Follow the manufacturer's instructions for adjusting the timer. If those problems occur with a water softener that uses a hardness sensor instead of a timer, the sensor may need service, a job for a technician.

2. If you have decreased the frequency of regenerations but still get insufficient soft water between regenerations, check that your water system is providing the 3-gallon- (12 liters) a-minute flow that most softeners need for proper regeneration. As a guide, 1 pound (½ kilogram) of softener salt can regenerate some 2000 grains of hardness, enough to soften 400 gallons (1,700 liters) of water at 5 grains-per-gallon (1 grain per liter) hardness.

3. If the brine level is too high or too low, adjust the brine-control setting. If regenerations kick in at the wrong time of day, reset the clock for the correct time. Most other water-softener problems are best handled by a technician.

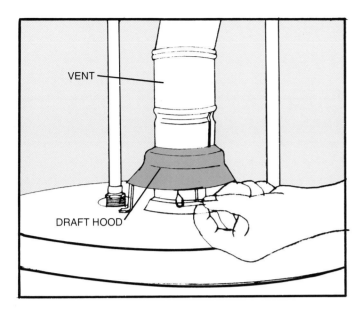

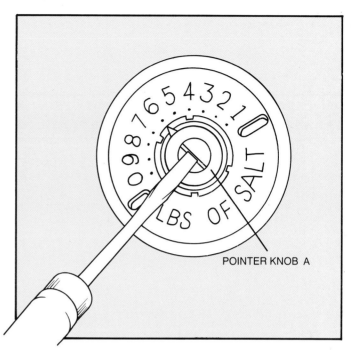

Fig. 51. Deadly carbon monoxide can back up into the basement if a gas water heater isn't drawing properly. To test the draft, hold a lighted match under the draft hood when the burner has been firing for 10 minutes. If the flame is pulled inward, the vent system is working properly. If the flame blows outward or is extinguished, the vent may be blocked; call a technician.

Fig. 52. Setting the timing of regeneration cycles is much like programming a light timer. Softeners vary somewhat from model to model, so consult the owner's manual.

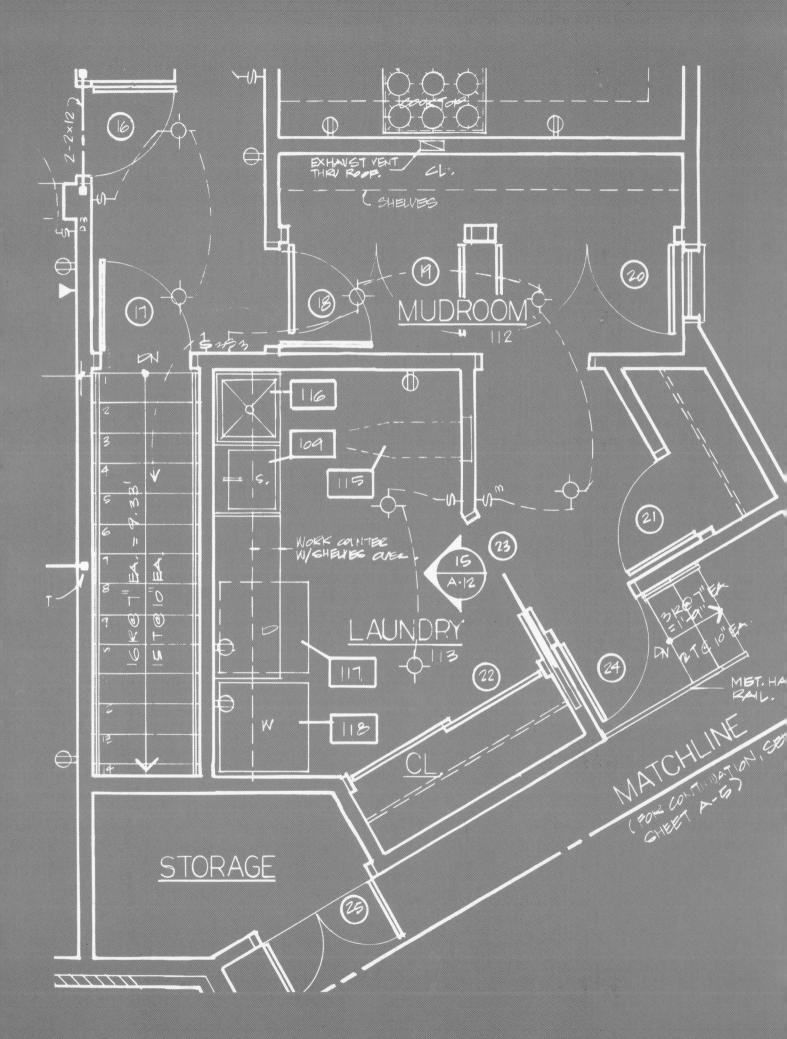

ELECTRICITY AND WIRING

Of all do-it-yourself jobs, electrical repairs seem to intimidate homeowners the most. That's not hard to understand when you consider the dangerous consequences of making a repair improperly. But if you observe and master the precautions outlined in this chapter, you can be confident about basic repairs such as replacing switches, receptacles, light fixtures, and doorbells.

SAFETY FIRST

❑ For all but the voltage-tester checks, turn off electricity at the fuse box or circuit-breaker panel. It's wise to determine which fuse or circuit breaker serves which switch or outlet right now, before any problems arise. Loosen fuses or flip off circuit breakers one at a time and make a note of which lamps or light fixtures go out.

❑ If you haven't charted the fuse or breaker-switch panel beforehand, kill current throughout the house by turning off the main electric switch. That's the one between the fuse or circuit-breaker panel and the service entrance, where the electric cable from the outside enters the house.

When using a voltage tester, protect yourself from shock as follows:
❑ Wear rubber, not latex, gloves.
❑ Be sure your hands are dry.
❑ When inserting the probes into the receptacle, hold the probes by the insulation.
❑ Don't stand in water.

Checklist

❑ Make a chart that identifies which breakers or fuses control which circuits. Taping the chart inside the circuit-breaker box or fuse box will save you time when you need to make an electrical repair.

❑ Before replacing a wall switch, make sure it's the switch and not the light fixture or appliance that's faulty.

❑ Before replacing a receptacle, make sure a faulty appliance or wall switch isn't the culprit (see the Troubleshooting Guide in this chapter).

❑ Inspect the plugs on lamp and appliance power cords and replace any that appear to be damaged.

❑ If you live in an older home with two-slotted receptacles, consider having an electrician install new, three-slotted receptacles which are grounded.

Using a Continuity Tester

This device can test whether a switch is sound. First, remove the switch from the wall, as described in "Replacing Wall Switches," page 67. Attach the alligator clip at the end of the continuity tester's wire to one of the switch terminal screws. Then hold the continuity tester's probe to the other terminal and flip the toggle on and off. If the switch is sound, the continuity tester's bulb will light when the toggle is turned on **(Figure 1)**.

Note: Before using the tester, check the battery by touching the alligator clip to the probe. If the battery is charged, the bulb will glow. A weak or dead battery could make a sound switch appear to be defective.

Using a Voltage Tester

For safety's sake, never work on a live receptacle. To determine whether power to a receptacle has been shut off, use a voltage tester. Insert its probes into the hot and neutral slots of the receptacle **(Figure 2)**. If the receptacle is live, the voltage-tester bulb will glow.

The hot slot holds the wire carrying electricity to the receptacle from the fuse or circuit breaker panel. The neutral slot holds the neutral wire, which completes the circuit. Hot and neutral wires also complete the circuits of switches and light fixtures.

The hot slot is the smaller of the two. As you face the receptacle, the hot slot is on your right, providing the receptacle was installed correctly.

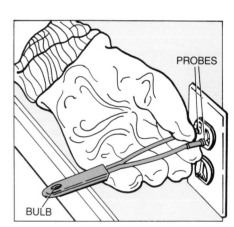

Fig. 2. To test for live wires, insert one probe of the voltage tester into the hot slot of a receptacle and the other probe into the neutral slot. If the wires are live, the voltage tester will glow. If you insert the probes in the neutral and ground slots, the voltage tester shouldn't glow. For safety, wear rubber gloves and hold the probes' insulation.

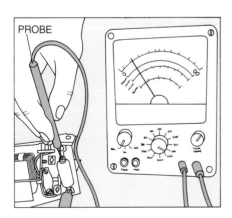

Fig. 1. A continuity tester lets you check whether a switch has failed.

In homes built since the late 1950s, the receptacles have a third, half-round ground slot below the other two slots. If a short circuit occurs in the receptacle, the current will flow harmlessly through the ground wire to the earth (or ground). Without that safety feature, the short circuit could start a fire or expose anyone plugging in a lamp or appliance to an electric shock.

Checking a Receptacle

A voltage tester can determine whether wires have been connected correctly to a new receptacle.

1. Insert one of the tester probes into the ground slot of the outlet.
2. Insert the other probe into the neutral slot. If an outlet has been connected properly, the tester bulb won't glow **(Figure 3)**.
3. Switch the probe from the neutral slot to the hot slot while leaving the other probe in the ground slot. The tester bulb should glow.

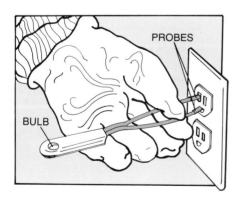

Fig. 3. To see whether a new outlet has been installed correctly, insert the probes in the neutral and ground slots; the tester shouldn't glow.

AVOID THESE PITFALLS
❑ Using a dimmer switch to control the flow of current to a power tool or appliance can damage the switch, receptacle, tool, or appliance.

REPLACING WALL SWITCHES

Tools and Materials:

Screwdriver; needle-nose pliers; adhesive labels; crayons; wire nuts (solderless connectors); electrician's tape.

Toggle switches and rotary dimmer switches both control the flow of electricity to a receptacle or a light fixture. This section covers both.

The most commonly used toggle switch is a single-pole switch. Several other types of toggle switches are available, including three- and four-way switches. Using the information on single-pole switches as a guide, you can replace the other varieties as well. You can also replace rocker-arm switches, which use panels rather than toggles.

If a lamp fails to go on, the toggle switch controlling the receptacle may be faulty. A loose toggle is one indication of a faulty switch.

First try plugging the lamp into an outlet not controlled by the suspect

---

switch. If the light still doesn't go on, it's the lamp, not the switch, that's faulty.

If the switch doesn't control an outlet, remove the switch and test it with a continuity tester (see ''Using a Continuity Tester,'' page 66), or simply replace the switch with another.

Replacing a Toggle Switch

1. Flick off the circuit breaker or remove the fuse to turn off the electricity.
2. Remove the screws that secure the cover plate and take off the plate.
3. Remove the screws that hold the switch in the switch box **(Figure 4)**.

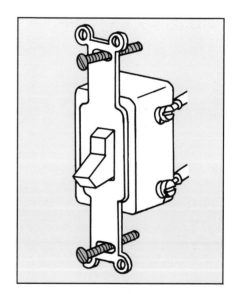

Fig. 4. Free the switch from the box by removing the retaining screws.

4. Carefully pull the switch out of the box until the two or three terminal screws holding the wires are accessible. Some switches, known as ''back-wired'' switches, give you a choice of

terminal screws or slots into which the wires can be inserted **(Figure 5)**.

5. With a screwdriver, loosen the terminals to release the wires, **(Figure 6)**. Use adhesive labels and crayons to identify which wire goes to which terminal. Release only the wires from the terminal screws. Don't touch other wires attached to the switch box.

6. If wires are inserted into the slots of a back-wired switch, insert the end of a paper clip or a tiny screwdriver into the small hole next to each slot, and press against the tang as you pull the wire loose.

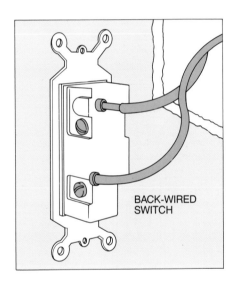

Fig. 5. A back-wired switch lets you attach the wires either with terminal screws or by pressing them into slots. Either way works well.

7. Leaving the electricity off, take the switch to a hardware or home-supply store for a replacement. The amperage and voltage ratings stamped on the new switch should match those on the old switch. In the United States,

the switch should have "UL" (Underwriters Laboratories) embossed on it. In Canada, it should bear the letters "CSA" (Canadian Standards Association).

8. Position the new switch so the word "off" on the toggle is at the top and the word "on" is at the bottom.

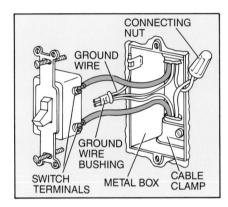

Fig. 6. Release the wires from the terminal screws, but don't tamper with connections inside the box. Note the colors of the insulation on the wire. Black or red identifies the hot wire; white, the neutral wire. The third, green wire on some switches is a ground wire.

9. Place the loop of one of the wires around the terminal it's supposed to attach to. Make sure the loop goes around the screw in a clockwise direction; that way, the loop won't open up as you tighten the screw. Use needle-nose pliers to squeeze the loop around the screw, if necessary, and then tighten the screw. Make sure the wire is securely connected by tugging it with some force. Attach the other wires the same way.

10. When installing a back-wired switch, push the end of the wire into its proper slot as you press the tang in the slot; then release the tang. Tug the wire gently to make sure it's locked in place.

11. Slip the switch into the box and secure it with screws. The switch has two ears on top and two on the bottom to hold it flush with the wall if the switch box is recessed. If the box isn't recessed, the ears may prevent you from installing the cover plate. Remove the ears by bending them back and forth with pliers until they snap off.

12. Reinstall the cover plate and turn on the electricity.

Replacing a Dimmer Switch

Test for a failed rotary dimmer switch the same way as for a toggle switch. Replace the switch as follows:

1. Turn off the electricity.

2. Pull off the rotary dial.

3. Remove the cover screws and cover.

4. Remove the screws holding the switch in the switch box.

5. Carefully pull the dimmer switch out of the box.

6. The wires of a rotary dimmer switch are connected with wire nuts **(Figure 7)**. Color-code each dimmer-switch wire and its connecting house wire, using adhesive labels and crayons.

7. Unscrew each wire nut, and untwist the spliced wires carefully with needle-nose pliers.

8. Buy a replacement dimmer of the same rating, bearing the "UL" or "CSA" logo.

9. Reattach each house wire to the proper dimmer-switch wire and twist the ends together, making sure the splice is secure.

10. Screw on the wire nut so none of the bare wire is exposed, and wrap a layer of electrician's tape around the bottom of the wire nut to seal the opening. (If you replace a wire nut, use one of the same size.)

11. Install the dimmer switch in the switch box, replace the cover, and turn on the electricity.

12. Set the rotary control so the switch is off and press the dial onto the switch, making sure the dial is in the off position.

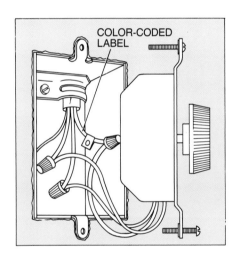

Fig. 7. You'll find a wiring arrangement such as this when you withdraw a dimmer switch from the wall. Use adhesive labels and crayons to color-code the proper connections for easier reassembly.

REPLACING OUTLETS AND PLUGS

Tools and Materials:
Screwdriver; pliers; adhesive labels; crayons; scissors.

Outlets

There are two basic types of outlets. In an end-of-the-run outlet **(Figure 8)**, the electricity terminates instead of proceeding on to a second outlet. That type of outlet has a hot wire and a neutral wire attached to the terminal screws. If the outlet is grounded, it has a third, ground wire as well.

A middle-of-the-run outlet **(Figure 9)** connects to a second outlet. That type of outlet has either four or five wires (again, depending on whether it's grounded) attached to its terminal screws. There are two hot wires, two neutral wires, and usually one ground wire.

If you examine the outlet you're replacing, you'll see that the terminal screws are different colors, as are the coated wires that connect to them. Those colors identify the following:

❏ The green terminal screw accepts the green ground wire.

❏ The brass terminal screw or screws are on the hot side of the outlet and accept the black or red wire or wires.

❏ The silver terminal screw or screws are on the neutral side of the outlet and accept the white neutral wire or wires.

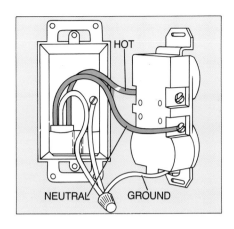

Fig. 8. In an end-of-the-run outlet, electricity does not go on to a second outlet. The hot wire connects to the hot terminal screw of the top outlet and the neutral wire connects to the neutral terminal of the bottom outlet.

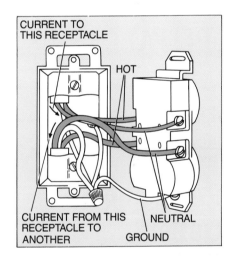

Fig. 9. In a middle-of-the-run outlet, electricity continues to flow to the next outlet. All terminal screws are occupied.

SAFETY FIRST

- Before taking off the cover plate, make sure the electricity to that outlet is off. Either shut off the house electricity with the main switch, or flick the circuit breaker or unscrew the fuse that serves that outlet.
- In older homes with two-slotted outlets, the outlets generally don't have ground terminal screws. For safety reasons, consider having an electrician install grounded, three-slotted outlets.

AVOID THESE PITFALLS

- Wind wires clockwise around their terminal screws. That way, the wire loop won't open up as you tighten the screw.

Replacing an Outlet

1. Turn off the electricity.
2. Remove the cover screws and cover.
3. Undo the two screws that hold the outlet in the box and gently pull out the outlet.
4. If it's an end-of-the-run outlet, the hot wire should be connected to the top brass terminal screw and the neutral wire should be connected to the bottom silver terminal screw. To

make sure you connect the wires to the new outlet in the same way, mark the wires and terminal screws with adhesive labels and crayons.
5. Unscrew the terminal screws and detach the wires.
6. Attach the wires to the proper terminal screws of the new outlet. Each wire should wrap around its terminal screw in a clockwise direction so the loop doesn't open up as you tighten the screw.
7. Place the receptacle into the outlet box and secure it with screws.
8. If the outlet box is flush with the wall, the ears on the receptacle may make it protrude too far for the cover plate to fit on. Use pliers to bend the ears back and forth until they snap off.

Replacing a Standard Plug

1. Loosen the terminal screws and release the wires.
2. Push the cord through the plug until the knot is accessible.
3. Undo the knot and pull the power cord free from the damaged plug.
4. Insert the power cord into the new plug and make an Underwriters' knot to secure the cord **(Figure 10)**.
5. Loosen the two terminal screws of the new plug and fit the looped wire ends of the power cord clockwise around the terminals. Push the wires under the screws with a screwdriver, and tighten the screws.
6. Slip the cardboard insulator that comes with the new plug over the prongs.

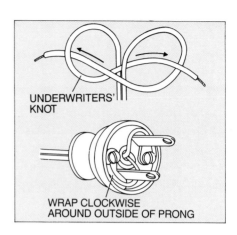

Fig. 10. The power cord going to the terminal screws wraps around the prongs of the plug. That keeps the cord from coming loose.

Replacing a Clamp-Type Plug

1. Cut the wires to free the damaged plug.
2. Open the lever of the new plug.
3. Press the power cord into the plug and snap the lever closed **(Figure 11)**. The prongs in the plug will pierce the insulation of the power cord and make contact with the wires.

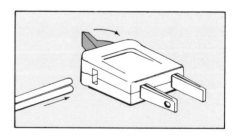

Fig. 11. To attach a power cord to a clamp-type plug, simply insert the cord into the plug and press the lever closed.

Power Cord Plugs

Plugs come in various shapes and sizes, but in only two basic types: standard type, which have terminal screws for attaching the wires; and clamp type, with sharp prongs that make the contact with the wires.

If the power cord is to be plugged in and unplugged frequently, replace the damaged plug with a standard type, which is stronger. If the plug is to stay put, use a clamp type replacement, which is easier to install. (To prevent damage to either type, always unplug the cord by grasping the plug, not the wires.)

TROUBLE-SHOOTING WALL OUTLETS

Troubleshooting Guide

Problem	Causes	What to Do
Lamp or appliance doesn't work	Faulty lamp or appliance	Plug the appliance into another outlet; if it works, the outlet is faulty
	Tripped circuit breaker or blown fuse	Reset circuit breaker or replace fuse; if failure recurs, call electrician
	Faulty outlet	Replace outlet (see "Replacing Outlets and Plugs," page 69)
	Wall switch damaged	Replace switch (see "Replacing Wall Switches," page 67)
Lamp or appliance plug can't be inserted in outlet slots	Faulty outlet	Replace outlet (see "Replacing Outlets and Plugs," page 69)
Lamp or appliance plug too loose in outlet slots	Prongs of plug don't make contact	Spread prongs slightly so they secure themselves in outlet; if that doesn't work, replace the plug (see "Replacing Outlets and Plugs," page 69)
	Faulty outlet	Replace outlet (see "Replacing Outlets and Plugs," page 69)

Most homes built since the 1950s use three-slotted outlets that are grounded and accept three-prong plugs; those built earlier generally have two-slotted outlets that are not grounded. The information in the Troubleshooting Guide in this section applies to both two- and three-slot outlets.

A duplex outlet assembly consists of two outlets fed by the same current. If one outlet of a duplex assembly becomes defective, you must replace the whole assembly.

Duplex outlets come in two types: live-all-the-time and switch-to-life. Live-all-the-time outlets have current available at all times, as their name implies. In a switch-to-life duplex outlet, a wall switch turns the electricity on and off.

Beyond those basics, special-purpose wall outlets include:

❏ **120/240-volt outlets.** Those are used with major appliances such as clothes dryers and electric ranges, which require 240-volt current for heating elements and 120-volt current for clocks and lights.

❏ **240-volt outlets.** Those are used by major appliances such as electric water heaters and heavy-duty air conditioners.

❏ **Ground-fault circuit interrupters (GFCIs).** A sensing device in the outlet instantaneously turns off the flow of current when it detects a fault. It protects you even when current leakage is too insignificant to trip the circuit breaker or blow the fuse. Use GFCIs outdoors and in rooms such as the kitchen, bathroom, garage, and laundry room, where current leakage and dampness might create a deadly combination.

Changing Ceiling-Mounted Light Fixtures

Tools and Materials:

Pliers; screwdriver; wire coat hanger; wire nuts.

SAFETY FIRST

❏ Before you install or remove a fixture, turn off the electricity to the fixture at the circuit breaker or fuse panel. Simply turning off the wall switch isn't enough; with some wiring arrangements, current will still flow through the hot wire of the fixture. If you're not sure which circuit breaker or fuse is the correct one, first turn on the old fixture at the switch. Then flip off each circuit breaker or remove each fuse in turn until the bulbs go out.

❏ The ladder you work on should be fully opened and locked. Make sure the ladder is high enough so you needn't stand on the top step.

AVOID THESE PITFALLS

❏ Don't try to take down a chandelier by yourself. Have a helper hold it from below as you disconnect the wires.

To replace a ceiling-mounted light fixture, proceed as follows:

Disengaging the Old Fixture

1. Make a cradle from a wire coat hanger **(Figure 12)** to hold the fixture while you work. Hold the portion of the coat hanger just below the hook with one hand and pull down on the straight bottom section of the wire with the other hand to form a loop.

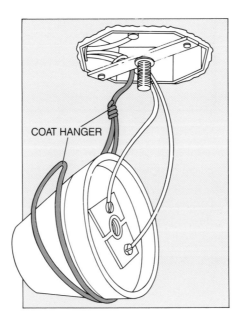

Fig. 12. Make a cradle from a coat hanger to support the fixture as you work. The cradle frees your hands and prevents strain on the wires.

Then bend the loop in half to form the cradle, which will support the old fixture as you disconnect its wires.

2. Remove the screws or nuts that secure the fixture to the junction box in the ceiling, using pliers or a screwdriver. Hold the fixture so it doesn't drop and tear the wires as it comes loose.

3. Ask a helper to hand you the coat-hanger cradle. Place the loop of the coat hanger around the fixture and position the hook over the hanging strap in the junction box.

4. Note the color of the insulation on the wires of the fixture, and mark the house wires with labels if necessary. Red or black insulation identifies the hot wire; white insulation identifies the neutral wire; a wire with green insulation (if there is one) is the ground.

5. Disconnect the house wires from the fixture. If they're connected to the fixture with wire nuts **(Figure 13)** unscrew the nuts and untwist the house wires from the fixture wires. Or, if the fixture

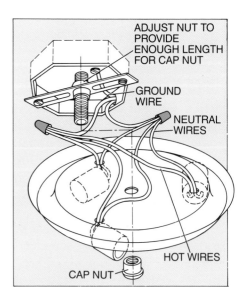

Fig. 13. To release a fixture, remove the wire nuts and untwist the wires.

has terminal screws, loosen them with a screwdriver to disengage the wires. Don't tamper with any other wires inside the junction box.

6. When the wires are disengaged, take down the fixture and the coat-hanger cradle.

Disengaging a Chandelier

The fastening hardware that holds a chandelier in place is often a knurl that extends through the cover plate and is screwed to a threaded nipple in the junction box **(Figure 14)**. Unscrew the knurl to release the fixture. Have a helper hold the chandelier from below as you undo the wires; the coat-hanger cradle won't work with a chandelier.

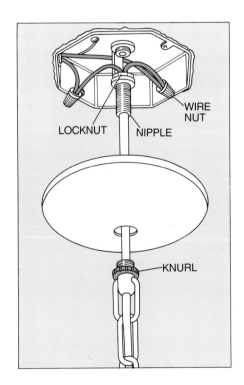

Fig. 14. To release a chandelier, unscrew the knurl, untwist the wires, and carefully draw the chandelier down, pulling the wires through the threaded nipple.

Hanging the New Fixture

Use the coat-hanger cradle to hold the fixture as you connect the wires.

To connect a fixture with terminal screws, loop each house wire in a clockwise direction around its proper terminal—that is, the red or black hot wire around the brass screw, the white neutral wire around the silver screw, and the green ground wire (if there is one) under the green screw.

If the new fixture has wires attached to it, use wire nuts to secure those wires to the house wires of the same color. Twist the ends of the wires together securely in a clockwise direction. Then screw a wire nut over the ends and wrap electrician's tape around the open end of the wire nut to seal it.

Supporting the fixture with your hand, bring it up to the junction box. As you do so, tuck the wires carefully into the box. Make sure the wires aren't caught between the fixture and junction box. Then attach the fixture with fasteners.

Frequently, the new fixture won't line up with the old hardware. Examine the fixture to determine how it should connect to the junction box.

If the fixture has a mounting screw on each side while the old fixture hung by a threaded stud that extended through its center, see whether the mounting strap now in place has slots through which the screws of the new fixture can extend. If so, you can probably retain the old mounting strap.

If the fixture and the mounting strap don't line up, you'll have to replace the strap **(Figure 15)**. Junction boxes have provisions for attaching new straps.

If the new fixture has a hole in the center for a threaded mounting stud

that extends from the junction box, and the present setup has no such stud, install a center-mounting strap and a stud with nuts. When the fixture is mounted, screw a threaded cap nut onto the stud to hold the fixture to the junction box **(Figure 16)**.

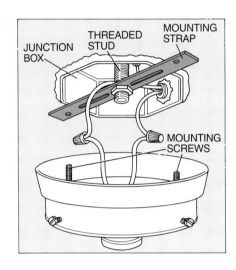

Fig. 15. Since this fixture is hung by two mounting screws, you need a mounting strap that has holes or slots to accept the screws.

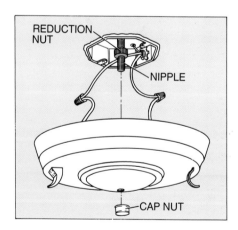

Fig. 16. A fixture with a hole in the center requires a center-mounting strap and a nipple with nuts.

TROUBLE-SHOOTING AND REPAIRING DOOR SIGNALS

Tools and Materials:
Voltmeter; screwdriver; sandpaper.

Although doorbells, door chimes, and door buzzers make different sounds, they're all wired the same way. And all three require a transformer and a push button **(Figure 17)** to work. While we refer only to doorbells in this section, our comments apply to chimes and buzzers as well.

Pressing a push button closes a set of contacts, allowing current to flow from the transformer to the bell. The transformer reduces the 110/120 volts of house current to 10 to 16 volts.

If a transformer fails, the current can't get to the signaling device, and the doorbell doesn't work. Except for the transformer, the low voltage used by these systems is unlikely to cause a tickle, much less a shock.

When a doorbell doesn't work, the problem most often is a bad push button or a burned-out transformer. A loose or broken wire may also be the cause. The doorbell itself is less likely to fail.

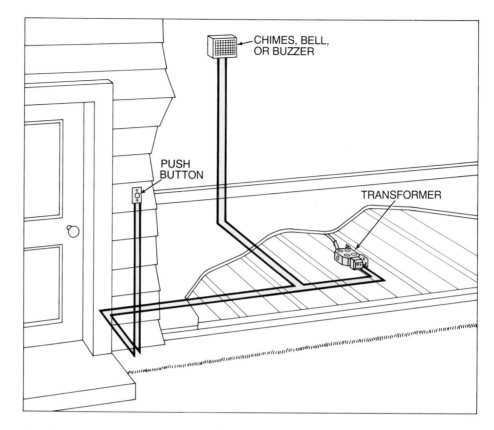

Fig. 17. Doorbell, chime, and buzzer systems have three main components: the push button, the transformer, and the sounding device—the bell or buzzer.

Troubleshooting the Push Button

1. Remove the screws holding the push button to the door frame.
2. Pry the push-button housing off the frame with a screwdriver until the wires and terminal screws are accessible **(Figure 18)**. Don't pull on the wires.
3. Tighten the terminal screws to make sure the wires are secure. Then press the push button to test the doorbell.
4. If the doorbell still doesn't work, hold a screwdriver firmly across the two metal contacts of the push button. If the doorbell rings, the push button is causing the problem—possibly because its wires and terminal screws are corroded. Loosen a terminal screw to free the wire and clean

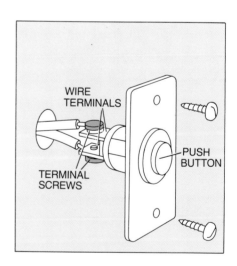

Fig. 18. Undo the retaining screws and pry out the push-button housing to expose the terminal screws. Make sure the screws are tight.

the terminal screw and the ends of the wire with a piece of sandpaper. Reattach the wire tightly to the screw. Then repeat the process with the other wire and terminal screw.

5. If the doorbell still fails to sound, install a new push button.

Testing the Doorbell

1. Remove the cover. Using a screwdriver, make certain the terminal screws are tight.

2. If a loose connection isn't the problem, determine whether the current is reaching the doorbell. Attach the voltmeter leads to the terminal screw for the wire from the transformer and the terminal screw for the wire from the push button, and have a helper press the push button.

3. If the voltmeter registers 10 to 16 volts, replace the doorbell. Otherwise, there's probably a break in the wiring. Call an electrician.

SAFETY FIRST

❑ Before you replace a transformer, turn off the house current. If you know little about handling electricity, leave that job for an electrician.

Testing the Transformer

Most likely your transformer looks like the one in **Figure 19**. If your home has a basement, the transformer is probably attached to a junction box that is screwed to one of the joists. A thick wire coming to the junction box from the fuse or circuit-breaker panel carries current to the transformer. Thin wires emerging from the transformer complete the circuit between the push button and the doorbell. One transformer may serve doorbells at several doors, or each doorbell may have its

own transformer. If your home doesn't have a basement, the transformer or transformers may be in the attic or in a utility room.

Connect the leads of a voltmeter to the terminal screws of the transformer, and have a helper press the push button of the doorbell. The voltmeter should register 10 to 16 volts. If it doesn't, call an electrician.

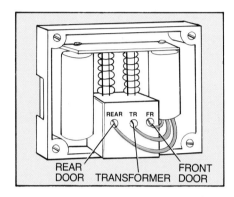

Fig. 19. To test the transformer, attach voltmeter leads to terminal screws holding the thin wires. Before you replace a transformer, make sure the house current is off.

Fig. 20. This illustration identifies the components of a typical home electrical system.

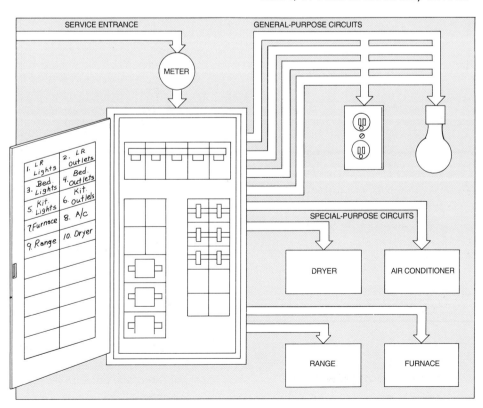

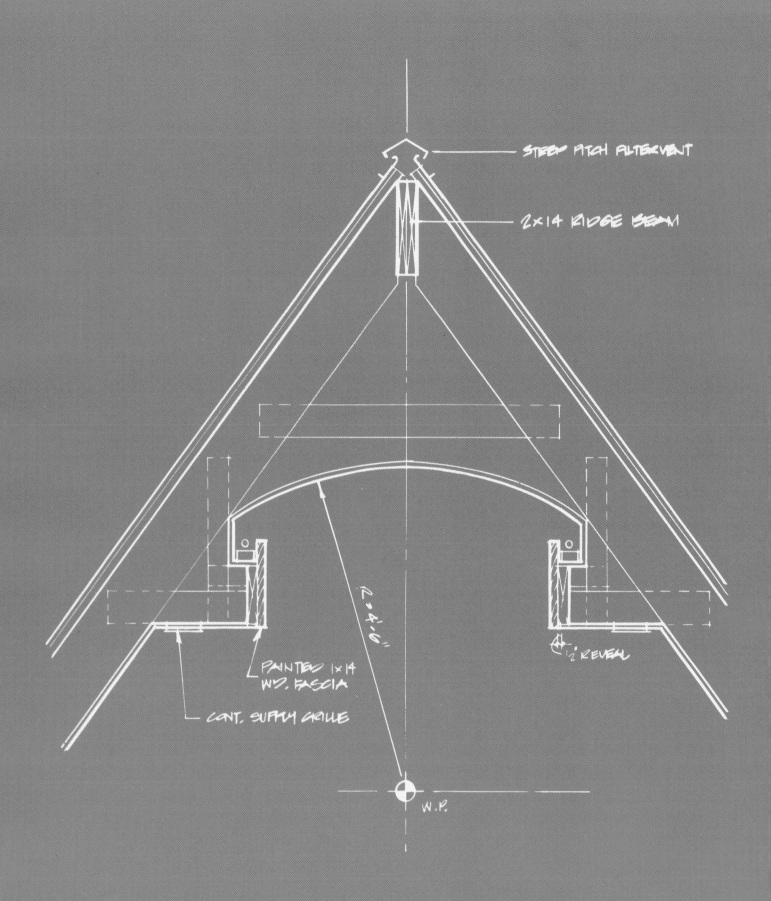

STEEP PITCH FILTERVENT

2×14 RIDGE BEAM

R=4'-6"

PAINTED 1×14 WD. FASCIA

CONT. SUPPLY GRILLE

½" REVEAL

W.P.

Chapter Five

ATTICS AND BASEMENTS

Proper maintenance of attic and basement spaces protects your home from serious structural damage that can result from leaks, condensation, and seepage. Further, it can save you money in heating and cooling costs, and it can protect you from breathing air that is laden with indoor pollutants. This chapter tells you how to keep those two critical areas dry, and how to insulate and ventilate them.

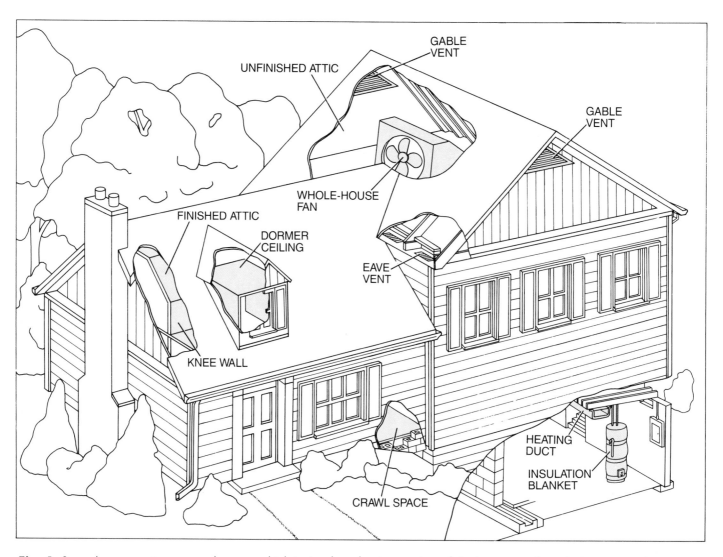

Fig. 1. Some homes rest on a crawl space, which is simply a shorter version of the basement foundation pictured, or on a concrete slab. And some homes are capped by a shorter version of a full attic, also called a crawl space.

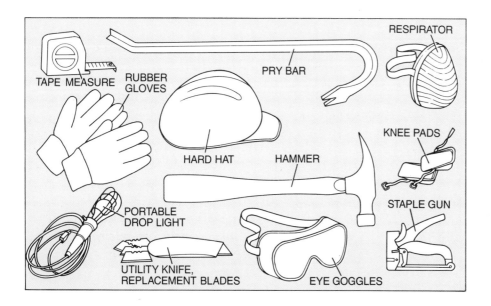

Fig. 2. These are the basic tools and materials you'll need to install insulation.

Insulating Materials

The best insulating materials are lightweight and rely mostly on trapped air to do their job. Most commonly used are fiberglass, foam, cellulose, and vermiculite. Each has advantages and disadvantages.

R-value is a convenient measure of how well a material insulates. Insulation can increase the R-value of a wall or ceiling considerably. An uninsulated roof, for instance, might have an R-value of less than 5, while the same roof with 6 inches (150mm) of fiberglass insulation would have an R-value of about 24.

R-values for common insulating materials are shown in the chart; those are for 1-inch (25mm) thicknesses. Roughly speaking, doubling the thickness doubles the R-value.

R-value, though, isn't the only consideration. Ease of installation, fire hazards, environmental and health hazards, and cost are other factors to consider.

Blankets and batts. The most common type of insulation is a fluffy blanket of fine fibers made from fiberglass, cellulose, or rock wool. It comes in widths that fit snugly between standard stud spacings in walls, ceilings, and floors.

You can buy blankets in rolls of 16 to 64 feet (5 to 20 meters) and thicknesses of 3 1/2 and 6 inches (90 and 150mm). Blankets are available either with or without a foil vapor barrier already attached to one side. Batts are sections of blanket, cut into 4- or 8-foot lengths for easier installation.

Loose-fill materials. These are the same fibrous materials used for blankets, but they come in short chopped lengths that can be poured or blown into cavities. Loose fill generally comes in large bags and is convenient for insulating finished walls (a

How Insulating Materials Compare

Type	Form	R-value per inch (25mm)	Comments
Vermiculite	Loose fill	2.1	Pours easily into small spaces
Perlite	Loose fill	2.7	Pours easily into small spaces
Fiberglass	Blankets, batts	3.1	Convenient for open spaces
	Loose fill	2.5–3.3	Blown into closed spaces or poured into open horizontal floors
Rock wool	Batts	3.7	Convenient for open spaces
	Loose fill	2.7–3.5	Blown into closed spaces or poured into open horizontal floors
Polystyrene	Foam boards	3.5–5	Moisture-resistant; requires noncombustible cover for indoor use
Cellulose	Loose fill	3.6	Blown into closed spaces or poured into open horizontal floors

job for a contractor) or for filling open, horizontal spaces. If you use loose fill, you'll usually have to provide a separate vapor barrier.

Light-weight mineral granules such as vermiculite (an expanded mica) and perlite (a porous volcanic rock) are sometimes used as loose fill. Those materials are fire-retardant, but they tend to absorb moisture, which further lowers their already low R-values.

One disadvantage of loose-fill insulation is that it settles with time, losing some of its effectiveness.

Plastic foams. They make up another major class of insulating materials, often called foam-in-place insulation. They are introduced as liquid chemicals into a wall cavity, where they flow around obstructions, expand, and then harden to a rigid foam. They require professional installation. Their formaldehyde content, which may present an air-pollution

Checklist

- Check existing insulation on the attic floor to make sure there's a vapor barrier between the insulation and the floor.
- Review R-value recommendations and add insulation, if necessary.
- Seal the base of the chimney where it enters the attic, using a nonflammable caulking.
- Seal around the base of the plumbing stack.
- Weatherstrip the attic door.
- Keep attic fans connected year-round.
- Disconnect whole-house fans before the weather turns cold.
- Inspect whole-house fans for air leakage; make or buy a cover to eliminate winter drafts.
- Check the ends of roofing nails on the roof's underside; condensation on the nails indicates the need for more attic ventilation.
- Check attic vents to make sure the screens are intact and the vents are free of grime and debris that could block airflow.
- Make sure vents aren't blocked by insulation or stored objects.
- Periodically check the attic for condensation or leaks in the roof.
- Lubricate vents with movable louvers.
- Lubricate the fan bearings; adjust the tension of belts on belt-driven fans.
- Caulk basement and crawl-space areas where the house framing meets the foundation.
- Check basement walls for water seepage.

hazard, has made foam-in-place materials less popular in recent years.

Board insulation. Preformed polystyrene boards are easy to install, and their resistance to moisture makes them suitable for exterior and below-grade applications. However, they are fairly fragile and require careful handling during installation. In addition, they are highly flammable and, when used indoors, must be covered with a noncombustible material such as gypsum board.

Vapor Barriers

Although not really an insulator, a vapor barrier is an important part of any insulation project. It's needed to protect insulation from moisture.

Warm air can retain more moisture in the form of water vapor than cold air can. In the winter, the heated air inside the house holds a good deal of moisture, supplied by dishwashing, bathing, and the people living there. If that air comes in contact with a cold surface (a window, for example), it becomes chilled and some of its water vapor condenses into water.

If warm, moisture-laden air passes through an insulator that's exposed to cold outside air, water will condense inside the insulation, soak it, and destroy its insulating ability. In worst cases, it even can damage the house framing.

The solution is a foil or plastic layer that won't let the damp air into the insulation. Locate the barrier on the warm side of the insulation: the interior surface, if you're insulating against the cold. Installing the insulation with the barrier on the outside would keep the damp air inside the insulation, virtually guaranteeing moisture problems.

If you stack two layers of blanket or batt insulation and both layers have vapor barriers, slash the vapor barrier on the outer layer with a knife to

prevent accumulation of any moist air that might leak past the inner barrier.

If the insulation you buy doesn't have a vapor barrier, buy a separate roll of plastic film or paper-backed metal foil.

INSULATING AN ATTIC

Any surface that separates a heated interior from a cold exterior or an air-conditioned interior from a hot exterior can benefit from insulation. Exterior walls are difficult to insulate, because there's usually no convenient access to the space inside. But an attic provides easy access to joists and rafters, espe-

AVOID THESE PITFALLS

- If the attic is unheated and only the floor is to be insulated, don't block the vents in other areas of the attic with insulation.
- If you're adding a second layer of insulation to existing insulation, don't install a second vapor barrier. If the new insulation has a vapor-barrier backing, slash it with a knife to avoid trapping moisture.
- Don't stuff insulation into the eaves. That area doesn't connect to the rest of the house, so the insulation is of little value. Worse, you may block the vents under the eaves and interfere with attic ventilation.

cially if it's unfinished. Unlike exterior walls, which typically have room for only 3½ inches (90mm) of insulating material, attics can accommodate at least 6 inches (155mm), and if there's no attic floor, twice that.

SAFETY FIRST

- ❑ Don't leave foam-board insulation exposed indoors; it's a fire hazard. Cover it with gypsum board.
- ❑ Don't run insulation directly up to a chimney; install aluminum flashing around the chimney as a heat shield and use loose fiberglass to insulate that area. While fiberglass won't burn, the backing paper and moisture barrier usually will.
- ❑ Wear gloves, goggles, and a dust mask whenever handling insulation, especially fiberglass. Also wear a long-sleeve shirt and ankle-length pants to protect your skin. A barrier skin cream that you can wash off later can reduce itching if your skin is sensitive.
- ❑ In an unfinished attic, wear a hard hat to protect your head from roofing nails protruding from the sheathing.
- ❑ In many attics, footing isn't secure, so wear shoes with non-skid soles.

Unheated Attics Without Floors

Tools and Materials:
For an unheated attic: Batt or blanket insulation with a vapor barrier; utility knife with replaceable blades; nails; hammer; stapler; 3/8-inch staples; aluminum foil or flashing; gloves; hard hat; goggles; dust mask; knee pads; drop light.

The idea is to let the attic stay cold in the winter, but to isolate it from the living space by adding insulation in the attic floor. If the attic is unfinished, simply lay batts of insulation between the floor joists **(Figure 3)**.

Fig. 3. When installing insulation in an attic without a floor, use batts or blankets with a vapor barrier attached. If the batts have none, staple strips of polyethylene plastic to the spaces between the joists before laying the batts.

Today, virtually every attic has at least some insulation in its floor. Pick up a portion of the existing insulation to make sure a vapor barrier has been installed underneath. If there's no barrier, you can either replace the old insulation with new insulation, making sure the vapor barrier faces downward, or leave the old insulation in place and install a vapor barrier on top. A less-effective approach is to apply several coats of low-permeability "barrier" paint to the ceiling directly below the attic.

If you add insulation to existing insulation, make sure the insulation you add doesn't have its own vapor barrier. If it does, slash it with a knife so it doesn't trap moisture.

The question of how much insulation to install in an unheated attic is a difficult one. Although federal agencies and insulation manufacturers have published maps with R-Value recommendations for different parts of the country, the best advice probably remains: as much as you have room for, and as much as you can afford. Even though the benefits of more insulation drop off as the thickness increases, installing R-38 insulation, which consists of two 6-inch (155mm) layers of fiberglass, is almost always a good idea.

Install the insulation as follows:
1. Lay the first layer of insulation between the joists **(Figure 4)**.
2. Install the second layer at right angles to the batts in the first layer. To provide a place to work when installing the second layer, nail short 2x6 uprights at 4-foot (1¼-meter) intervals to the middle pair of joists; those should extend over the top of the new layer and provide a place to put down a walkway **(Figure 5)**.
3. Trim the insulation to fit as closely as possible around pipes and vents that come through. But don't run the insulation directly up to a chimney; install a layer of heavy foil or aluminum flashing around the chimney as a heat shield, and then insulate with loose fiberglass. Fiberglass doesn't burn, but backing paper and moisture barrier can.

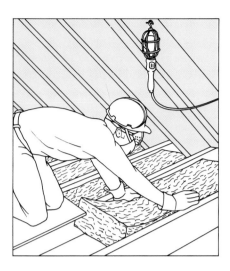

Fig. 4. In an unfinished attic, lay the batts between the joists, vapor barrier side down. Start the insulation at the eave, being careful not to shove the insulation into the eave itself and block airflow in the attic. Dress for the job; wear protective clothing, rubber gloves, a hard hat, goggles, a dust mask, and knee pads.

Fig. 5. To provide a place to work when installing a second layer of insulation, nail short 2x6 uprights at 4-foot (1¼ meter) intervals to the middle pair of joists. They should extend over the top of the first layer and provide a place to put down a new walkway.

Unfinished Attic With Floor

If your unfinished attic has a floor that blocks access to the joists, your best option is to insulate the rafters and the end walls.

Don't make the mistake of running the insulation up to the ridge beam. Instead, install "collar beams" **(Figure 6)** made with 2x4s or 2x6s. That method provides a ventilating channel at the ceiling that, in combination with the roof or peak vents, helps get rid of heat in the summer and water vapor in the winter.

1. Measure and cut collar beams to bridge the rafters.
2. Nail the beams to the existing rafters to a point about 2 feet (²/₃ meter) or so below the roof peak. Make sure they all line up.
3. Staple the insulation, barrier side down, between the collar beams.
4. Staple separate batts between the rafters from the collar beam to the floor.
5. Insulate the end walls. Trim carefully around obstructions.

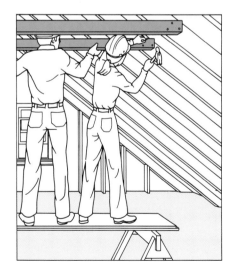

Fig. 6. If you can't get at the joists, fasten the insulation to horizontal collar beams below the roof peak.

Heated Attic Room

Tools and Materials:
For a heated attic: Friction-fit batt insulation; plastic vapor barrier; foamboard insulation; gypsum board; utility knife with replaceable blades; nails; hammer; stapler, ³/₈-inch staples; gloves; hard hat; goggles; dust mask; knee pads; drop light.

A finished attic should be insulated at the walls and ceiling, rather than at the floor. The basic techniques are no different than those used for insulating an unfinished attic, except for the problem of gaining access to the area behind the walls. The only way to do that is to cut the knee walls and ceiling and resign yourself to refinishing those surfaces when you're done.

1. Cut access holes into the knee walls and ceiling.
2. Buy friction-fit batts for the knee walls. That type of batt generally doesn't have a vapor barrier, so you'll have to staple a foil or plastic barrier to the batt before pressing it into position. Or, in place of a vapor barrier, paint the inner walls of the room with several coats of a low-permeability paint.
3. Install the friction-fit batts in the knee wall. They're designed to be installed between the vertical studs without staples.
4. Staple standard batts or blankets, vapor barrier facing down, in the spaces in the ceiling.
5. Insulate the end walls. While you can use batt or blanket insulation, your best bet is to install

foam boards and then cover them with gypsum board for fire protection. That approach usually requires that you modify the window moldings.

ATTIC VENTS AND VENTILATION

Tools and Materials:

Lubricating oil; stiff wire brush; sponge; water; all-purpose cleaner.

With the current emphasis on insulation, it's easy to forget an important rule: A house shouldn't be airtight. Ventilation is necessary to remove odors, smoke, gases, and water vapor. Attic ventilation in particular prevents excessive heat buildup during the summer.

SAFETY FIRST

❑ Shut off the electric power to an attic fan before working on or near it. Many have thermostat and/or humidistat controls that can start the fan unexpectedly, exposing you to possible injury.

Attic Vents and Windows

An attic should have 1 square foot ($1/10$ square meter) of vent openings for every 150 square feet (15 square meters) of floor area.

However, the actual space the vents occupy should be more than that; grilles, screens and louvers take up a surprisingly large amount of the available vent area. A vent covered with a fine mesh window screen, for example, has only half the actual opening area of an uncovered vent. Even a coarse mesh screen, installed to keep out animals, cuts the effective area by 20 percent, while a combination of insect screen and louvers reduces the effective vent area by two-thirds.

The two most common types of attic vents are eave vents, in the underside of the eaves, and peak or gable vents, in the end walls of the attic near the peak of the roof. Using the two in combination results in a natural convection current that helps provide effective ventilation for the attic.

Attic windows are also useful for venting, especially when used with large electric fans. Other types of vents are roof vents and ridge vents **(Figure 7)**.

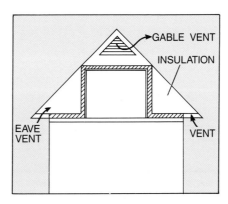

Fig. 7. Though many types and styles of attic vents are available, they all serve to replace hot and moist air in uninsulated attic areas with fresh, drier air. A venting system works most effectively if the intake and exhaust vents are at different heights (with a combination of eave and gable venting). Adding a fan also helps to move the air.

Attic and Whole-House Fans

A standard attic fan ventilates only the attic, while a whole-house fan draws air up to the attic from the lower levels of the house and discharges it through the attic **(Figure 8)**. The latter type can

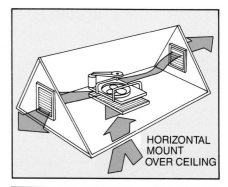

HORIZONTAL MOUNT OVER CEILING

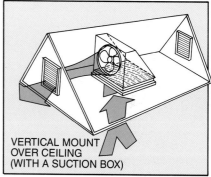

VERTICAL MOUNT OVER CEILING (WITH A SUCTION BOX)

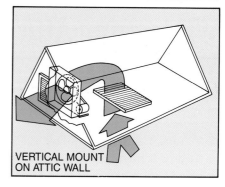

VERTICAL MOUNT ON ATTIC WALL

Fig. 8. A whole-house fan keeps your house more comfortable in the summer. If your system doesn't have movable louvers that close tightly, cover the fan opening in the top-story ceiling with insulation during the heating season.

be an effective alternative to air-conditioning when nights are cool and humidity is low.

It's easy to appreciate the value of attic ventilation in hot weather; the difference in temperature is dramatic. The need for ventilation doesn't diminish in cold weather, though. An insufficiently insulated attic collects moisture-laden air. The resulting condensation can ruin insulation and cause water stains on ceilings. In extreme cases, condensation can rot a home's structure.

Go into the attic on a cold day and look carefully at the protruding roofing nails. If you see considerable condensation or even a coating of frost on the nails, the attic needs more venting. In severe cases, you may find icicles on the nails.

AVOID THESE PITFALLS

❏ Don't pile stored cartons in front of vents.
❏ Make sure insect screens in front of vents are clear of debris and grime.

Winterizing Attic Vents and Fans

Don't close or cover attic vents when the weather gets chilly. True, a well-ventilated attic will be cold, but adequate insulation in the floor should keep that from becoming a problem. Nor should you disconnect the attic fan at the end of the summer. Besides thermostatic controls, most such fans have humidity-sensing devices that turn on the fan whenever moisture levels become excessive. So don't be surprised if an attic fan goes on in the dead of winter; it's only doing its job.

Whole-house fans, on the other hand, should be disconnected at the end of the warm weather. If air leakage is noticeable around the fan, install a cover to eliminate winter drafts.

Maintenance

Attic ventilating systems don't need much attention; a yearly inspection usually suffices:

1. Make sure that screens over the vent openings are intact and not clogged with grime. Carefully clean them with a wire brush, and wash with an all-purpose cleaner.
2. Check the attic for wasps' nests or other signs of pests.
3. Make sure that neither insulation nor stored items are blocking the vents.
4. If the vents have movable louvers, check that they move freely; if not, lubricate them with heavy oil.
5. Check the fan manufacturer's recommendations on lubricating fan bearings and adjusting tension belts.

Caution: Be sure to turn off the electric power or disconnect the fan before working on or near it. Many have thermostat and/or humidistat controls that can start the fan unexpectedly.

INSULATING PIPES, DUCTS, AND WATER HEATERS

While attics and walls readily come to mind when you think of insulation, they're by no means the only places where insulating can save you money. Any area you want to keep warm amidst cold surroundings, or vice versa, is a candidate for insulation. What's more, insulation can prevent costly disasters such as burst pipes.

Insulating Water Heaters

Tools and Materials:
For water heaters: Precut insulation kit for water heaters.

Your water heater has to store water that's been heated to 60° to 100°F (15° to 38°C) over the surrounding air temperature. Newer tanks and "energy-saver" models are already insulated to some extent, but the amount of insulation manufacturers can use is limited by cost and space requirements. Fortunately, adding insulation is inexpensive and simple. It will often pay for itself in a short time, particularly if the water heater is in an unheated area. Although you could improvise an insulating cover for your water heater, it really doesn't pay—commercial kits are inexpensive and simple to install. They come precut to fit most popular sizes and generally have complete instructions **(Figure 9)**.

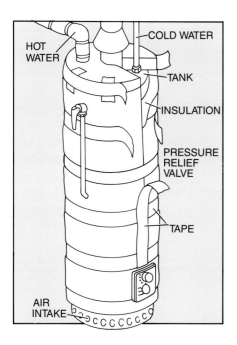

Fig. 9. Water-heater insulation kits are precut to provide a good fit, and they include a plastic sheet cover and installation tape. Follow instructions exactly; don't block the vent or air intake on a gas water heater or interfere with the operation of the thermostat.

SAFETY FIRST

- ❏ Don't cover the heater's thermostat, pressure-relief valve, or control knobs with insulation.
- ❏ If you have a gas- or oil-fired water heater, make sure the air inlets at the heater's base are unobstructed.
- ❏ Follow the manufacturer's instructions to make sure you don't block the stack.
- ❏ Be extremely careful when using a propane or butane torch to thaw frozen pipes: It's easy to start a fire.

Insulating Hot-Water Pipes

Tools and Materials:

For pipes: Foam-tube pipe insulation; utility knife; vinyl tape; electric heat tape.

The pipes that carry hot water between your water heater and the rest of the house can benefit from insulation, as can the pipes that carry hot water between the boiler and the radiators or convectors. Several types of insulation are available, but the most convenient consists of foam tubing slit lengthwise so it can slip over the pipes. **(Figure 10)** Foam tubes come in various diameters to match the pipes.

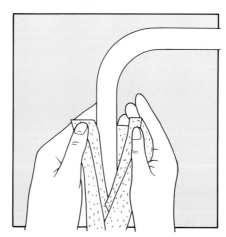

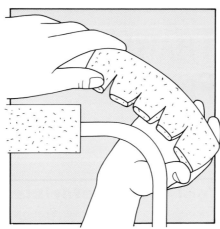

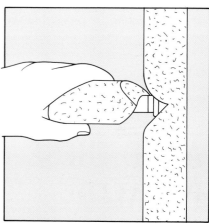

Fig. 10. Flexible foam tubing is generally best for pipe insulation. It's slit lengthwise so it can slip over pipes. Buy tubing that is the proper size for the pipes you're insulating. Fasten the foam with vinyl tape, and fill any voids between joints with scraps of insulation cut to fit.

1. Cut the lengths of foam to size.
2. Slip the sections over the piping and butt them together.
3. Join them with vinyl tape.
4. Tees and elbows are best handled by cutting the tubing into miter joints with a utility knife. For large-diameter bends, notch a section of foam tubing to fit and wrap the outer surface of the bend with tape.

Insulating Cold-Water Pipes

Cold-water pipes that run through an unheated crawl space or inside exterior walls need insulation to keep them from freezing. Be sure you interpose a layer of insulation between the pipe and the cold area without. If that's not feasible, consider protecting vulnerable pipes with electric heat tape. A thermostat generally controls those tapes, so you won't use electricity unless temperatures approach freezing.

AVOID THESE PITFALLS

- ❏ Don't leave gaps between lengths of pipe insulation.
- ❏ Don't overlook pipes in out-of-the-way locations such as crawl spaces and attics.
- ❏ If you buy foam pipe insulation, get the right size for the pipe: A snug fit reduces loss of heat.

Insulating Heating Ducts

Tools and Materials:

For ducts: Duct insulation or insulation batts; utility knife; duct tape; heavy-duty stapler.

Insulated heating ducts can save considerable heat, particularly if they pass through an unheated crawl space or basement. You can purchase specially cut sections of duct insulation or cut your own batts from an insulation blanket **(Figure 11)**. Seal the joints with duct tape. If the ducting is recessed between the joists, staple the batts to the joists to cover the duct. That way, any lost heat will travel upward and heat the living space above.

Caution: Some basements rely on heat loss from ductwork to prevent water pipes from freezing. If you insulate the ducts and then find that the basement temperature approaches freezing on cold days or nights, remove some of the insulation.

Fig. 11. Use batts of insulation, cut to fit, around exposed ducts. Wrap the ducts with the insulation, barrier side out, and fasten the batts with duct tape. If the duct is recessed between joists, staple insulation batts directly to the joists, isolating the duct from the unheated basement. Don't neglect ducting that passes through crawl spaces.

THAWING FROZEN PIPES

Tools and Materials:

For thawing frozen pipes: Propane or butane torch; blow dryer; vacuum cleaner.

Ideally, you should keep pipes from freezing in the first place. Failing that, you have to apply enough heat to the pipe to thaw the plugs of ice that have formed inside.

If the pipes are exposed, use a propane or butane torch to warm them. Be careful, though; it's easy to start a fire. A blow dryer is slower but safer.

For pipes that are buried in the wall, blow air from the exhaust end of a canister-type vacuum cleaner onto the pipe. That's a slow but safe process, and you don't have to be there all the while the vacuum is running.

Start the thawing process at elbows, tees, and valves, where pipes usually freeze first. Also open a faucet at the end of the line you're working on. Once a trickle of water starts, the water flow will generally melt the rest of the ice. If you have a section of plumbing that freezes frequently, allow a faucet at the end of the section to trickle slowly at the onset of a cold spell. Once spring comes, you can take more permanent steps.

HOW TO SOLVE WET BASEMENT PROBLEMS

Tools and Materials:

Downspouts; tin snips; carpenter's level; shovel; fill dirt; miscellaneous elbows for ground pipes.

Most wet basement problems are caused by rain running into the basement from the roof or lawn. If water collects near a basement wall, it often finds its way through the foundation.

SAFETY FIRST

❏ Don't use electric tools when working on wet concrete walls or floors; they pose a shock hazard. Use a hammer and star drill or a battery-powered drill.
❏ Wear goggles when drilling or chiseling concrete.

You can solve most basement water problems by adding or altering a roof gutter system or by correcting the slope of the lawn so water flows away from the house. Often, a few wheelbarrow loads of dirt, properly placed, solve the grading problem.

Infrequently, a high water table is the culprit. (The water table is the depth at which the ground is totally saturated with water.) To check, call your city building inspector or a local excavating contractor familiar with the water table in your neighborhood. If the water table is not the problem, you can move on.

Check all around your house for one or more of the problems shown in the illustrations. If the house has a gutter system, the solution may be as simple as adding a pipe at the bottom of a downspout to divert the water from the basement wall. Conduct your inspection while it's raining so you can observe whether the water flows toward or away from the house.

Most houses on small city lots have gutters because lack of space makes it difficult to change the slope of the lawn. But not all houses have or need gutters. Many suburban houses, for example, have wide soffits or overhanging eaves that deflect the rain far enough from the basement walls for it to run off down a sloped lawn.

But conditions change over time, and the original judgment on whether to install rain gutters may need rethinking. If your house doesn't have a gutter system, adding one may cure a basement water problem.

AVOID THESE PITFALLS

❏ Waterproofing paint or coating products are a temporary fix. Put your energy and money into providing better drainage so water won't seep through the walls in the first place.
❏ You won't find the cause of water problems by watching where water enters from inside the basement. Inspect the outside perimeter of the house during a rainstorm and note water-flow patterns. Prevent standing water near the basement or streams of water flowing to the basement by adding fill dirt to improve slope and drainage.

Solving a Grade Problem

When ground pipes are too short or absent **(Figure 12)**, roof water can fall against the basement walls and run into the basement. If you have a similar situation, you can make the following simple changes:

1. Spread a couple of yards of dirt around the perimeter of your basement. Distribute the dirt so the lawn slopes away from the basement wall on all sides of the house.

2. Check the new grade with a carpenter's level and a section of downspout **(Figure 13)**. Use the downspout as a straightedge and place the carpenter's level on top of it. To measure the slope, raise the outside end of the downspout until the bubble

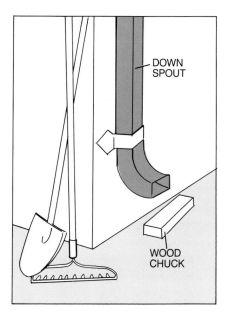

Fig. 12. Two common mistakes are poor slope away from the foundations and a ground pipe so short that it deposits water close to the foundation. Shovel dirt against the foundation to improve the slope

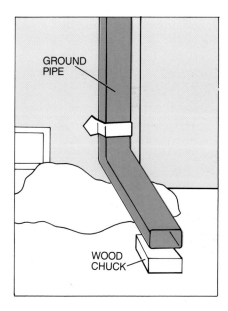

Fig. 13. Check the slope frequently as you grade fill dirt around the foundation. A length of downspout is a useful straightedge; a carpenter's level indicates slope when placed on the downspout. To measure slope, raise the outer end until the bubble shows level, then measure the space from the downspout to the ground.

shows level, then measure the space from the downspout to the ground.

3. Install longer ground pipes on all downspouts and redirect them, if necessary, to flow toward street gutters or elsewhere **(Figure 14)**.

4. Move plantings away from basement walls. Plants that are too close to the foundation can cause the soil to hold water, which eventually seeps through the basement wall. After moving the plants, check the new grade with a level to be sure the soil slopes away from the basement wall. When the grade is established and the soil becomes compacted, water will run off rather than soak in.

If you need help establishing a new grade on the lawn, call an excavating contractor. If all else fails, or if the water table is high in your area, you face the expensive prospect of excavating around the house and installing drain pipes and sump pumps to control the water.

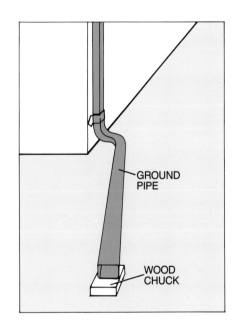

Fig. 14. Add 90-degree elbows to change the flow of water from the side of the house to the front or vice versa.

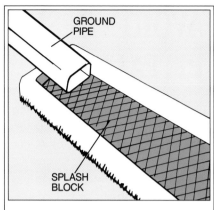

Fig. 15. A splash block placed under a ground pipe extends its reach and diverts the water from the foundation.

INSPECTING FOR TERMITES AND CARPENTER ANTS

Tools and Materials:
Pen knife or wood chisel; mortar compound; flashlight.

Inspecting your home for termite or carpenter ant damage requires some knowledge of the life cycles of these insects. Termites, for example, need constant moisture as well as a regular diet of cellulose (found in wood and wood products). Give them those two vital elements and they can literally chew a house to the ground.

Carpenter ants, on the other hand, don't eat wood. They merely use it to create concealed nests, similar to those of termites. Favorite foods of carpenter ants include sugar, honey, bread products, fats, and oils, all of which can be found in pantries and kitchens.

Identifying the Enemy

You rarely see termites or carpenter ants because they do their dirty work inside wood. Termites can't expose themselves to the air or they dehydrate and die. Instead, they create enclosed shelter tubes to form a bridge from the soil to the wood under attack.

Because both insects take the path of least resistance, the sections of homes that first come under attack are foundation supports, sills, basement windows, ceiling joists and rafters, and other sections that are in direct contact with the soil. Other favorite targets include wood steps, trellises, porch supports, sheds, and other outbuildings.

Unlike termites, carpenter ants can't travel from an outside nest in a rotting tree or wood pile to a house up to 100 yards (100 meters) away. They can enter the home through a small crack in the mortar or siding, through a gap under a door, or through the windows. They may use overhanging tree branches or bushes close to the house as pathways.

Conducting an Inspection

Inspect your home for termites and carpenter ants in the spring or summer, when colonies become active. Start with the outside portions of the house that contact the soil.

1. For termites, look first for shelter tubes leading from the soil and along foundation walls. The

Checklist for Termites and Carpenter Ants

❏ You may notice little furrows along the outside of a piece of wood—a door saddle, or a basement window frame, for example. Those "galleries" allow passage through wood while protecting the termites from exposure to air. Carpenter ants also furrow through wood, but they frequently leave piles that resemble pencil shavings outside their nests.

❏ In time, the insects can hollow out a massive beam. Tap on the wood; a distinctive hollow sound means that termites are present in large numbers. Of course, by that stage, the wood must be replaced.

❏ Carpenter ants frequently make noises with their jaws inside wood. Stand in the middle of the room at a quiet time of day and listen for a dry rustling sound. The noise gets louder when the ants are disturbed.

❏ A key to the presence of termites is the appearance of the wood under attack. Most homeowners describe the wood as being "dirty." The "dirt" is actually termite excrement and soil that the insects have carried in with them.

tubes are up to ½ inch (12mm) wide and several inches long.

2. If you find a shelter tube, scrape it open with a penknife. If you find worker termites inside, you can be certain they've moved into your house.

3. Usually, the shelter tube is attached to a foundation crack.

Destroy the tube and seal the crack with dense mortar. Repeat that process if you find more shelter tubes. If you open a shelter tube and it's empty, destroy it and inspect the site a week or two later. If another tube has been constructed, you know termites are active in your house. Call an exterminator.

4. Inspect exterior wood around basement windows and doors. Because they're often close to the soil, they're a convenient food source for termites.

5. Inspect your basement or crawl space, particularly the outer edges of the foundation wall. If there are wood posts resting on the ground or on a small concrete footing, examine the footing and posts for shelter tubes.

6. If you find shelter tubes, take a wood chisel or pocket knife and expose the wood beneath. Chances are you'll extract some termites or ants if you have an active colony.

7. Do the same for exposed floor joists, beams, and sills.

8. If you find evidence of insects in the support structures, the infestation is probably advanced. Call an exterminator.

9. In a finished basement, detection is more difficult. You may have to remove a panel or part of the ceiling to expose floor

beams and joists or wall studs.

10. In the spring, look for insect wings or winged termite or carpenter ant bodies near basement windows and door saddles. That's a sign that the insects are spawning.

Moisture Is the Key

In your search for these pests, check for moisture and remedy the problem quickly.

For example, a brick house may have poorly pointed brickwork that allows rain to seep into the walls. Wet beams are prime snack food for termites. Carpenter ants find wet wood ideal for creating nests.

Inspect water pipes, from the water main to the heating unit and into the circulation system to the rest of the house. A pipe may be leaking just enough to provide the moisture that termites and carpenter ants need.

Blocked gutters and leaders can leak rain water onto eaves or splash water against a wooden section of your home. When water constantly hits a window or door frame, it eventually seeps through the wood and rots it. Clean all gutters to provide proper water flow to leaders. Repair or replace rotting wood.

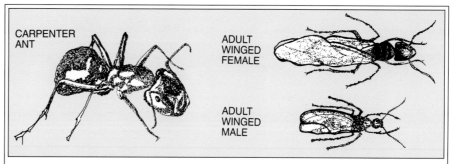

Figs. 16a and 16b. Winged reproductive carpenter ants are ¼ to ¾ inch (6 to 19mm) long. Finding them near windows and doors, or swarming, is a sure sign of infestation.

CARPENTER ANT

ADULT WINGED FEMALE

ADULT WINGED MALE

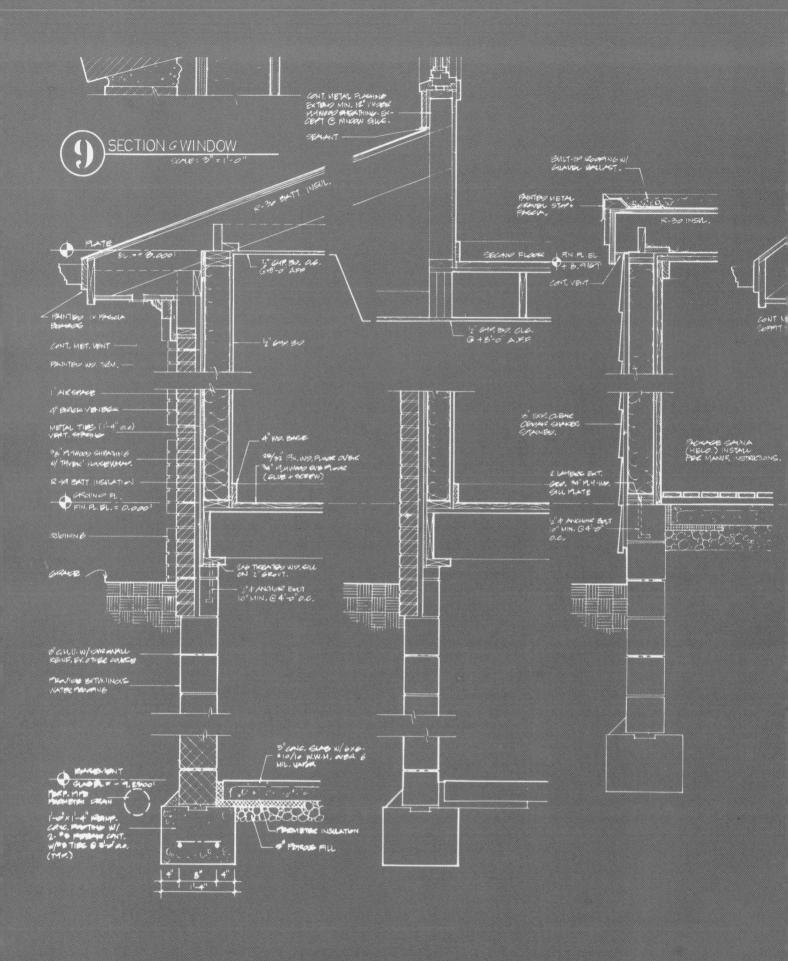

9 SECTION G WINDOW
SCALE: 3" = 1'-0"

CONT. METAL FLASHING
EXTEND MIN. 12" UNDER
PLYWOOD SHEATHING. EX-
CEPT @ WINDOW SILL.

SEALANT

BUILT-UP ROOFING W/
GRAVEL BALLAST.

PAINTED METAL
GRAVEL STOP +
FASCIA.

R-30 INSUL.

R-30 BATT INSUL.

PLATE
EL. = + 8.000'

SECOND FLOOR

FIN. FL. EL.
+ 8.969'

CONT. VENT

PLATE
EL. = + 8.000'

½" GYP. BD. CLG.
@ +8'-0" AFF

CONT. M
SOFFIT

PAINTED IX FASCIA
BOARDS

CONT. MET. VENT

PAINTED WD. TRIM.

½" GYP. BD.

½" GYP. BD. CLG.
@ +8'-0" A.F.F.

1" AIRSPACE

4" BRICK VENEER

METAL TIES (1'-4" O.C.)
VERT. SPACING

⅜" PLYWOOD SHEATHING
W/ "TYVEK" HOUSEWRAP.

R-19 BATT INSULATION

GROUND FL.
FIN. FL. EL. = 0.000'

RUNNING B

GRADE

4" WD. BASE

25/32 FIN. WD. FLOOR OVER
¾" PLYWOOD SUB FLOOR
(GLUE + SCREW)

2X6 TREATED WD. SILL
ON 2" GROUT.

½" Ø ANCHOR BOLT
10" MIN. @ 4'-0" O.C.

10" EXP. CLEAR
CEDAR SHAKES
STAINED.

2 LAYERS EXT.
GRD. ¾" PLYWD.
SILL PLATE

½" Ø ANCHOR BOLT
10" MIN. @ 4'-0"
O.C.

PACKAGE SAUNA
(HELO.) INSTALL
PER MANUF. INSTRUCTIONS.

8" C.M.U. W/ HORIZONTAL
REINF. EV. OTHER COURSE

PROVIDE BITUMINOUS
WATER PROOFING

BASEMENT
SLAB EL. = -9.3900'
TEMP. MTD.
PERIMETER DRAIN

1'-0" X 1'-4" REINF.
CONC. FOOTING W/
2-#6 REBARS CONT.
W/#3 TIES @ 30" O.C.
(TYP.)

5" CONC. SLAB W/ 6X6
#10/10 W.W.M. OVER 6
MIL. VAPOR

PERIMETER INSULATION

6" POROUS FILL

4"   8"   4"
1'-4"

HEATING AND COOLING SYSTEMS

Next to your mortgage and property taxes, you probably pay more each year for heating and cooling than for any other home-related expenses. For that reason, and for safety's sake, routine care of those systems should be at the top of your maintenance checklist.

Make sure, however, that you pay equal attention to all parts of your home's heating and cooling systems. Spending time and money to ensure that the burner is working efficiently is wasted if the furnace or boiler or the ducts or pipes aren't also properly maintained.

The following sections tell you how to maintain the most commonly used heating and cooling systems. Read the sections that apply to your home.

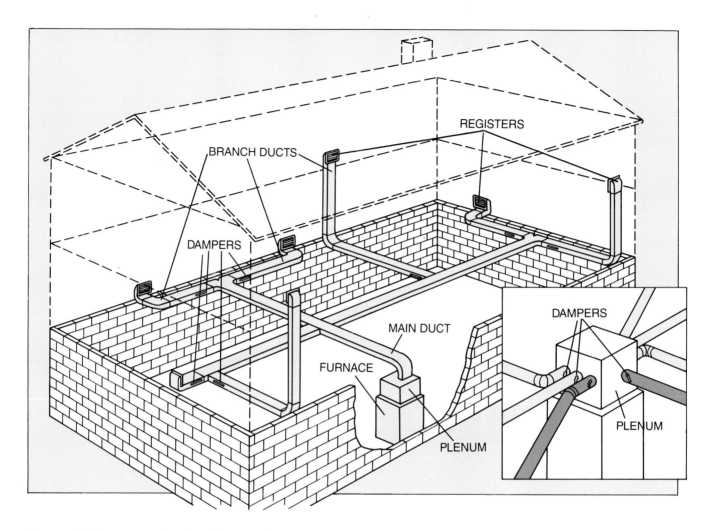

Fig. 1. This illustration identifies the parts of a typical forced-air heating system.

A Warning about Carbon Monoxide

While most people know that automobile exhaust contains deadly carbon monoxide (CO), they may be less aware that furnaces, stoves, gas-water heaters, and fireplaces produce large amounts of that gas. Normally, the CO from those appliances vents to the outside through a flue. However, if the flue is blocked or a vent pipe is dislodged, the CO can back up into the home. The gas is odorless, so its presence may go unnoticed until it is too late.

CO is the result of the incomplete burning of fuel. It's a menace to health because it blocks the blood's ability to carry oxygen. Low concentrations can cause drowsiness and lack of coordination; higher concentrations can cause death within a short time.

Until recent years, checking your home for CO was almost impossible. Laboratory measuring equipment was expensive and difficult to use. Today, however, you can buy less costly devices to monitor CO in your home and car.

The simplest and cheapest type is a badge that you clip to your clothing or place on the dashboard of your car. The badge holds a replaceable disk, or tablet, which darkens in the presence of CO. The higher the concentration, the faster it darkens. Such badges generally cost less than $5, and they need no batteries. Replacement disks are available.

You can also buy electronic CO monitors, which operate on AC current, standard batteries, or automotive batteries. Those detectors, ranging in price from $40 to $100, let you monitor the air you breathe on a regular basis. They're available from companies that distribute industrial safety equipment.

Inspecting Chimneys and Wood-Stove Pipes

Tools and Materials:
Flashlight; a small mirror taped to a broom handle; binoculars; furnace cement.

SAFETY FIRST

❏ A dirty wood-stove chimney is a carbon monoxide and fire hazard. Check for creosote buildup at least twice a year, and once a month if the stove is used frequently.

❏ If you're inspecting or cleaning a chimney from the roof, wear shoes that provide traction. Don't walk on the roof when it's wet. If the pitch of the roof is steep, call a technician to do the job.

AVOID THESE PITFALLS

❏ Don't "choke" a wood-burning stove—stuff it with wood and close off the air inlets; you'll only foul your chimney with soot and creosote.

❏ Don't neglect a brick chimney. Repoint badly weathered mortar before bricks start to loosen and fall into the chimney, blocking the flue.

A general rule of thumb: If you're burning wood, any problems with the chimney will start on the inside of the chimney; if you're burning oil or gas, whatever problems exist will come from outside.

No matter what fuel you burn, a chimney is essentially a heat-powered pump that pulls combustion gases out of the furnace, stove, or fireplace. It works because the heated air at the base of the chimney weighs less than the cooler air at the top. The lighter hot air rises, forcing the cooler air up and out.

If the chimney is serving a wood stove or a fireplace, the combustion gases traveling up the chimney deposit vaporized creosote, a tarry substance that results from incomplete combustion of wood. In addition, the burning wood gives off soot, dust, and ash. Soon, those deposits can reduce the chimney's effective diameter and allow deadly carbon monoxide gas to back up into the house. What's more, creosote is flammable, and an excessive accumulation poses the threat of a chimney fire. A chimney serving a wood-burning stove should be inspected at least twice yearly.

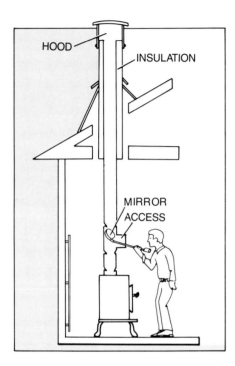

Fig. 2. Inspect a chimney for buildup of creosote at least twice a year; do it in the daytime so there's light at the top of the chimney. A mirror taped to a stick makes a convenient "periscope" for looking past awkward corners.

To see how much creosote has built up in your chimney, open the damper fully and shine a flashlight up the flue. If the chimney has a bend, check from both above and below. Most wood stoves have removable access caps to ease inspection and cleaning, while many outside chimneys have clean-out doors at their base. A mirror taped to a piece of broom handle may make inspection easier **(Figure 2)**.

If you have a buildup that's ¼ inch (6mm) thick or thicker, a cleaning is called for. Chimney sweeping isn't

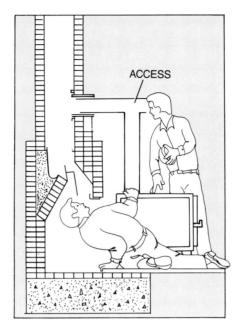

Fig. 3. If the stove's flue has several bends, inspect each section separately. If the stove shares a chimney with a fireplace, the job is easier. Make sure the damper in the fireplace is open.

difficult, but it's messy—not a task that most homeowners relish. If you decide to do the job yourself, you can buy wire brushes and rods from stove-supply catalogs or large hardware distributors. Open any cleanout openings outside the house, and cover fireplace openings with a sheet or similar cover to keep soot out of the home.

If your inspection reveals a clean chimney, you can keep it that way by operating the wood stove in such a way that creosote and soot production is minimized. Don't, for example, stuff the firebox full of wood and then close the air inlets down so far that the fire smolders, instead of burning brightly. That provides a long burn without refueling, but it also generates excessive smoke and creosote. When you first fire up a stove or fireplace, let it burn strongly with

dampers and glass doors open for the first half-hour or so; you'll burn out light creosote deposits before they become a fire hazard.

Gas- and oil-fired heating systems don't usually require chimney cleaning. However, a badly adjusted burner can cause soot buildup. A technician can advise you whether cleaning is necessary. A more common problem is blockage caused by bricks at the top of the chimney falling in or by birds or animals making a home at the top of the chimney. The most effective inspection tool for a chimney is a pair of opera glasses or binoculars **(Figure 4)**.

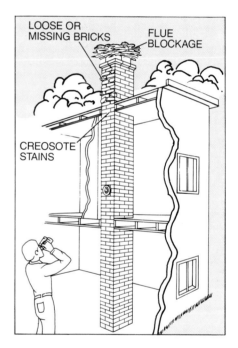

Fig. 4. You can learn much about a chimney's condition by stepping outside and looking at it, preferably from a nearby hill, with a pair of binoculars. Missing bricks may be partially blocking the chimney. Birds' nests, built over the summer, can present problems once the heating season starts.

Other points to check on a chimney serving a gas or oil appliance are the places where flue pipes from a furnace or water heater join the chimney. Caulk any gaps around the flue pipes with furnace cement.

Checklist for Wood Stoves and Fireplaces

❏ Inspect the chimney serving a wood-burning stove for creosote buildup at least twice yearly, or even oftener if you use the stove frequently. Have the chimney cleaned by a professional if you have ¹/₄ inch (6mm) or more buildup.

❏ Check the gasket around the door of a wood stove; if the gasket is frayed or broken, replace it with a nonasbestos gasket.

❏ After using your fireplace, close the damper to minimize heat loss up the chimney. Better still, have glass doors or a glass door insert installed. Those accessories let you see the fire without wasting expensive house heat.

MAINTAINING GAS- AND OIL-FIRED FORCED-AIR FURNACES

Tools and Materials:
Vacuum cleaner; electric-motor oil; screwdriver; wrench; hex wrench; carpenter's square; automotive grease gun (if fan has grease fittings); thermometer.

SAFETY FIRST

❏ Don't try to adjust your furnace's burner; you could cause a fire or explosion. Leave the job to a technician.

❏ Don't use the thermostat to turn off a furnace while you work on it. Turn off the main power supply to avoid nasty surprises.

AVOID THESE PITFALLS

❏ Don't economize by skipping a yearly furnace tune-up.

❏ Don't install filters backwards; they're marked to indicate proper orientation.

Home heating systems tend to fail at the least convenient time—usually, on Saturday night when the temperature is below freezing. Some timely preventative maintenance, however, can prevent such failures.

When most people think about forced-air heat, the first thing that comes to mind is the furnace. But any hot-air heating system, whether oil- or gas-fired, has certain other basic parts in common. The burner burns the fuel, converting its chemical energy to heat. Within the furnace, the burning fuel heats a section of metal duct called a heat exchanger, which in turn heats air passing through. Thus, the heated air needn't mix with combustion gases.

A large, electrically powered blower forces the air through a dust filter and into the heat exchanger; a network of warm-air ducts delivers heated air to the living areas of the house through hot-air registers in the rooms. As heated air enters the living areas, it replaces the cooler room air, which is forced back to the furnace through cold-air registers and cold-air ducts. It's fed into the suction side of the blower to complete the cycle.

One or more room thermostats control the furnace's operation; they switch on the furnace when room temperature drops too low. In addition, a secondary thermostat on the furnace duct delays the blower's operation until the air in the heat exchanger warms enough to heat the rooms, and it delays the blower's shutdown until after the furnace is turned off and the air cools off to near room temperature. That arrangement minimizes cold drafts when the furnace starts and avoids wasted heat because of hot air remaining in the furnace.

Routine Maintenance Chores

Most of a furnace's routine maintenance should be performed by a technician as part of an annual checkup. A modern furnace requires precise combustion adjustments, which require specialized tools and training. Incorrect adjustments will, at the very least, lower the furnace's efficiency. It can also make the furnace generate smoke, soot, or dangerous levels of carbon monoxide, and it can even cause a fire or explosion.

A homeowner can, however, deal with certain maintenance tasks, apart from furnace combustion adjustments, safely and effectively:

Check filters at least monthly, and replace them when they become coated with dust and dirt. Hold the filter up to the light; if you can't see the light through the filter, it's time for replacement. Use the proper size filter; stock up when they're on sale. Make sure you install them with the printed arrows pointing in the direction of the airflow.

Start the season by cleaning the heating system's registers. Otherwise, the heating system will scatter dust throughout the house. Vacuum the registers, using a brush attachment. Make sure the hot-air and cold-air-return registers aren't blocked by rugs or furniture. If you have a duct-mounted humidifier, inspect it every few weeks to make sure it's clean and free of scale; check the manufacturer's cleaning instructions.

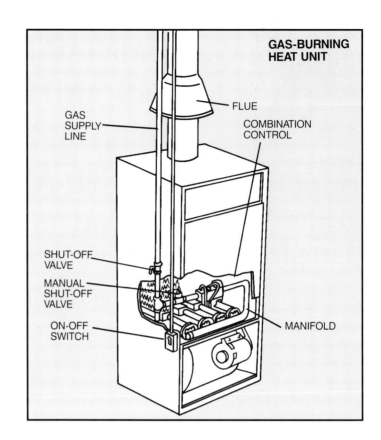

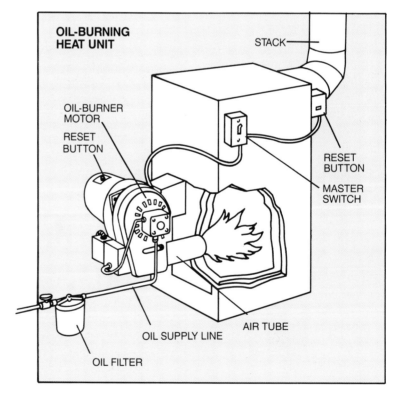

Figs. 5a and 5b. The parts of typical gas-burning and oil-burning forced-air heat units are shown here.

Checklist for Chimneys Serving Gas- or Oil-fired Heating Systems

☐ Before you turn on the heat for the season, check the chimney for blockages with a pair of binoculars.

☐ Check the joints for gaps where the flue pipes from the furnace or water heater join the chimney. Caulk the gaps with furnace cement.

☐ Inspect brick chimneys for loose mortar, and repoint if necessary.

Blowers and Motors

A technician should lubricate the furnace's blower and blower motor and adjust the tension of the drive belt as part of the annual tune-up. That's no guarantee, however, that the blower and drive belt won't need further attention that season. If the blower becomes noisy, or if the airflow from the hot-air registers seems weak, inspect those parts.

Blowers and blower motors are generally located behind an access panel at the base of the furnace. If the blower motor drives the blower directly, with no intermediate belt drive, there's not much you can do except lubricate. Turn off the furnace at its main power switch before you do any work on a blower; you wouldn't want it to start while you're

working. With a direct-drive blower, proceed as follows:

1. Partially remove the blower from its housing **(Figure 6)**; that's usually necessary to get at its oil cups, which are at the visible end of the blower motor.

2. Open the oil cups and add 6 to 8 drops of electric-motor oil into each (check the manufacturer's manual for the weight of oil recommended).

3. Slide the blower back into its housing and replace any screws you may have had to remove.

4. If there are no oil cups, the motor has a sealed lubrication system and doesn't require oiling.

Belt-driven fans require more maintenance **(Figure 8)** than do direct-drive models, but the task is easier to perform.

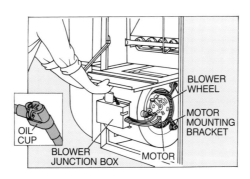

Fig. 6. To oil the motor of a direct-drive blower, turn off the power to the furnace, as well as the gas-supply valve if the furnace is gas-fired. Remove the access panels from the blower and the furnace. Loosen the screws securing the blower shelf, and slide the blower partially out, until you can see the end of the motor. Be careful not to damage or disconnect any wires. If there are oil cups, add six to eight drops of electric-motor oil to each cup. If there aren't, the motor is sealed and doesn't need lubrication.

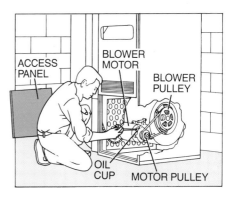

Fig. 7. Belt-driven blower motors are accessible for lubrication once you remove the blower access panel. If there are oil cups or grease fittings, they'll be at the ends of the motor. To lubricate grease fittings, use an automotive grease gun to deliver two full pumps of general-purpose automotive grease.

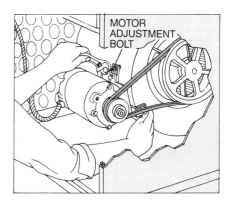

Fig. 8. To check the tension of the belt driving the blower, press hard with a finger at a point halfway between the two pulleys. The belt should deflect about ³/₄ inch (19mm). If it's too loose, turn the motor-adjustment bolt clockwise; if it's too tight, turn the bolt the other way. Replace a belt that's worn or frayed. Recheck the tension of a new belt after two weeks.

1. Make sure that the nuts and bolts securing the blower and motor are tight.

2. Check the belt's tension: Press on the belt about midway between the two pulleys **(Figure 8)**. You should be able to deflect it by about ¾ inch (19mm). If the belt is too tight or too loose, readjust it by means of a motor-mount adjustment bolt.

3. If the belt is worn, cracked, or frayed, replace it.

4. If the pulleys don't line up properly, loosen the setscrew of the pulley on the motor shaft, and slide it back and forth until the belt runs true **(Figures 9a and 9b)**. Retighten the setscrew.

Checklist for Forced-Air Systems

❏ Replace or clean the filter in forced-air furnaces monthly during the heating season.

❏ Before turning on the furnace for the season, have a technician tune it up and make precise combustion adjustments. Don't try to do that job yourself.

❏ Vacuum both the hot-air and cold-air return registers, using a brush attachment. Make sure registers aren't blocked by rugs or furniture.

❏ Every few weeks, make sure duct-mounted humidifiers are clean and free of scale buildup.

❏ Inspect hot-air supply and return ducts for leaks; use duct tape for repairs.

❏ If heat is distributed unevenly from room to room, balance the system by adjusting the dampers within the ducts.

Belt-driven fans and their motors, like their direct-drive counterparts, sometimes come with sealed lubrication. More commonly, though, there are oil cups or grease fittings at each end of the motor and blower. If there are oil cups, add 6 to 8 drops of electric-motor oil to each cup; if there are grease fittings instead of cups, lubricate them with an automotive grease gun.

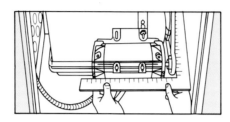

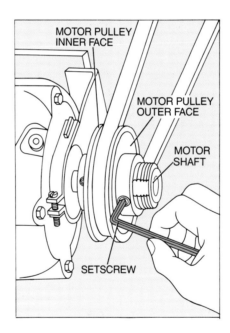

Figs. 9a & 9b. The pulleys on the motor and the blower should line up along the same plane to avoid excess wear on the fan belt. Use a large square or yardstick to check alignment. If the pulleys need adjustment, loosen the set screw locking the pulley to the motor shaft, and slide the pulley along the shaft until it lines up with the blower-shaft pulley. Tighten the setscrew, and recheck the alignment.

Balancing a Hot-Air System

All too often, forced-air heat leaves some rooms too cold and some too warm. The process of reducing the flow of hot air to the overly warm rooms and increasing the flow to cooler areas is called balancing.

It's best done by adjusting dampers—metal plates that pivot inside the ducts, partially blocking airflow. You adjust a damper with a handle on the outside of the duct **(Figure 10)**. It's tempting to try to balance a system with the adjustable louvers found in most registers, but you're better off using those only to control the direction in which warm air leaves the register.

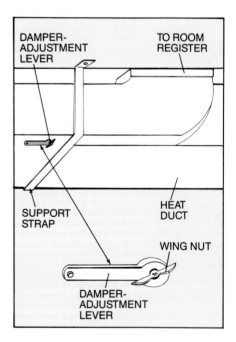

Fig. 10. Most forced-air heating systems have adjustable dampers in the ductwork between the furnace and the registers so you can balance the heat in various rooms. In some installations, the dampers are at the point where each duct leaves the furnace's hot-air hood, or *plenum;* in others they are in the ductwork near each room.

Balancing a heating system is an easy but time-consuming chore, since it may take as long as eight hours for a room's temperature to stabilize after an adjustment. If subsequent adjustments are necessary, a complete balancing job could take as long as a week. Luckily, it's usually a one-time job unless you perform a major house remodeling.

Do your balancing during cold weather, starting with the hottest room (probably the one closest to the furnace).

1. Partially close the damper in the duct supplying that room **(Figure 10)**. That will divert some of the hot air to other, cooler rooms.
2. Measure the temperature in that room after four hours, using a thermometer held at waist level; repeat the measurement every hour until the room's temperature has stabilized.
3. Repeat the process with the next overheated room, continuing until you've gone through the whole house, room by room.
4. If you reach a room that's still too cool, open the damper as wide as possible.
5. When you're done with all the rooms, go back to the first room you did, and repeat the process for all the rooms, making minor adjustments to fine-tune the system.
6. When you're done, mark each damper's final position with a marking pen.

When you're finished and you no longer have any overheated rooms, you may still have a room that doesn't receive enough heat. Two solutions are possible: Install a booster blower in the duct feeding that room; or, if you have a belt-driven blower, increase the blower speed (and the airflow) by changing the size of one of the pulleys. Call a technician to do either of those tasks.

MAINTAINING HOT-WATER AND STEAM SYSTEMS

Tools and Materials:

Screwdriver or radiator key; vacuum cleaner; wide-jaw locking pliers; blocks or shim material; garden hose.

Hot-water or steam systems, collectively referred to as hydronic systems, provide reliable and draft-free heat. However, they are much less common than they once were, before the introduction of central air-conditioning in the 1950s. That's because central air-conditioning is much cheaper to install in a house that already has ductwork in place for a forced-air heating system.

Like any heating system, hydronic systems benefit from regular maintenance. An annual checkup or tune-up of the gas or oil burner unit and the boiler, performed by a technician, is the cornerstone of a regular maintenance program, taking care of the portion of the system that converts fuel to heat. However, you must still deal with those parts of the system that deliver the heat to the house.

SAFETY FIRST

❑ Don't try to adjust the flame or draft in a gas or oil furnace. The job requires the special tools and skills of a technician.

AVOID THESE PITFALLS

❑ When cleaning convectors, don't bend or damage the fins.
❑ Even small leaks in hydronic-system plumbing can cause major damage. If you notice a leak, or if the automatic water supply valve feeding your boiler operates frequently, call a technician.

Hot-Water Systems

Hot-water systems are the most popular type of hydronic system. The burner's flame heats water that's pumped out of the boiler by a circulator pump. The hot water travels through pipes to radiators or convectors, which heat the air in the various rooms. The cooled water is piped back to the boiler, where the cycle begins again.

If a radiator is cooler at the top than at the bottom, trapped air is probably blocking circulation of hot water. Release the trapped air by loosening the air-bleed valve near one of the radiator's top corners **(Figure 11)**. Use a screwdriver or special wrench called a radiator key to turn the valve until you hear the hiss of escaping air. Loosen the valve slowly and not too wide; the water in the radiator is under pressure, and a flood could result. Close the valve tightly when air no longer escapes.

Convectors—the long heat-exchangers usually mounted on a room's baseboard—consist of finned sections of pipe inside a housing. Dust that collects on the fins can seriously reduce heating efficiency; vacuum them at least once a year. If the fins are bent, straighten them with locking pliers **(Figure 12)**.

Most convectors have a built-in damper that you can use to balance the heat throughout the house. For more complete control, many hot-water systems also provide flow-control valves in the pipes supplying the convectors. If your convectors don't have flow-control valves, ask your technician whether such valves can be installed in your system.

Fig. 11. A radiator that's hotter at the bottom than the top needs bleeding to remove trapped air at the top. Use a screwdriver or a special key sold at hardware stores to loosen the bleeder valve. When the air is eliminated, water will start to spurt out. When that happens, close the valve.

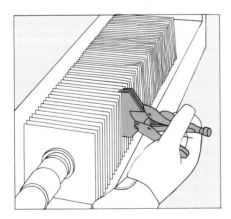

Fig. 12. Under the removable covers of baseboard convectors are finned copper pipes. If the fins are bent, carefully straighten them with wide-jaw locking pliers.

Checklist for Hot-Water Systems

- ❏ Before the start of the heating season, have a technician tune up the gas or oil burner unit and the boiler.
- ❏ If radiators or convectors heat unevenly, release trapped air by carefully loosening the air bleed valve.
- ❏ Vacuum convectors to remove dust at least once a year.
- ❏ If your convectors don't have flow-control valves, have a technician install them.

Steam Systems

A steam-heat system doesn't require a circulator pump since the steam reaches the radiators through its own pressure. Most steam radiators use a single pipe both to carry steam from the boiler to the radiator and to carry condensed water back to the boiler. Instead of a bleed valve, a steam radiator has an automatic vent valve at one end. It allows air to escape, but not steam or water. If a steam radiator isn't uniformly hot, remove the vent and listen for escaping air **(Figure 13)**; if you hear the characteristic hiss, replace the vent. If you don't, it means the steam isn't getting into the radiator. Make sure the inlet valve is open.

Many steam radiators bang and clang when the boiler starts operating. That's because accumulated water in the radiator interferes with steam circulation. To drain the water, slip shims under the vent end of the radiator until the radiator is pitched downward toward the supply pipe

(Figure 14). That allows water to drain into the supply pipe.

In a steam-heat system, the most effective way to balance the heat output from room to room is with ther-

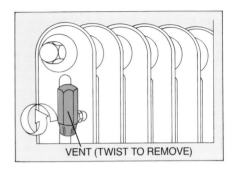

VENT (TWIST TO REMOVE)

Fig. 13. A steam-radiator vent should allow air to escape while retaining the steam. If the radiator heats unevenly, air is probably trapped inside. Unscrew the vent shortly after the heat is turned on to release the air. If air escapes, followed after a short while by steam, the vent is faulty. Take the old vent to a plumbing-supply store to make sure you get the right replacement.

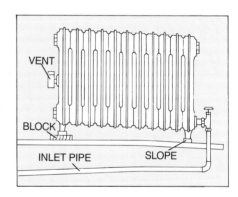

Fig. 14. Clanging in a steam radiator is usually caused by condensed water trapped in the radiator. The cure is simple: Raise the vent end of the radiator with shims until the slope toward the inlet valve is sufficient for the water to run out.

mostatic valves. They shut off the flow of steam to individual radiators when the room temperature reaches a preset level. Most large heating-supply distributors sell them.

Checklist for Steam Systems

❏ If a steam radiator doesn't become uniformly hot, remove the vent and listen for escaping air. If you don't hear a hiss, check to see that the inlet valve is open.

❏ Check that radiators are pitched downward toward the supply pipe; if they aren't, slip shims under the vent end of the radiator.

❏ Have thermostatic valves installed on radiators that don't already have them. They shut off the flow of steam to individual radiators when the temperature in a room reaches a preset level.

Zoned Systems

Since you may not need to keep all the rooms in the house at the same temperature at all times, a house is frequently divided into different heating zones controlled by separate thermostats. Most zoned heating systems use a single circulating pump; they control the flow of water to the various zones with electrically operated zone valves at the boiler. If you have a zoned heating system and one of the zones is cold, turn the thermostat serving that zone all the way up to make sure it's calling for heat. If it is, and the boiler is operating, the problem is probably in the zone valve supplying that particular zone.

Maintaining the Boiler

While burner and draft adjustments are best left to a technician, you can handle some routine maintenance of the boiler and its associated equipment.

Look for a draincock near the base of the boiler. Once a year, at the beginning of the heating season, draw a little water from that draincock into a glass jar and examine it. If the water appears unusually rusty, flush the boiler **(Figure 15)**.

1. Turn off the main power switch to an oil burner. If you heat with gas, turn off the gas-supply valve and the pilot light (or the power switch, if your unit has electronic ignition).

2. Screw one end of a garden hose to the draincock and lead the other end to a drain.

3. Open the draincock fully. Water will enter the boiler from the

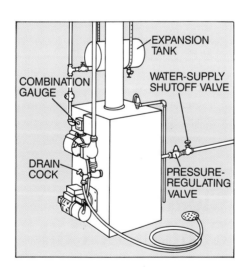

Fig. 15. To flush a boiler, turn off the power to the system and wait until the water in the boiler cools to 80°F (27°C), as shown on the combination gauge. Run a garden hose from the draincock to a floor drain or sink, and flush the boiler until the water from the hose runs clear.

automatic fill valve, pass through the boiler, and out through the drain.

4. When the water leaving the hose is free of rust, close the draincock to allow the boiler to fill completely.

5. Restart the furnace.

Because water expands when heated, a boiler system has an expansion tank that's partially filled with air. It acts as a cushion to accommodate variations in water volume. On older boilers, it's simply a cylindrical tank that's about half full of water. With time, such tanks may fill with water and lose their effectiveness. Water on the floor beneath the boiler's pressure-relief valve means it's time to drain the expansion tank. Shut off the inlet valve to the expansion tank and open the draincock at the bottom of the tank. Catch the water in a bucket or lead it to a nearby drain with a garden hose.

Many new boilers use a smaller expansion tank with a rubber diaphragm separating the water from the air. If one of those fills up with water, the diaphragm is ruptured and the tank must be replaced.

Checklist for Boilers

❏ At the beginning of the heating season, draw water from the boiler's draincock and check for unusual amounts of rust. Flush the boiler, if necessary.

❏ Inspect the boiler floor beneath the pressure-relief valve. If water is present, drain the expansion tank.

❏ Periodically check the water-level gauge and add water to the boiler, if necessary.

MAINTAINING AIR CONDITIONERS

Tools and Materials:

For central air-conditioning systems: Screwdriver; soft paintbrush; vacuum cleaner with brush attachment; putty knife; wire brush; fresh filters (if required); mineral spirits; steel wool.

Air conditioners are remarkably trouble-free appliances. Maintenance consists mainly of simple cleaning and replacement of filters. Newer air conditioners have permanently lubricated fans and motors, but older ones—those with oil cups—can benefit from a yearly oiling. If you live in a climate with a winter season, you should also winterize the air conditioner in the fall and prep it for start-up in the late spring. This section covers maintenance of both central-system and room air conditioners.

Central Air-Conditioning Systems

Tools and Materials:

For systems with condensate pumps: Condenser cover.

If you have a central air conditioner, odds are it shares ducting, blower, and filter with your forced hot-air furnace. A condenser unit is mounted outside the house, and an evaporator coil is located in the ductwork, or plenum, immediately above the furnace. The condenser and evaporator are connected by runs of metal tubing.

Checklist for Central Air-Conditioning Systems

- ❏ Keep condenser-unit vents free of leaves and grass. Make sure nothing blocks the top grille.
- ❏ Once each season, open the condenser and clean the coils, after making sure the power of the unit is switched off. Also, clean the evaporator coil inside the furnace plenum.
- ❏ Change or clean the furnace filters monthly during the cooling season.
- ❏ Cover the condensing unit in the winter to keep out dirt, ice, and vermin.
- ❏ In the spring, turn on the power to the unit at least 24 hours before you start it up; that vaporizes any refrigerant that has condensed and prevents damage to the compressor.

Cleaning the Condenser Coil

The condenser unit generally has a fan that exhausts through a grille on top of the case, and one or more mesh side panels that let in air. Make sure the side vents are

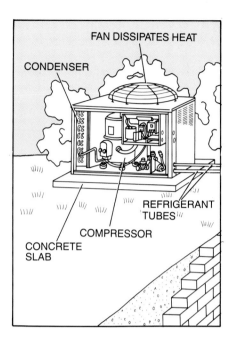

Fig. 16. This illustration shows a typical central air-conditioning system.

free of leaves and grass and nothing blocks the top grille. If air can't flow freely through the condenser, the air conditioner's effectiveness drops drastically.

Once a season, open the condenser and clean the coils: The covers either snap off or are fastened with screws. Before you open any enclosure, though, make sure the power to the air conditioner is switched off. Besides the hazard of spinning fan blades, central air conditioners operate at much higher voltages than do most home appliances, and exposed live wiring poses the threat of electrocution.

Coils have delicate fins to help cool them. Treat the fins gently when you clean them; use a soft paintbrush to loosen the dirt, and vacuum away the debris. Caked grime on fans and blowers calls for harsher measures such as a putty knife or wire brush.

Maintenance at the Furnace

Clean the evaporator coil with a soft brush and vacuum. To reach the coil, remove the access panel on the furnace plenum. Again, use a careful touch to avoid damaging the fins.

Next, change or clean the filter—the one you deal with during the heating season. If it's the washable type, wash it in warm, soapy water and rinse. Check the manufacturer's recommendations; permanent filters can often be washed in the dishwasher.

Changing the filter will be the last maintenance step for most homeowners—unless your system isn't hooked into a condensate drain. The condensate drain disposes of the water that condenses when warm, moist air from the house passes over the cold evaporator coil. While most installations direct that water to a floor drain, a few collect the water in a catch container equipped with a pump that's controlled by a float switch. When several inches of water collect in the container, the switch actuates the pump, which pumps the water out through a hose to a remotely located drain.

Condensate pumps are reliable, but they require occasional cleaning and oiling. Proceed as follows:

1. Turn off the power to the pump (often, that's simply a matter of pulling the plug).
2. Remove the screws that secure the pump, and lift out the entire pump and switch assembly.
3. Clean the fan with a rag soaked in kerosene or mineral spirits.
4. If the plate attached to the pump calls for oiling, do so, following the instructions.
5. Make sure the float moves up and down freely; if it binds, pol-ish the rod with steel wool.
6. Reassemble, making sure the power cord doesn't dip into the condensed water.

Winterizing the Unit

Cover the condensing unit of a central system to keep out dirt, ice, and vermin. In the spring, when you put the air conditioner back into service, turn on the power at least 24 hours before you start up the unit. That activates an automatic heater in the air conditioner that vaporizes any refrigerant that may have condensed over the winter. Running an air conditioner with liquid refrigerant in the compressor can damage the compressor.

Window Air Conditioners

Tools and Materials:

For room air conditioners: Replacement filters (if required); covers for both outside and inside; spirit level; foam insulation strips; floor fan.

SAFETY FIRST

- ❑ Room air conditioners are heavy; make sure they're supported securely in the window opening. If you're not sure you can handle the weight, get some help.
- ❑ Make sure the main power switch for a central air conditioner is off before you open any enclosure. The 240 volts these units operate on present a severe shock hazard.

Checklist for Window Air Conditioners

- ❑ Change or clean the filter once a month during the cooling season.
- ❑ At the end of the cooling season, remove the air conditioner from the window, or cover the outdoor portion of the air conditioner with a snug-fitting cover. Also, cover the inside portion of the air conditioner with a snug-fitting cover to keep out cold air. In the spring, remove the covers before starting up the unit.
- ❑ When reinstalling the air conditioner in the spring, check the support brackets to make sure they are securely fastened.
- ❑ Use a spirit level to ensure a slight tilt downward toward the outside. That prevents condensed water and rain from dripping inside the room.
- ❑ Insulate the installation with a strip of foam between the lower sash and the top of the air conditioner. Also, fill any large gaps around the case of the air conditioner.

Maintenance of these units is generally limited to changing or cleaning the filter, though the exposed condenser coils at the back can benefit from an occasional cleaning if you can reach them.

To keep your air conditioner in good working order, remove it from the window at the end of the cooling season and store it in a safe place. If that isn't possible, cover the outdoor portion with a snug-fitting waterproof cover. A cover protects the air conditioner, and it keeps out cold drafts through the air conditioner's vents. Even when the vents are closed, most window air conditioners are far from airtight. It's wise to cover the inside portion of the air conditioner, too, to further reduce drafts. In the spring, remove the covers before you start up the unit.

If you take the air conditioner out of the window for the winter, there are a few things to remember when you reinstall it in the spring:

❏ Make sure the support brackets are solid and securely fastened **(Figure 17)**.

❏ Use a spirit level to adjust the air conditioner so it has a slight tilt downward toward the outside; that way, condensing water won't drip into the room.

❏ Slip a strip of foam insulation between the lower sash and the top of the air conditioner before you lower that sash **(Figure 19)**.

❏ To close large gaps around the air conditioner, cut wood filler pieces **(Figure 20)**. Stuff any remaining gaps with flexible foam insulation.

While most window air conditioners have enough cooling capacity to handle more than one room, they lack the ability to circulate cool air effectively enough to reach the far corners of a second room. If the capacity of your unit is sufficient to cool an adjacent room, try using a floor fan as a booster to get more effective air movement. Or, if you have a forced-air furnace, you may be able to use a large window air conditioner as a "central" cooler by locating it near a return register. Turning on the furnace blower will distribute cool air through the heating ducts to the entire house.

AVOID THESE PITFALLS

❏ Tilt a window air conditioner downward slightly, away from the house, so condensation doesn't drip into the room.

❏ Don't let leaves and debris or weeds block the air vents of a central air conditioner's condenser.

❏ When you clean the coils of an air conditioner, don't bend the delicate fins.

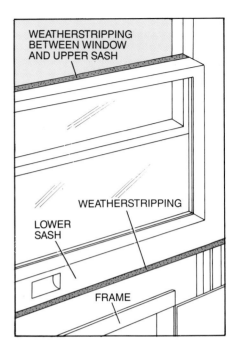

Fig. 19. Install foam insulation between window and upper sash and below lower sash.

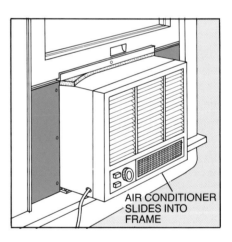

Fig. 20. If side panels supplied with air conditioner leave gaps, cut wood filler pieces to fit.

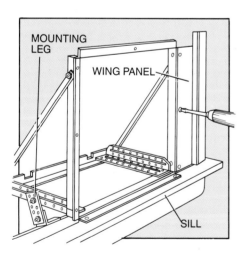

Fig. 17. Air conditioners that extend more than a foot beyond the sill require mounting brackets (usually supplied with the unit) for a secure installation. Use a spirit level to adjust the air conditioner so it tilts downward slightly toward the outside.

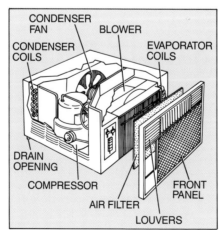

Fig. 18. This illustration shows a typical window air conditioner.

Dealing With Thermostat Problems

Tools and Materials:

Brush or vacuum; emery paper; spirit level; screwdriver.

SAFETY FIRST

❏ Most thermostats handle only very low voltages, but some—particularly those controlling electric heaters or attic fans—carry dangerously high voltages. Turn off the power at the circuit breaker before you open a thermostat's case.

If the furnace is the heart of a home heating system, the thermostat is the brain. It senses the temperature in a room, and it turns the furnace on or off to maintain a predetermined temperature.

Most thermostats "anticipate" when the furnace should be shut down and do so before the set temperature is reached; similarly, they start the furnace before the room temperature drops below the set point, to compensate for the heating system's delay in supplying heat once the furnace is on. Some thermostats incorporate clocks to automatically lower the temperature during parts of the day when heat isn't required. And some thermostats control both heating and air-conditioning.

Despite the many tasks they handle, most thermostats have relatively few parts. Aside from an occasional dusting, they don't need much routine maintenance. If something does go wrong, your living area will become too hot or too cold.

Most thermostats use a bimetallic coil—a thin two-layered metal band wound into a spiral, like an old-fashioned clock spring. The two layers are made of different metals; since different metals expand and contract at different rates when heated and cooled, the coil loosens or tightens as the room temperature changes. One end of the coil is permanently attached to the thermostat's body; the other end operates an On/Off switch as the coil opens or closes.

Problems With the Switch

Some thermostats, older ones in particular, have one contact on the coil and another on the thermostat body. When the coil expands, the contacts open. That design allows dust and dirt to settle on the contacts. If you have a thermostat of that type, remove the cover every month or so and brush or vacuum the interior **(Figure 22)**. If the thermostat stops working, the contacts may be corroded. Turn off the power, remove the cover, and clean the contacts with a piece of emery paper or an automobile point file. The contacts may need cleaning even if you dust regularly.

In modern thermostats, a sealed mercury switch usually replaces the open contact switch. The sealed switch consists of a small glass vial containing a bit of liquid mercury into which two wires protrude. Tipped one way, the mercury flows away from the wires, breaking the circuit; tipped the other way, the mercury touches both wires and allows electric current to pass.

Mercury switches are immune to contamination by dust and grime. They have one problem, however, that isn't shared by the open contact switches: A mercury-switch thermostat that isn't precisely level will activate the switch too early or too late, depending on which way the thermostat is tilted **(Figure 21)**. If a mercury-switch thermostat seems to maintain an incorrect temperature, turn off the power, remove the thermostat cover, and check for level mounting with a spirit level or plumb line. You can make a plumb line by holding one end of a thin string and tying a small weight to the other end. The weight will pull the string straight down to a vertical position, making a vertical line against which to align the thermostat case.

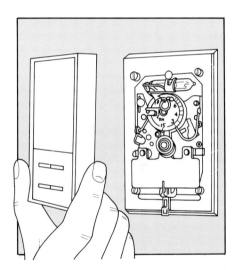

Fig. 21. A mercury switch must be mounted absolutely level if it's to maintain the proper temperature.

AVOID THESE PITFALLS

☐ Don't treat the inner parts of a thermostat roughly; a delicate touch is needed for dusting and cleaning.

☐ If you're filing the points on an open-contact thermostat, don't bend the contacts.

☐ Don't buy an automatic clock thermostat with more programming capability than you need. You'll pay more and have to deal with more complex programming.

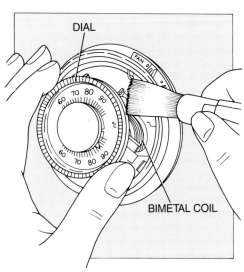

Fig. 22. If your thermostat isn't one of the new all-electronic models, it has a bimetallic coil. It will benefit from cleaning every month or so. Remove the cover, and gently brush dust and grime from the coil. Rotating the thermostat from its lowest to its highest setting will help loosen dirt, but don't forget to return it to its previous setting.

Checklist for Thermostats

☐ With a bimetallic-coil type thermostat, remove the cover every month and vacuum the interior. If the thermostat stops working, turn off the power; then clean the contacts with a piece of emery paper.

☐ If you have problems with a mercury-switch thermostat, check the level of the mounting with a spirit level.

☐ If room temperatures never reach the preset level or if the furnace cycles on and off frequently, turn off the power and adjust the anticipator.

☐ Check for loose wires; if necessary, tighten the screw terminals.

☐ Move lamps and TVs away from air-conditioning-system thermostats; the heat from those appliances could make the air conditioner switch on unnecessarily.

☐ Make sure furniture doesn't block the registers.

Problems With the Anticipator

Thermostats turn the furnace on at one temperature and off at another, higher temperature. That temperature difference—called "deadband"—is necessary for effective thermostat operation. Without the deadband, the furnace would be chattering on and off rapidly as the room temperature varied by tiny amounts.

Besides a deadband, many thermostats have an anticipator—a small electric heater in the thermostat that goes on whenever the furnace does. As a result, the thermostat coil senses a temperature somewhat higher than the room temperature whenever the thermostat is calling for heat. The result is that the thermostat's switch turns off the furnace a bit before the room reaches the desired temperature. Even after the furnace goes off, though, the blower or pump continues to supply heat to the room for a while, allowing the room temperature to rise to that set on the thermostat.

Many anticipators are adjustable to compensate for differences in heating systems. If the anticipator in your thermostat is set too high, the room may never reach the desired temperature. If the anticipator is set too low, the furnace may "short-cycle," switching on and off every few minutes. Thermostats come with anticipators preset for a typical heating system. Making adjustments isn't difficult, but it calls for a bit of trial and error.

1. Turn off the power to the furnace.

2. Open the thermostat cover and look inside for a lever that moves a metal slide along a flat coil of wire **(Figure 23)**. There will generally be a label indicating which direction to move this lever to achieve longer cycles. (If you can't find an anticipator adjustment, there may not be one. Some thermostats use fixed anticipators.)

3. Move the lever a quarter-inch (6mm) or so in the appropriate direction: toward "longer" if your furnace is short-cycling or the other way if the room doesn't reach the preset temperature.

4. Replace the cover, turn on the power, and see what happens.

5. Repeat as necessary.

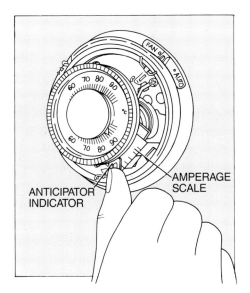

Fig. 23. The anticipator controls how long the furnace remains on when heat is called for. If your home cools down too much before the furnace goes on and heats up too much before it shuts off, move the anticipator's control lever toward the end of the scale labeled "shorter." If your furnace cycles on and off frequently, use a "longer" anticipator setting.

Other Problems

Most other problems with simple thermostats are caused by improperly placed covers that jam the coil or by loose wires. If wires are loose, tighten the screw terminals.

A thermostat that's mounted on a cold wall may respond to the wall temperature instead of the room temperature. The best solution is to relocate the thermostat. If that isn't feasible, insulate the thermostat with a pad of foam plastic or rubber 1/4-inch (6mm) thick and mount it with longer bolts.

Thermostats don't usually wear out; many home thermostats are still going strong after 25 years or more. You may want to replace an old thermostat, though, just to take advantage of some of the features the newer ones offer.

Automatic Clock Thermostats

Automatic clock thermostats let you turn down the heat at night and wake up to a warm house. More sophisticated ones, called electronic setback thermostats, let you set different heating schedules for weekdays and weekends, while still fancier ones permit a different program—each involving several different on/off periods—for each day of the week. If you have central air-condi-tioning, you can buy an automatic thermostat that offers the same kinds of programming for both heating and cooling.

Older clock thermostats were a problem to install; they needed four wires: two to power the clock and two to control the furnace. (The old non-automatic thermostats had only two control wires.) Newer automatic models use a battery to run the clock, and they're installed with two wires. If you decide to buy one, make sure batteries are readily available. Some models require special batteries that must be mail-ordered from the manufacturer.

An automatic clock thermostat can easily reduce your heating bill by 15 to 30 percent, depending on how many hours each day you keep the temperature down. For years, debates have raged about whether turning down the temperature sharply at night wastes energy because of the severe demands on the system to reheat the house. The answer is simple: As long as your heating system can rewarm the house adequately, the lower you set the nighttime temperature and the longer you leave it lowered, the more money you'll save.

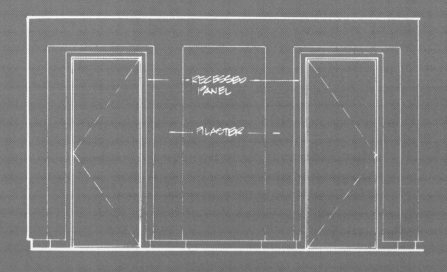

RECESSED
PANEL

PILASTER

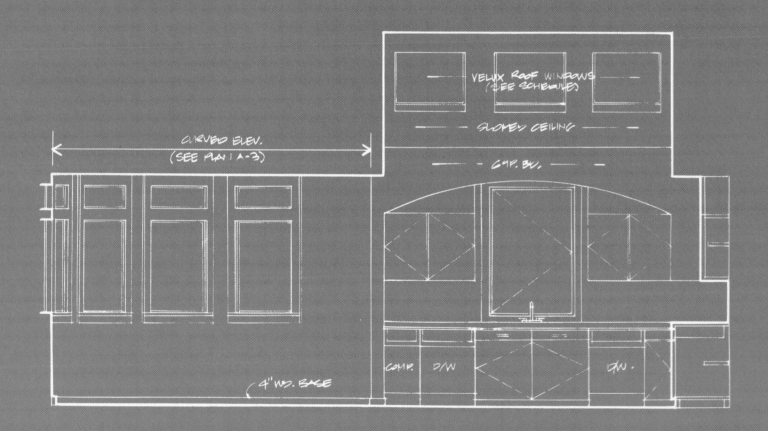

VELUX ROOF WINDOWS
(SEE SCHEDULE)

SLOPED CEILING

GYP. BD.

CURVED ELEV.
(SEE PLAN A-3)

4" WD. BASE

COMP.   D/W   OV.

Chapter Seven

WALLS AND CEILINGS

Maintaining and repairing walls may seem straightforward and obvious, but it helps to know the tricks of the trade. Read the relevant sections in this chapter before you undertake a project. Using the right materials and techniques for a painting or wall-covering job or for a wall repair will extend the life of the project and possibly save you a repeat performance a year or two down the line.

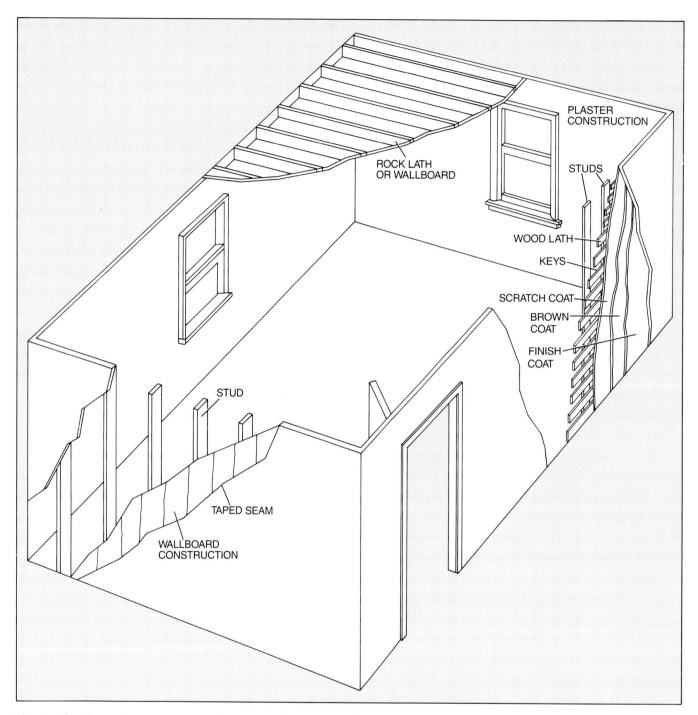

Fig. 1. This illustration shows the various types of wall and ceiling construction.

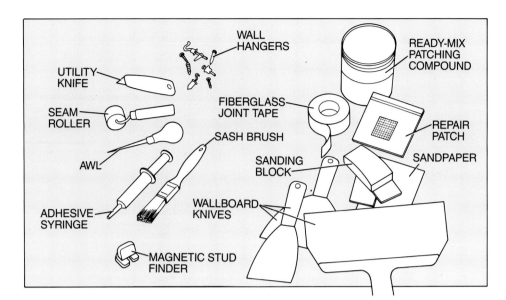

Fig. 2. Basic tools and materials for patching plaster and wallboard.

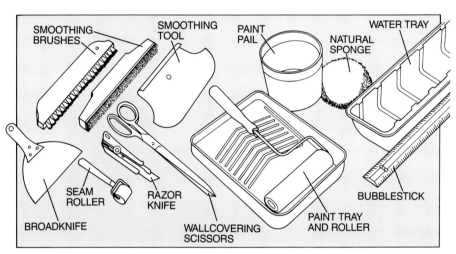

Fig. 3. Basic tools for installing wall coverings.

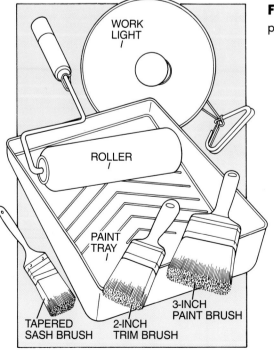

Fig. 4. Basic tools for interior painting.

TOOLS AND MATERIALS

The tools and materials you choose can greatly affect the quality of your work. Bargain tools may break or bend in midproject; cheap materials may be difficult to work or apply. For example, a patching product that is not "plasticized" may be less expensive, but it may not slip as smoothly over trowels or knives.

The difference between the cheapest and the best hand tools is usually just a couple of dollars. If you intend to do any amount of decorating and repair work, invest in quality tools.

Shop at full-service decorating stores that feature a contractor's counter, and ask for advice. Some materials are so difficult to apply that even some pros stay clear of them.

Plastering trowels, for example, are used by professionals who are adept in the use of a flat material holder called a hawk. The hawk has a bottom handle, and the blade can be piled with mortar or plaster—if you know how to handle it. For the beginner, flat tools or taping knives are a better choice. Taping knives range from a 1-inch (25mm) putty knife up to the 12-inch (1/3 meter) finish knife. When you work with those knives, you can carry the patching compound in a device called a mud pan, which looks like a bread pan with a scraper edge attached.

Use 10- and 12-inch (1/4 and 1/3 meter) knives for finishing coats of wallboard joint compound. Use a 4-inch (100mm) wide knife to tape and finish the inside corners on wallboard. A corner tool for finishing both sides of the corner at once is available, but it's difficult for an amateur to use. Instead, apply compound to one side of an inside corner, let it dry, and then apply compound to the other side.

When you select taping knives, push the tip of the knife blade against a wall and put pressure on the handle. The blade should flex without bending permanently; an overly stiff knife can't feather the edges of joints in wallboard. Look for riveted handles; the spot welds on cheaper models tend to crack when you apply pressure on the knife. Look for a tight-fitting, molded knife handle. Loose handles fill with water when you wash them, causing water to drip as you work with the knife.

Look for paintbrushes that are a blend of polyester, nylon, and natural bristles. Those all-purpose brushes are a good choice for the homeowner. Pure hog or ox bristles are necessary only for very fine varnishing or enameling, such as on furniture. Also, choose a ferrule—the metal band that secures the handle to the brush—that is noncorrosive; chrome is the most common choice. And finally, buy a brush with a handle secured by brads.

Quality brushes have bristle tips that are split on the ends to hold more paint and make application smoother. The end of the brush should be tapered or chiseled for better cutting in at corners. To test the brush, hold it in one hand and bend the bristles with the other, looking for thick, tight bristles that don't show open spaces and don't come loose.

Roller covers should have a plastic center or core; cardboard cores soften in water or latex paint and may come apart. For an all-around applicator, buy 9-inch-(1/4 meter) wide rollers, and buy roller covers with a 3/8-inch-(10mm) long synthetic nap. For very smooth surfaces, choose a 1/4-inch-(6mm) long wool or mohair nap. For painting rough or textured surfaces, buy a cover with a 1-inch-(25mm) long nap.

The roller frame should be a wire-cage construction that grips the cover without trapping paint inside. The handle should be threaded so you can attach an extension handle to reach ceilings. Spin the roller cage to be sure it moves freely; nylon bearings ensure easy operation.

Many other specialty painting tools can make your job easier: rounded paint rollers for painting pipes; mitts for painting wrought iron or for staining trim; corner rollers to eliminate brushwork; paint pads that let you cut a straight edge; and foam disposable brushes for odd touch-up jobs.

It's best to touch up paint while it's still fresh, using the same tool you used initially. Surfaces that were painted with a roller have a slightly textured finish, and touching up a spot with a brush leaves a flat patch that is noticeable.

Take the time to check out the new crop of patch products. Ready-mix patching compounds are lightweight and fast-drying and end the mess and waste of mixing. Caulks that come in preformed ropes eliminate the need for a messy caulk gun, and pre-gummed fiberglass wallboard tape goes on fast and eliminates the drying time between taping and the finish coat.

For filling a hole in the wall—once a tough job, because you had to install a backer material to prevent the patching material from falling out of the hole—there are now peel-and-stick adhesive patches with a steel-mesh center to provide strength and patching speed. Smart professionals install those steel-mesh patches on the walls, in line with the doorknobs, to prevent the knobs from banging through the walls.

INTERIOR PAINTING

Tools and Materials:

Paintbrushes; rollers and roller covers; putty knife; paint scraper(s); ladders or a scaffold; screwdrivers; paint-stir sticks (free from the paint store); liquid-sander type product; paint; masking tape; paint thinner, if required; brush cleaner, if required (latex paints need only water cleanup); canvas tarps for covering furniture, floors, or walls.

Painting is a job you can do well even if you have no experience. Latex paints, rollers, and spray-painting tools have given the do-it-yourselfer a professional edge. Still, an informed approach can make the job easier and yield better results.

AVOID THESE PITFALLS

- ❏ The most common cause of paint problems is failure to follow the application instructions on the label.
- ❏ To slow paint drying and extend working time, place a humidifier in the work area. That prevents unsightly laps in the paint that develop when paint edges dry too quickly.

SAFETY FIRST

- ❏ Don't stand on chairs or make-shift scaffold when painting. Buy, rent, or borrow ladders or scaffolding as needed.
- ❏ Observe safety notes on the paint label.
- ❏ If you paint an older house, check with the local Environmental Protection Agency or health office for advice on determining whether previous coats may be lead-based. If they are, ask those agencies for advice on safe removal of the lead-based paint.
- ❏ To avoid dust from sanding, use a liquid sander rather than sandpaper to prepare wood for painting.
- ❏ Wear a mask or use a fan for ventilation.

Latex or Oil-Base: Which Is Best?

Professional painters once scoffed at the thought of using water-base paints. But today's latex paints are the equal of oil-base paints in almost every way. Latex paints are easy to apply. And you can clean them up with water, so you don't have to buy a thinner or brush cleaner. Alkyd or oil-base paints are still preferable for wood cabinets or furniture, but for any other use, stick with the latex paints.

Paints come in a variety of sheens, or gloss ratings. Flat paints that don't reflect light are best for ceilings and problem surfaces. The other sheens, in order of glossiness, are eggshell, semigloss, and high gloss. The greater the sheen or gloss, the better the washability. High-gloss paints are used on woodwork or cabinets to stand up to frequent washing; in halls or other high-traffic areas, a washable gloss finish holds up the best.

Checklist for Interior Painting

- ❏ Choose paint that's right for the job. Paints come in a variety of sheens, or gloss ratings, as well as in oil-based or latex formulations.
- ❏ Determine whether the surface you plan to paint requires a primer coat.
- ❏ Calculate the amount of paint you'll need so you won't run out midproject.
- ❏ Keep a room-by-room painting record. List the manufacturer, the color code, its gloss rating, and whether primer was used. Save the color chip, if you have one. That information can be useful if you need to touch up or repaint a wall.
- ❏ Prepare walls thoroughly.
- ❏ Mask everything you don't want painted and move everything that's unattached out of the room.
- ❏ Use a roller with the appropriate nap for the surface you're painting and the paint you're using, as well as the proper brushes.

How Much Paint?

Measure the length and width of the room and add them. Double that number and multiply it by the ceiling height. That will give you the total area of the room. If you intend to paint the trim with a different product, such as aklyd, subtract the area (height times width) of the windows and doors.

When you have figured the space to be covered, look at the estimated coverage listed on the paint label. Most paints cover 350–400 square feet (36–40 square meters) of surface per 1 gallon (4 liters) when used on a surface that has been previously painted. Unprimed surfaces require more paint. Apply paint at the spread rate indicated on the label to be sure of long wear and complete coverage.

When to Prime?

Primers are formulated to provide a superior base for paint application. When in doubt, prime. Primer is cheaper than finish paint, and it can be tinted to match the finish paint you'll be using. So you can usually save money and get superior results by using primer for the first coat.

It's absolutely essential to prime over textured ceilings: Use a flat latex for the finish coat.

Preparing to Paint

1. Move everything that isn't nailed down out of the room: furniture, rugs, wall hangings, and drapes. It's easier to move those items than to protect them.
2. Spread a drop cloth on the floor; use a painter's canvas tarp, not lightweight plastic. When you paint a ceiling, cover the walls and furniture with plastic.
3. Use masking tape to protect surfaces such as window glass **(Figure 5)**. Consider removing double-hung windows **(Figure 6)**.
4. Remove picture hangers or nails, cabinet or door hardware, and light fixtures before starting to paint. Hardware and nails can trap paint and cause runs down the wall or door.
5. To avoid paint runs, remove doors and lay them flat for painting.
6. Use sandpaper to remove dirt and grime from the old paint finish. Use a paint-prep product or liquid sander to prepare most woodwork for painting.
7. Check roller covers to make sure the nap is appropriate for the surface and for the paint you're using. Use long-nap rollers for latex paint or for rough or textured surfaces. Use mohair or short-nap rollers for applying alkyd or varnish finishes.
8. You can use paintbrushes with synthetic fibers or bristles with any paint. For very fine finish work—when using lacquers, varnishes, or oil-base paints—you may prefer a pure-bristle brush made from hog or other animal hair.

Fig. 5. Mask anything you don't want painted. The masking paper shown has a pregummed edge for easy application. To prevent paint from soaking under the edge of the tape, press down the edge with a putty knife.

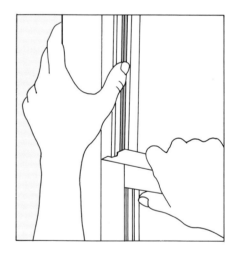

Fig. 6. Double-hung windows are removable: press against the spring-loaded side and pull outward on the sash to remove it for painting. Set the sash on a bench or sawhorse.

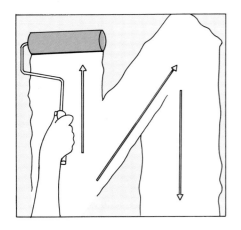

Fig. 7. Apply paint by moving the roller in a W-pattern, then roll horizontally to distribute the paint evenly. Finish by rolling in one direction, from the top of the wall downward.

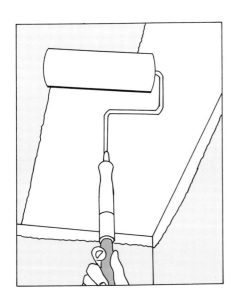

Fig. 8. Use a roller and extension handle to roll the ceiling while standing on the floor. That's faster and safer than using a ladder or scaffold.

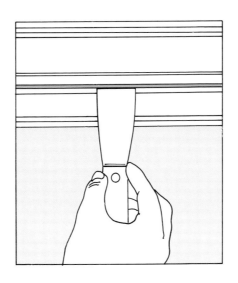

Fig. 9. To prevent windows from sticking, move them while they're drying. Move the wet upper sash with a putty knife.

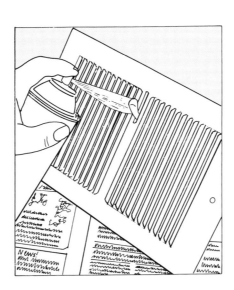

Fig. 10. Remove and spray-paint outlet covers and registers. Aerosol paint provides a smoother finish than rolled or brushed-on paint.

PATCHING PLASTER AND WALLBOARD

Tools and Materials:

Premixed wallboard taping compound; adhesive patches with foil centers; wallboard tape; scraps of wallboard; latex bonding agent; assorted taping knives; sponge or wallboard wet sander.

AVOID THESE PITFALLS

- ❑ Most wall and ceiling cracks are caused by movement of the framing as humidity and temperature change. Simply filling cracks with patch plaster or spackle will allow cracks to recur. For a permanent patch, tape and finish cracks as you would joints in wallboard.
- ❑ Match the width of the patching tool to the job. Using a patching tool that is too wide spreads the patch area beyond the damage and makes it hard to conceal with paint. Using a patching tool that is too narrow leaves extra tool marks as you move the tool over the patch area.

Checklist for Patching Walls and Ceilings

- ❏ Buy materials that make wallboard patching jobs easy. Use premixed taping compounds and peel-and-stick adhesive patches with metal foil centers for repairing holes.
- ❏ Use a latex bonding agent to patch holes in plaster. The bonding agent helps the new patch stick to the old plaster.
- ❏ When installing wallboard, use wallboard adhesive along with wallboard screws driven by a screw gun.
- ❏ Install wallboard perpendicular to the framing.
- ❏ Avoid placing wallboard joints at the corners of windows or doors so the joints don't crack.
- ❏ Maintain an even temperature in the work area when installing and finishing wallboard.
- ❏ Use joint tape when finishing joints.
- ❏ Prime new wallboard only with latex primer.
- ❏ Work with a partner when installing wallboard.

P lastering a wall is a difficult skill to learn, but patching it is easier than ever, thanks to new repair materials developed for the novice.

Premixed wallboard taping compounds, for example, are available in 1-, 2-, and 5-gallon (4-, 8-, and 20-liter) pails, for large patching projects. They eliminate the mess associated with mixing powder compounds. Another boon for beginners is the peel-and-stick adhesive patch with metal foil center for repairing holes **(Figure 11)**. Once the patch is in place, you simply cover it with one

SAFETY FIRST

- ❏ Wear a dust mask when removing plaster or wallboard. Older wall materials may contain substances that are dangerous to inhale. If you suspect that the wall or ceiling material may contain asbestos, call your regional Environmental Protection Agency for advice.
- ❏ Don't use sandpaper to smooth repair areas. Use a sponge or wallboard wet sander.

or two coats of spackle or wallboard compound and smooth it with a damp sponge **(Figure 12)**.

Holes in plaster or wallboard that are too large for adhesive patches require the following patching technique:

1. Cut away the damaged area **(Figure 13)**.

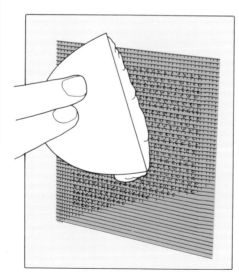

Fig. 11. Adhesive patches are available in a variety of sizes. Peel off the backing and position the patch over the hole. The metal foil center prevents the patch from sagging. Spread spackle or wallboard compound over the patch; allow it to dry, and apply a second coat, if necessary.

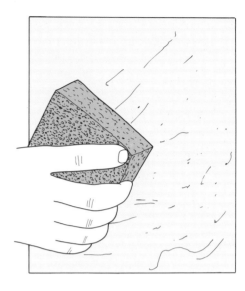

Fig. 12. When the patching compound is firm but not completely dry, smooth the repair area with a damp sponge or wallboard wet sander.

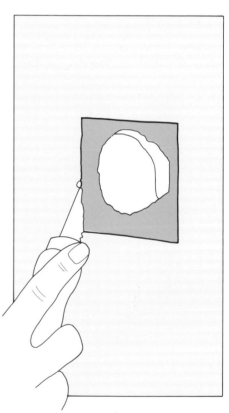

Fig. 13. If the hole is large, mark a square around the damaged area. Cut away the damaged portion with a wallboard saw or a saber saw.

2. Cut a backing strip or strips from scrap wallboard and install them in the hole, behind the damaged area **(Figure 14)**.

3. Cut a patch from scrap wallboard, and use hot glue or taping compound to hold the patch against the backing strip **(Figure 15)**. You can buy wallboard in half-sheet sizes at home centers. Or ask at any construction site; you can usually have scrap wallboard for the asking.

4. Tape and finish cracks as you would finish joints in wallboard **(Figure 16)**. If you don't reinforce the cracks with wallboard tape, they'll open up when the temperature or humidity level changes.

Holes in plaster often occur when the plaster breaks loose from the lath. Simply patching the hole doesn't work, since the patch will break loose while it's drying. To prevent that,

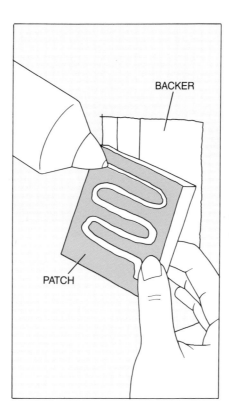

Fig. 15. Apply adhesive to the back of the patch and press it against the backing strip.

paint the lath and the edges of the plaster with a latex bonding agent, available from home centers **(Figure 17)**. Then trowel spackle or patch plaster into the hole until the patch is level, and smooth it with a wet sponge **(Figure 18)**.

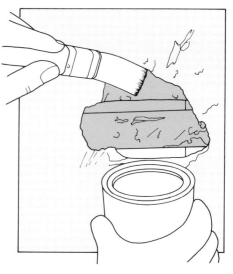

Fig. 17. When you patch a plaster wall, brush latex bonder on the lath and edges of the plaster to prevent excessive shrinking and cracking.

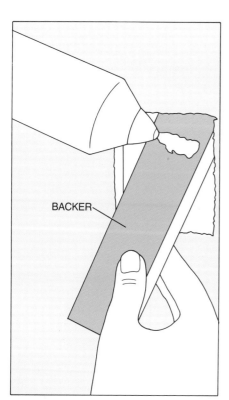

Fig. 14. Use a hot glue gun or construction adhesive to secure a backing strip in the hole. The backing strip will hold the patch in place.

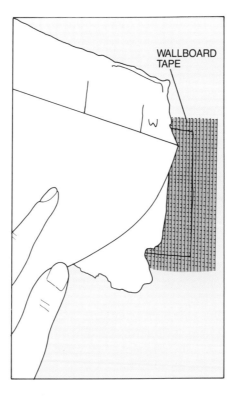

Fig. 16. Place wallboard tape over the cracks around the repair area, then apply wallboard compound.

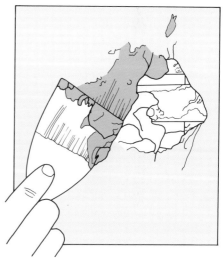

Fig. 18. Use a knife or trowel to fill and smooth the hole with patching compound. Apply extra coats of compound, as needed, to level the patch area. Smooth with a damp sponge.

BASIC WALLBOARD TECHNIQUES

Tools and Materials:

Wallboard T square; 12-inch-long (⅓ meter) measuring tape; sharp pencil; razor knife with extra blades; straightedge; wallboard or saber saw; wallboard hammer or screw gun; nail/screw apron, nails or screws; goggles; scaffold; wallboard; ready-mixed all-purpose taping compound; wallboard joint tape; taping knives in 4-, 6-, and 10-inch (100, 150, and 250 mm) widths; all-steel nail-on corner bead; mud pan; compound; sanding block and 100-grit sandpaper or a wet sander.

SAFETY FIRST

❑ Wear goggles for eye protection when cutting, sanding, or taping wallboard. Wear a dust mask when sanding, or use a wet sander to prevent dust.

❑ Choose your ladder or scaffold carefully. It must bear your weight, your helper's weight, and the weight of the wallboard panels.

❑ Always work with a helper when installing wallboard. The heavy panels can injure you or they can suffer damage if they slip off makeshift props or if they slip from your grip.

When working with wallboard, as with any task, there's a good way and a better way to do the job. For example, you could use just nails to attach wallboard; for years that was the only method available. But the new way is to use wallboard adhesives along with wallboard screws that are driven in by a screw gun. That method reduces the number of fasteners needed and makes walls and ceilings straighter. Using screws and a screw gun is better than using a hammer and nails, because the screws pop less and the screw gun doesn't damage the wallboard as a hammer can.

Some texts suggest that one person can install wallboard with the help of props. But handling these heavy, awkward panels alone can be very tiring and can lead to minor catastrophes. Mishandling a panel, for example, can make it crack under its own weight. Work with a helper.

While you can install 4 × 8-foot wallboard panels vertically, installing them horizontally is better. If you use panels longer than 8 feet (2½ meters), horizontal mounting results in fewer feet of joints to finish, and it creates a much stronger wall because it ties together many framing members—both studs and joists. In addition, horizontal joints are easier to finish because they're a convenient 4 feet (1¼ meters) up from the floor. And they're easier to conceal; they run in the same direction as the light streaming in through the window, and the sidelighting won't show up minor flaws as readily.

Planning where the joints occur is important. Joints that are placed at the corners of windows or doors will crack; use 12-foot (4-meter) panels and cut out the area for the window or door so there are no joints.

Maintain an even temperature in the work area when installing and finishing wallboard. Using heaters temporarily may make you comfortable in the daytime, but allowing the temperature to fall at night results in temperature variations that cause ridges in the joints due to expansion, rusting of screws, and delayed drying of the taping compound. When working with room additions, install the heating system first so you can maintain the temperature at a minimum of 55°F (13°C) until the wallboard is installed and painted.

AVOID THESE PITFALLS

❑ Use ½-inch-thick wallboard panels for all single-layer applications. Use ⅜-inch-thick wallboard as a new surface over old plasters, or as a backer or base for paneling. Use ⅝-inch-thick fire-rated wallboard where required by local building codes.

❑ Don't use ordinary wallboard as a base for ceramic tile. Wallboard deteriorates when exposed to water or moisture. Use special green-board panels or cement/fiberglass panels designed for such installations.

❑ Wallboard adhesives help bridge minor framing irregularities and reduce the number of screws or nails needed. Use them to attach wallboard wherever possible. (There are instances when you can't use adhesives, as over plastic moisture barriers. Follow the directions on the adhesive label.)

❑ Many job failures can be traced to using taping compound that's too thin or too thick. Amateurs should use ready-mixed wallboard compound to avoid mixing errors.

❑ Use a wallboard screw gun and screws to apply wallboard. A hammer can damage the wallboard.

Finishing Wallboard

A void using taping compounds with instructions that suggest you don't need to use reinforcing tape. Tape is good insurance against job failure and cracks in the future.

When applying compound to joints, allow each coat to dry completely before applying the next coat. Wallboard joints, nails or screws, and outside corner bead require three coats of compound to overcome the shrinking that occurs with drying.

Inside corners require a tape coat for reinforcement. Apply it as follows:

1. Spread the compound along both sides of the corner.
2. Cut the tape to length, fold it down the middle, and press it into the corner.
3. Apply another coat of compound to one wall and let it dry.
4. Apply compound to the other wall. (Two-sided corner tools are available to do that job in one step, but they are awkward to handle.) Use a 4-inch-(100mm) wide taping knife for finishing inside corners.
5. Wipe away excess compound with your taping knife, cleaning up spills and drips as you go. Those blobs of compound are much easier to remove while they're wet.
6. Apply a heavy-bodied latex paint or latex primer to new wallboard. Don't use alkyds as a first (priming) coat on new wallboard.

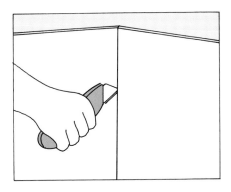

Fig. 19. To cut wallboard, slice through the face paper with a razor knife, then bend and break the plaster core. Finish with a cut through the back paper, and set the cutoff section aside.

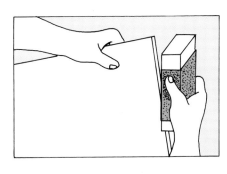

Fig. 20. Fold coarse sandpaper over a wood block and move the block along the cut edges of the wallboard to smooth them.

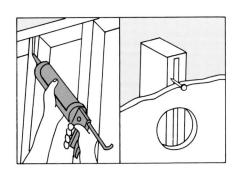

Fig. 21. Apply panel adhesive to studs or joists, according to the instructions on the adhesive label. Adhesive is useful where nails or screws would be difficult to use.

Fig. 22. Install ceiling wallboard first, the top panel on the wall next and the bottom panel last. Props such as these, made of scrap lumber, are a poor second choice to having a helper assist you.

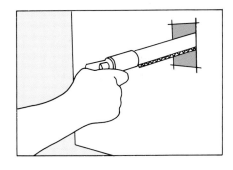

Fig. 23. Measure and mark the location of light boxes, outlet boxes, and heat-duct openings on the wallboard. Use a wallboard saw or a saber saw to make the cutouts.

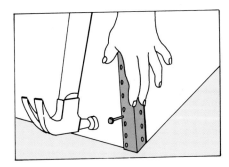

Fig. 24. Be sure corner beads are seated squarely on the corner. Drive a wallboard nail or screw through the corner bead, into the corner stud, about every 5 inches (125mm).

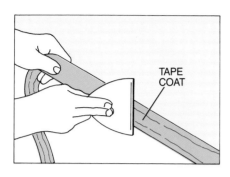

Fig. 25. Spread taping compound with 4- or 6-inch (100 or 150mm) taping knife, treating only one joint at a time. Imbed the tape, smooth it, and let it dry.

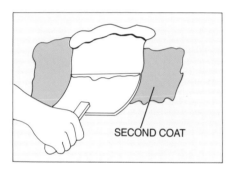

Fig. 26. Apply compound over the tape coat, using a 10-inch (¼ meter) taping knife. Don't build up a mound with the compound; keep treated joints flat. Apply a first coat to nail or screw heads.

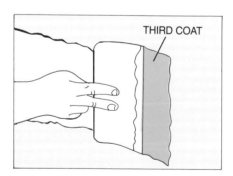

Fig. 27. When the second coat is dry, apply a thin third coat, feathering the edges out past the edges of the second coat.

Fig. 28. Apply compound to both sides of an inside corner. Then fold the tape and press it into the corner. Wipe away excess compound and smooth along each side. Apply a second coat to nail or screw heads.

Fig. 29. When the corner tape is dry, apply compound to one side of the corner. Let that side dry, then apply compound to the opposite side. Apply a third coat to nail or screw heads.

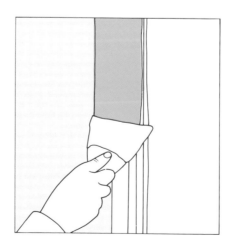

Fig. 30. Outside corner beads require three coats of compound. Wet-sand to smooth between coats

WALL COVERING

Tools and Materials:

Wall covering; adhesive, if needed; pencil; primer-sealer; scissors; water box; table; razor knife; bubblestick or level; seam roller; smoothing brush; sponges; floor covering (canvas tarp or newspapers); rubber gloves; goggles.

SAFETY FIRST

- ❑ Observe all warnings on package labels.
- ❑ Keep plastic garbage pails or bags handy for depositing wet wall covering as you trim it. Soggy covering can be slippery. Keep the soles of your shoes clean and dry when climbing a ladder.
- ❑ Turn off the electricity before papering; damp wall covering, especially metallic flocks, can conduct electricity.
- ❑ Wear rubber gloves and goggles when mixing and applying wallpaper remover.

As with many home improvement projects, doing your own wall covering has gotten easier as manufacturers have improved their products to remove the common pitfalls. Mixing and spreading adhesives was once a messy business. Bubbles and loose edges resulted from using adhesives that were too thin. Today, the adhesive is already on the covering and needs only a little soaking to be activated. And for those coverings that must be pasted on site, ready-mix adhesives of just the right consistency are available.

Another source of irritation was the task of removing the old wallpaper when we tired of it. Most modern wall coverings are strippable. Either the adhesive offers easy release from the wall surface or the vinyl finish coating tears free from a base paper that can easily be soaked and washed away. If you find either the wall covering or adhesive hard to remove, add wallpaper remover to the wash water and apply the mixture with a sponge, sponge mop, or garden sprayer. (You can adjust the sprayer nozzle to a very fine mist for less mess.)

The secret of removing wall covers is patience. Let the water or the remover solution do its job. If necessary, scratch the surface of the vinyl so water can reach the adhesive **(Figure 31)**. Don't start stripping until the adhesive is completely soft.

If you're a beginner, keep these basics in mind:

- ❏ Buy prepasted, strippable vinyl for your first effort.
- ❏ Avoid fancy metallics, flocks, and grasscloths until you've practiced a bit.
- ❏ Avoid bold patterns that are hard to match.
- ❏ Buy extra wall covering to be sure you don't run out, and allow an extra roll for mistakes.

Checklist for Wall Covering

- ❏ Inspect existing wall coverings for tears, loose seams, and bubbles. Repair according to instructions in this chapter.
- ❏ When applying wallpaper, use ready-mixed adhesive or prepasted wall coverings. Either one makes the job easier.
- ❏ If you're a beginner, use prepasted, strippable vinyl. Avoid using metallics, flocks, and grasscloths, as well as patterns that are hard to match.

AVOID THESE PITFALLS

- ❏ Keep the temperature low and the humidity high in the work area to slow drying time and avoid loose spots and bubbles.
- ❏ Apply a latex primer/sealer to the wall surface before applying wall covering.
- ❏ Consider the condition of your walls or ceiling before choosing a wall covering. Surfaces that are badly out of square will be difficult to cover, particularly if the wall covering has a bold pattern.
- ❏ Don't use a chalkline or ballpoint pen to mark walls or wall coverings. Chalk and ink can bleed through.

Removing Wall Covering

Fig. 31. If wall covering isn't strippable, use an abrading tool to make small holes in the surface. The holes will let steam or water reach the adhesive and soften it.

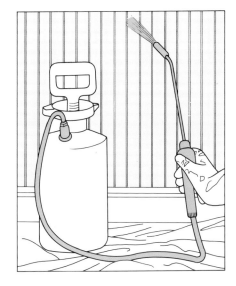

Fig. 32. Cover the floor and apply hot water to the wall covering. Use a garden sprayer, sponge mop, or paint roller to apply the water. Let the water soak the wall covering for several minutes.

Fig. 33. With a wall scraper, try to peel the covering away from the wall. If the adhesive is still firm, apply more water and let it soak in until the adhesive softens. After you've removed the wall covering, use a sponge and hot water to wash away any bits of backing and old adhesive. Rinse with clean water.

Hanging Wall Covering

Fig. 34. Use a carpenter's level or a bubblestick to establish a plumb line along the width of the wall covering minus ½ inch (12mm). Start the measurement from a corner.

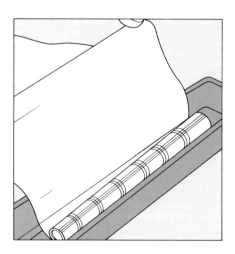

Fig. 35. Cut the wall covering strip so there's a surplus to trim on both ends. Place prepasted covering in a plastic water tray and let it soak according to the manufacturer's instructions.

Fig. 36. Fold (book) the covering and position the top edge at the ceiling. Adjust the covering so the outside edge is on the plumb line and the corner edge is folded around the corner. Smooth the wall covering.

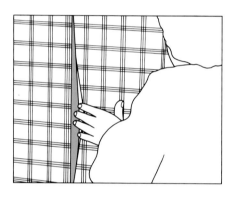

Fig. 37. Proceed down the wall, matching the edges and pattern at the seam. Use a sharp razor knife and a guide, such as a metal ruler, to trim the covering at the ceiling and base. Use a special vinyl-over-vinyl adhesive wherever the wall covering overlaps, as at inside corners or borders.

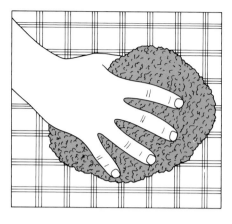

Fig. 38. Use a natural sponge and clean water to wash adhesive from the face of the wall covering. Rinse the sponge often and change the water in the bucket to keep it clean.

Fixing a Tear

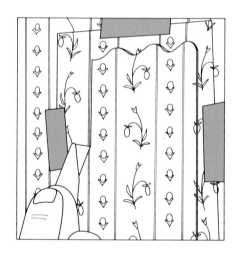

Fig. 39. Select a piece of scrap large enough to cover the damaged area. Position it over the torn spot, so that pattern marks align. Secure with masking tape. Use a sharp knife or razor blade to cut through the patch and the wall covering. Make the cut along a pattern line; if there's no pattern, make a wavy-cut line. Remove the patch and set it aside. Soak the wall covering to remove the damaged area. Wet or paste the back of the patch and carefully position it in the hole, then smooth the patch with a wet sponge.

Fixing a Seam

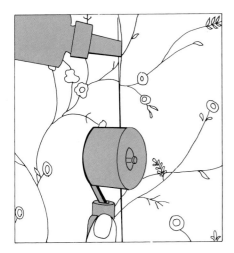

Fig. 40. Lift the loose edge and insert the adhesive nozzle. Apply adhesive to the loose spot, then roll the edge gently to rebond it. Sponge away excess adhesive.

Fixing a Bubble

Fig. 41. Make an incision with a razor knife at the center of the bubble.

Fig. 42. Insert the nozzle of the adhesive tube into the cut and apply adhesive. Then, press the loose covering in place and sponge away excess adhesive.

HANGING OBJECTS

Hanging objects on your walls or from the ceiling is easy if a stud or joist is in the wall directly behind where you mount the fastener. You can find the wood framing with an electronic stud sensor that senses the mass of the stud or joist in the wall or ceiling. Stud sensors really work, but you may have to practice a bit to get the knack of reading them accurately. Or you can use a magnetic stud finder to find the framing: A magnetized arrow on a swivel base lets the magnet turn when it passes over a nail in the wallboard or plaster lath. When you've located the framing member, simply drive a nail or screw into the framing.

More difficult is finding a way to hang objects between framing members, where there's no wood to anchor your fastener. Plaster-wall houses built before 1945 usually have a base of wood lath under the plaster, with small spaces between the lath: Test-drill a hole ⅛-inch (3mm) and check for wood particles in the plaster dust to be sure you've hit a lath. A nail or screw driven into the lath will support almost any weight you may want to hang.

Wallboard or plaster applied over rock lath provides a base that's too soft to support a nail or screw and the weight of the hung object. For those fastening jobs, a variety of new fasteners are available. Some work by gripping with deeper screw threads; some have threaded or expansion anchors that grip through a hole in the wall or ceiling when the screw is driven home; and some clamp against the back side of the wall or ceiling via a collapsible shaft or a spring-loaded toggle device that spreads the weight of the object over a larger area.

The dealer who sells you the object you're hanging often sells the proper fasteners as well. Mirror dealers, for

---

Checklist for Hanging Objects

❑ Consider buying an electronic stud sensor to take the guesswork out of finding studs from which to hang heavy objects.

❑ If you plan to hang a medium- or heavyweight object between the studs, buy the proper fastener for the wall type.

❑ Hanging really heavy objects always requires a stud for adequate support; if you're in doubt, choose another means of displaying the object.

example, usually offer mirror clips and anchors.

Check the instructions on a package of hanging fasteners. Most manufacturers list recommended uses and weight limits for their products. If the object to be hung weighs more than the suggested limit, use more than one hanger or select a different type of hardware.

Lightweight Hangers

These hangers **(Figure 43)** include hooks with adhesive peel-and-stick backs intended for hanging objects such as small pictures. A picture hanger, a hook-shaped device with a nail set through the hanger at about a 45-degree angle, is somewhat stronger. Use a small hammer and drive the nail carefully so you don't chip the plaster around the nail. Those hangers will support small pictures and craft items when driven into the soft core of plasterboard or wallboard.

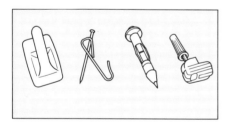

Fig. 43. Hang lightweight objects with adhesive-backed hooks, picture hooks, small molly screws, or mirror clips.

Small molly screws can also be hammered into wallboard. Once the screw penetrates the wallboard, hold the head with a small wrench (supplied with molly screws) while turning the screw with a screwdriver. As you turn the screw head, the flanged shaft

of the molly screw collapses against the back side of the wall or ceiling, spreading the weight over a larger area. Molly screws are quite sturdy when properly installed.

Another common fastener is the plastic anchor and mirror clip **(Figures 44 and 45)**. You drill a hole in the wallboard or plaster, insert the plastic anchor into the hole, then tighten the screw on the mirror clip to expand the anchor. A plastic anchor

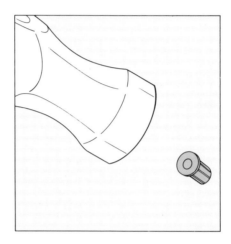

Fig. 44. To install mirror clips, first position the mirror and mark the clip locations at all four corners. Drill the necessary holes and install the plastic screw anchors.

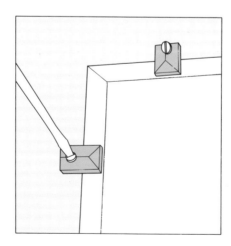

Fig. 45. Screw the bottom mirror clips in place and position the mirror on those clips. Use a screwdriver to attach the top and side clips.

and screw are useful for hanging items on concrete or on ceramic tile. Drill the hole using a carbide bit, insert the plastic anchor, and drive in the screw. The plastic anchor is, of course, rustproof—an added advantage in damp areas such as bathrooms.

Medium-Weight Fasteners

These include larger molly bolts **(Figure 46)**, Grip-It hangers that combine a threaded anchor base with screws, and automotive-type fasteners called Grabbers.

Molly bolts come in various sizes to accommodate anything from 3/4-inch-thick (19mm) plaster to hollow-core veneer doors.

Grip-It screws feature anchors with wide threads for better holding power in soft material such as wallboard. First, turn the base into the wall or ceiling, then attach the object using the screws, driven into the base anchor. Grab-It and Gripper fasteners are especially useful for installing drapery hardware when a stud isn't available.

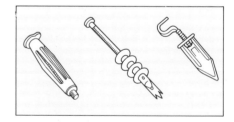

Fig. 46. Molly bolts are available in a variety of diameters and lengths to fit most common applications. The Grip-It screw anchor has wide threads to hold in soft wallboard, while the Grabber has a drivable base that expands when you tighten the screw.

Heavy-Duty Fasteners

A heavy object hung between studs or joists should be supported by a toggle bolt **(Figure 47)**. The toggle end is a spring-loaded folding device that springs open once inside a cavity. You drill a hole, insert the toggle bolt, and turn the bolt until the toggle presses securely against the back of the ceiling or wall panel **(Figures 48–50)**. Toggle bolts come with hooks for hanging potted plants or other objects from ceilings.

Remember that for hanging really heavy objects, there's no substitute for driving the hanger into wood framing. If you need a shelf to hold heavy objects such as books, consider using freestanding bookshelves.

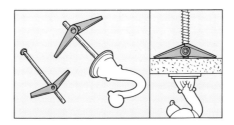

Fig. 47. Toggle bolts with screw heads or hook terminals are used for hanging heavy objects between studs or ceiling joists.

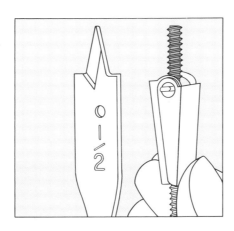

Fig. 48. To hang a plant, choose a drill bit with a diameter equal to the diameter of the toggle bolt. Drill a hole at the desired location.

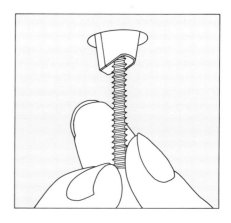

Fig. 49. Collapse the toggle bolt wings and insert the bolt into the hole. Pull down gently to be sure the wings have spread open.

Fig. 50. Screw the hook to the toggle bolt. While pulling downward on the hook, turn it clockwise to tighten it.

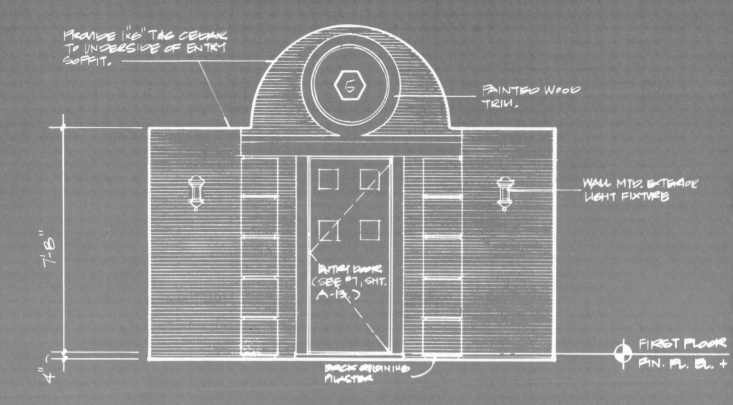

PROVIDE 1"x6" T&G CEDAR
TO UNDERSIDE OF ENTRY
SOFFIT.

PAINTED WOOD
TRIM.

WALL MTD. EXTERIOR
LIGHT FIXTURE

ENTRY DOOR
(SEE #7, SHT.
A-13.)

FIRST FLOOR
FIN. FL. EL. +

7'-8"

4"

BRICK REMAINING
PILASTER

1/2" REVEAL

5'-2"

GYP. BD.

BUILT-UP WOOD BASE

Chapter Eight

DOORS AND WINDOWS

Doors and windows stick during high humidity; locks break and require replacement; panes of glass are shattered by straying baseballs; and screens are torn or pierced by mysterious forces. Further, gaps between doors or windows and their frames require weatherstripping to keep winter drafts at bay.

Common as those problems are, it's often difficult to find a handyman willing to undertake such small jobs. Learning to make such repairs yourself may require less effort in the end than finding someone to make them for you.

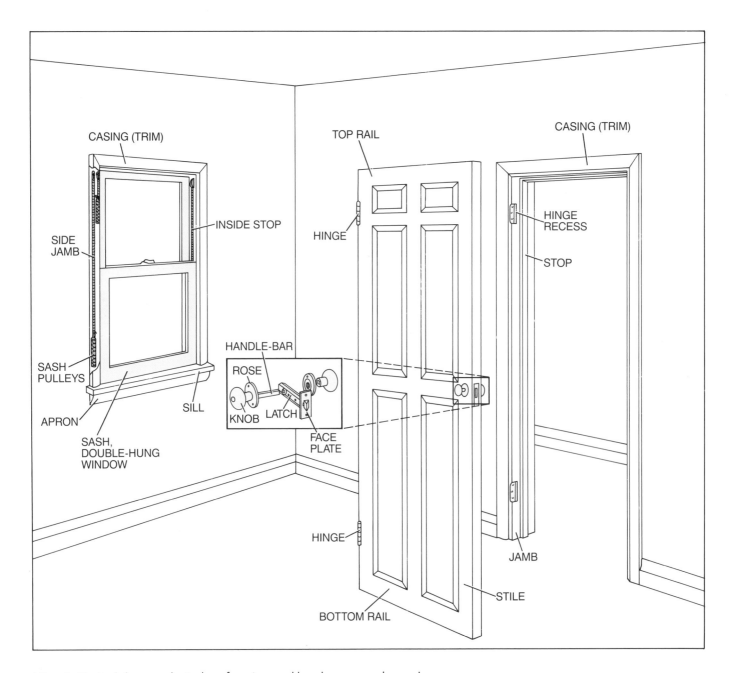

CASING (TRIM)

INSIDE STOP

SIDE JAMB

SASH PULLEYS

APRON

SILL

SASH, DOUBLE-HUNG WINDOW

HANDLE-BAR

ROSE

KNOB   LATCH

FACE PLATE

TOP RAIL

HINGE

CASING (TRIM)

HINGE RECESS

STOP

JAMB

HINGE

STILE

BOTTOM RAIL

Fig. 1. Typical door and window framing and hardware are shown here.

REPLACING A BROKEN WINDOW

Tools and Materials:

Soldering iron; putty knife; screwdriver or thin chisel; hammer; heavy work gloves; goggles; needle-nose pliers; sandpaper; linseed oil (for wood windows); glazing compound; sash paint.

SAFETY FIRST

- ❏ Wear work gloves and goggles when removing old glass and scraping the channels.
- ❏ Don't shatter the old glass. Doing so can make slivers of glass go flying.
- ❏ Before you discard old glass, wrap it in layers of newspaper to prevent injury to the refuse collector.

AVOID THESE PITFALLS

- ❏ If you cut the new glass yourself, be precise. If the glass is too large, shaving off a narrow area is practically impossible.
- ❏ Use a rafter square to make sure the edges are straight. An ordinary straightedge might slip and go askew as you're making the cut, or it may not be positioned straight across the pane of glass.

Checklist

- ❏ For security, exterior doors should have deadbolt locks.
- ❏ All windows, including casement and basement windows, should be secured with some sort of locking mechanism. If they aren't, see the recommendations in the section on installing door and window locks (page 132).
- ❏ Inspect window screens in spring for holes. Patch the holes, or if a screen is badly damaged, replace it.
- ❏ To keep double-hung windows from sticking in their frame, lubricate the window channels. If necessary, widen the channels, using the technique described in the section on freeing windows that stick (page 135).
- ❏ If windows are stuck because of dried paint from a recent paint job, insert a putty knife in the joint where the sash and frame meet. Work from the outside of the house. (To prevent binding in the first place, move each sash several times before the paint hardens.)
- ❏ Check for drafts by moving your hand along the edges between the windows and doors and their frames. Make the check on a cold day. Install weatherstripping where necessary.
- ❏ Check for drafts at the threshold of exterior doors. Again, install weatherstripping wherever it's needed.

A pane of glass that's cracked or broken is easily repaired as follows:
1. To remove the old glass in large pieces, use a soldering iron, if necessary, to soften the old glazing compound **(Figure 2)**.

2. Scrape the compound out of the channels with a putty knife.
3. To free the glass, pull out the glazier points or spring clips, using needle-nose pliers. Spring clips, which are used in aluminum windows, can be reused if they aren't damaged. Glazier points are usually bent or covered with too much glazing compound to reuse.
4. Brush debris from the channels. If the channels are wood, sand them until they're smooth. Make

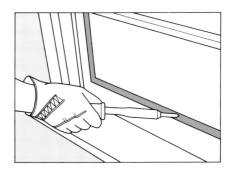

Fig. 2. The heat from a soldering iron can soften old glazing compound, easing the removal of broken glass.

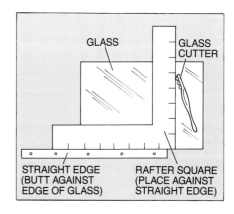

Fig. 3. Follow this diagram to cut glass straight. After scoring the glass hard with a glass cutter, position the score mark over the edge of the workbench and lightly tap the part you want to remove with a ball-peen hammer until it snaps off. Wear work gloves and goggles.

certain no slivers of glass or particles of old glazing compound remain.

5. Measure the length and width of the opening and deduct 1/8 inch (3mm) from each measurement. Then, cut the glass, using a rafter square **(Figure 3)**, or let the hardware store or glazier cut it for you.

6. Apply a coating of linseed oil to wood channels. Otherwise, the dry wood will absorb the oil in the glazing compound, making the compound lose its resiliency and crumble.

7. Apply a thin layer of glazing compound to all four sides of the

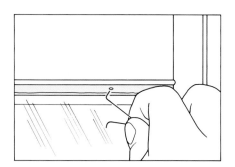

Fig. 4. Metal windows have holes in the channels for the spring clips that hold the glass to the channel.

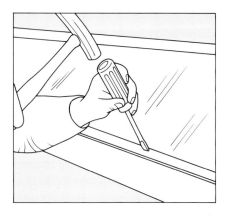

Fig. 5. Place a screwdriver or narrow chisel on top of the glazier points and tap until the sharp edge of the point penetrates the wood by 1/8 to 1/4 inch (3 to 6mm).

channel to help cushion the new glass.

8. Lay the new pane of glass into the channel and press it forward.

9. If the frame is metal, insert the end of each spring clip into the hole in the channel **(Figure 4)**. Press the lower part of the clip up and over the edge of the glass so the clip holds the glass to the channel. If the window is wood, slide glazier points down along the glass and into the channel. Secure the points by tapping them into the wood, using a screwdriver or thin chisel and a hammer **(Figure 5)**.

10. Scoop up a handful of glazing compound and roll it into a rope 1/4 to 1/2 inch (6 to 13mm) in diameter; then, press the rope into the channel on all four sides, so it contacts the glass.

11. Use a putty knife to smooth the glazing compound into a neat triangular edge.

12. After the glazing compound has cured for a week or two, paint it with trim and sash paint to keep it supple.

INSTALLING WEATHER-STRIPPING

Tools and Materials:

Hammer; screwdriver; wood saw or hacksaw; wood plane; tin snips or shears; brads; weatherstripping.

Putting up weatherstripping isn't difficult. However, the variety of available weatherstripping materials can be confusing.

Weatherstripping seals the edge where windows and doors meet their frames, preventing cold drafts. To inspect for air leaks, move your hand slowly along the edges between the window or door and its frame—preferably on a cold day.

AVOID THESE PITFALLS

- ❏ Don't use a power saw to trim a door. A power saw gives less control than a hand saw. A slip may mean a ruined door.
- ❏ Don't let weatherstripping interfere with the pulleys of a double-hung window.

Selecting Window Weatherstripping

Self-adhering foam weatherstripping is the easiest to install and the least expensive, but it's not as durable as other types. It's suitable for sealing edges around casement and awning windows, as well as around doors **(Figure 6)**.

Use scissors to cut the strips to size. Then, press the adhesive side of the strips against the frame of a casement or awning window so the strip butts up against the inner window edges.

Tubular-vinyl weatherstripping and felt weatherstripping with a thin metal edge **(Figure 7)** will serve for many years. Either is suitable for sealing double-hung windows.

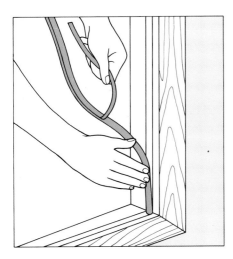

Fig. 6. To seal a door, apply self-adhering foam weatherstripping to the inner edge of the doorstop so the closed door presses against the material. Follow the same principle to seal casement or awning windows.

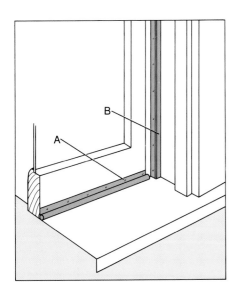

Fig. 7. To seal along the sides (A), nail tubular or felt weatherstripping to the window frame. To seal along the bottom and top (B), nail the metal border to the window so the vinyl or felt falls over gaps when the window is closed. To seal the gap formed where the top and bottom windows meet when closed, nail the strip under the bottom rail of the outer window.

Use scissors to cut the strips to size. Then, position each strip so the tubular or felt part of the strip aligns with the outside edge of the window and covers the crack. Secure the side strips to the frame and the top and bottom strips to the window. Most manufacturers put tiny holes in the vinyl strip of tubular weatherstripping and in the thin metal edge of felt weatherstripping to accept brads (small, slender nails). If predrilled holes aren't present, space brads about 12 inches (⅓ meter) apart.

Metal window weatherstripping sits inside the channels of a window frame and springs into position to seal the gaps between the window sash and the frame **(Figure 8)**. It's the most expensive window weatherstripping available, but it maintains its effectiveness indefinitely. If it loses its springiness, just pry under its lip with a screwdriver to reestablish its sealing ability. It comes in rolls or large strips and should be cut to size with tin snips or shears strong enough to cut through metal.

Nail the metal window stripping inside the channels of the frame so it's hidden from view when the window is

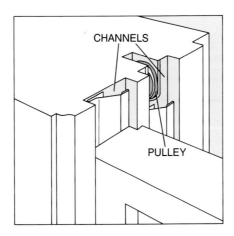

Fig. 8. To seal the gap along the sides of a double-hung window, nail metal window weatherstripping inside the channels. Don't cover the pulleys.

closed. When attaching the strip to the upper channel of a double-hung window **(Figure 8)**, be careful not to cover the pulleys.

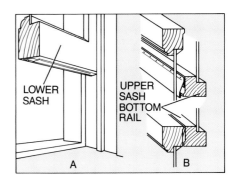

Fig. 9. To seal the edge along the bottom of the lower sash (A), nail metal window weatherstripping to the underside of the sash. To seal the edge along the top of the upper sash (not shown), nail metal window weatherstripping to the topside of the sash. To seal the gap where lower and upper sash meet (B), nail metal weatherstripping to the inside edge of the upper sash bottom rail.

Selecting Door Weatherstripping

Sealing the gaps between a door and its frame is similar to sealing gaps in a window, except for the space between the bottom of the door and the threshold. Around the frame, it's best to use foam materials with a wooden or metal edge, or vinyl materials with an aluminum edge.

Cut the weatherstripping to fit with a wood saw or, if you're cutting metal, a hacksaw. Then, with the door closed, stand outside and position the strip so the wood or aluminum is against the face of the doorstop and the foam or vinyl covers the gap **(Figure 10)**. Nail the wood or aluminum to the door. Often, the material is predrilled to accept nails. If it isn't, place the nails about 12 inches (⅓ meter) apart.

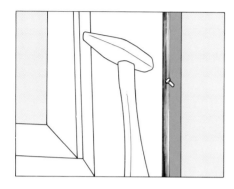

Fig. 10. When you nail weatherstripping with a wood or metal edge into position, be sure the foam or vinyl lies snugly against the door. This type is installed outside.

Selecting Threshold Weatherstripping

Vinyl flap weatherstripping screws to the bottom of the door so the flap falls over the gap when the door is closed **(Figure 11)**. When the door is opened, a cam screwed to the doorjamb pushes the vinyl up so it doesn't scrape against the floor.

It's easy to install, because the door doesn't have to be removed. However, it requires some fiddling. If it's too high, it won't seal the gap. If it's too low, it makes the door hard to open and close.

Vinyl and aluminum strip weatherstripping screws to the bottom edge of the door. To install the strip, you have to remove the door from its hinges **(Figure 12)**. Slide the vinyl

strip out of the aluminum channel and cut both sections separately, using a hacksaw for the aluminum and shears for the vinyl. Screw the aluminum channel to the bottom of the lower rail and slide the vinyl back in.

A vinyl threshold embedded in heavy aluminum is a replacement for the wooden or metal threshold you may have now **(Figure 13)**. Remove the old threshold and smooth the base. Then, install the new threshold. If it's too high for the door to open and close easily, remove the door from its hinges and trim its lower edge with a wood plane or handsaw.

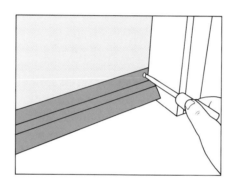

Fig. 11. Vinyl flap weatherstripping goes on the inside face of the door. You can do the job without taking the door off its hinges.

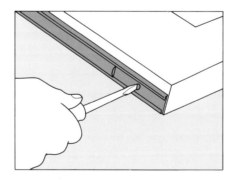

Fig. 12. You have to take the door off its hinges to install vinyl and aluminum threshold weatherstripping.

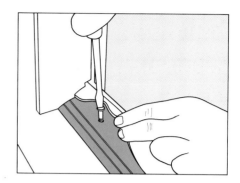

Fig. 13. Remove the old threshold to install a vinyl threshold that will seal the gap.

INSTALLING DOOR AND WINDOW LOCKS

Tools and Materials:

Masking tape; template; awl; hand drill with an expansive bit or hole saw; chisel; power drill with a bit to make a ¼-inch (6mm) hole.

Door locks come in various forms, from expensive and sophisticated electronic entry systems to simple chain locks. One of the most popular types is the deadbolt door lock, which secures the door to the thick wood of the doorjamb with a heavy metal bolt. Deadbolt door locks are difficult to pick and hard to break.

As for windows, you can buy special locks that screw to the window sash, or you can secure windows with simple nails or screws.

Selecting a Deadbolt Door Lock

To offer security, the bolt of a deadbolt lock should extend at least 3/4 inch (19mm) into the doorjamb. The longer the "throw" of the bolt into the jamb, the more difficult it is for a thief to break in the door.

You can open and close some deadbolt locks from inside with a lever or a key. A lever mechanism lets you get out quickly in case of a fire, but it's a poor choice if the door has glass panes; a thief can break the glass, reach in, and turn the lever. With such doors, a key-activated lock is better. Hang the key near the door, just out of reach of a thief, but where it will be accessible in an emergency—and within reach of every member of the household.

Installing a Deadbolt Lock

Use the following suggestions in conjunction with the directions accompanying the lock:

1. Using masking tape, mount the template that comes with the lock so the center of the cylinder is about 44 inches (slightly more than 1 meter) from the floor.
2. Using an awl, poke through the template to mark the spot on the door through which you must drill to accommodate the cylinder. Then, with the awl, mark the spot where the bolt will project through the door.
3. Holding an expansive bit or hole saw at a right angle to the door, drill through the face of the door at the mark you made for the cylinder **(Figure 14)**. As the bit or hole saw breaks the surface of the door on the opposite face, stop drilling and remove the tool. Complete the hole by drilling through the opposite face, to keep the door from splintering.
4. Drill the hole for the bolt, using the bit size specified in the lock's instructions.
5. Insert the bolt and its strike plate in the hole and mark the outline for the strike plate.
6. Using a chisel, carefully shave out wood to form a bed for the strike plate. Insert the bolt and its strike plate frequently to check depth. Stop chiseling when the strike plate lies flush with the surface of the wood.
7. Insert the bolt and its strike plate, and screw the strike to the door.
8. Insert the cylinder through its hole in the door so the rod intersects the bolt lever **(Figure 15)**, and screw the cylinder securely to the door.
9. Make a cutout in the doorjamb to accept the bolt. Drill a 1/4-inch-(6mm) diameter hole in line with the bolt to the depth that the bolt extends. If the bolt has a 1-inch (25mm) throw, for example, drill 1 inch into the jamb.

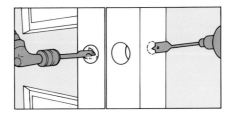

Fig. 14. Hold the drill at a right angle to the door and drill a hole for the cylinder of the deadbolt lock; then drill a hole for the bolt.

10. Position the strike plate over the hole and trace its position onto the jamb **(Figure 16)**. Guided by that outline, chisel out the wood to the depth of the hole. Then, screw the strike plate to the jamb.

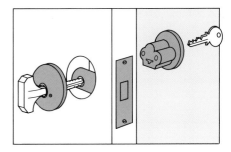

Fig. 15. Outline the strike plate and use a chisel to cut out the bed for the plate. Join the cylinder and deadbolt and screw the cylinder to the door.

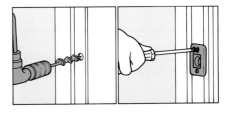

Fig. 16. Drill a hole in the jamb, center the strike plate over the hole, and outline the inner boundary. Chisel a bed for the bolt, and screw the strike plate to the jamb.

Securing Windows

To secure a double-hung window, use ordinary 12d nails. Close the window and, using an 11/64-inch-(4mm) diameter bit, drill a hole through the frame of the lower sash and into (but not all the way through) the frame of the upper sash **(Figure 17)**. Do the same on the other side of the window. Press nails into the holes, but allow the ends of the nails to protrude enough so you can pull them out when you want to open the window. If you want to leave the window open partway for ventilation but still have the security of a lock, open the lower sash halfway and drill through the holes already in the sash until the drill penetrates the upper sash. In the open position, press the nails into the new holes.

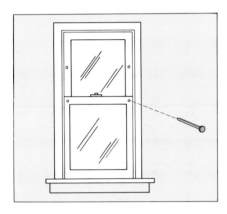

Fig. 17. To secure double-hung windows against burglars, drill through the frame of the lower sash and partway through the upper sash, and insert a nail.

The easiest way to secure casement and awning windows is to lock the windows and remove the handles with a screwdriver.

To secure a basement window that is wide enough for a thief to crawl through, fit 2x3 wood strips along the side walls adjacent to the window **(Figure 18)**. Position the strips about 2 inches (50mm) from the sash so the window can be opened for ventilation. Then, insert a No. 10 or 11 screw—2½ to 3 inches (64 to 77

mm) long—into each wood strip, letting the ends protrude about ½ inch (13 mm). If a thief jimmies the window, the screws will limit the size of the opening.

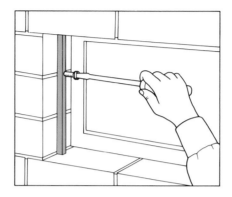

Fig. 18. To effectively secure basement windows, use strips of wood and screws.

REPLACING INSECT SCREENS

Tools and Materials:
Patching cement or wire-mesh patches; sawhorses; ¼-inch-(6mm) thick plywood base; putty knife; new screen; staple gun; C-clamps; drywall knife; tack hammer; brads; plastic wood; paint.

Patching an insect screen is much easier than replacing it. You can seal small holes with plastic cement, which dries clear. And patches made of fine mesh are avail-

able in hardware stores and home-supply outlets for larger holes. You fit the pronged ends of the patch through the mesh of the screen and bend them back to secure the patch.

If a screen is damaged beyond repair, it should be replaced.

Replacing an Insect Screen

1. Set up two sawhorses and lay a board across them. A piece of plywood ¼-inch (6mm) or thicker, and at least as long and wide as the window or door, is suitable. Lay the window or door with the damaged screen over the board.
2. Slide a putty knife under one of the moldings holding the screen in place, preferably next to a nail. Lift gently to loosen the molding. Do the same where other nails hold the molding, being careful not to split the molding. If the molding splits, you'll have to replace it. Remove all four moldings the same way.
3. Take off and discard the old screening.
4. Measure the opening (length and width) for the new screen. Add a few inches to the replacement screen as a safety margin.
5. Center and lay the new screen in place and staple the top to the wood **(Figure 19)**.

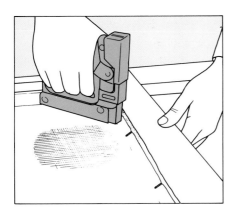

Fig. 19. Staple the new screen to one end of the window or door.

6. To make the screen taut enough to withstand heavy gusts of wind, place 2x4 blocks of wood under the top and bottom of the window or door to raise it off the board. Then, clamp the middle of the window or door to the board with C-clamps, one at each side **(Figure 20)**. Tighten the clamps to form a bow in the window or door.

7. With your hands, pull the bottom of the screen as tight as possible and staple it to the wood.

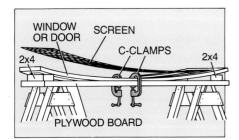

Fig. 20. Tighten a pair of C-clamps, one at each side, to form a bow in the window or door. That helps make the new screen taut when you remove the clamps.

Then, remove the clamps and the 2x4 blocks of wood.

8. Pull one side of the screen and staple it to the wood. Draw the other side taut and staple it to the wood as well.

9. If the window or door has a wood rail across its midsection, staple the screen to that, too.

10. Trim off excess screening with a sharp drywall knife.

11. Put the moldings in place and secure them to the window or door with brads.

12. To give the window or door a finished appearance, use a countersink to tap the heads of the brads below the surface of moldings. Fill the holes with plastic wood and let it dry. Sand the plastic wood level with the wood, prime the spots, and paint the window or door.

FREEING WINDOWS THAT STICK

Tools and Materials:
Bar of soap, paraffin, or silicone spray; narrow block of wood; hammer; 2-inch (50mm) putty knife; chisel; sandpaper.

Windows stick in their frames when humidity expands the wood or when paint seals the windows shut. Neither problem is difficult to overcome.

Freeing Swelled Windows

A double-hung wood window that swells because of humidity doesn't usually jam completely, but it can be hard to open. Lubricate the channels with dry soap, paraffin, or a silicone spray.

If the window remains tight, widen the channels a bit by holding a block of wood against one of the channels and tapping the wood **(Figure 21)** with a hammer. Do the same to the other channel. Tap *means* tap. Banging the wood block may open the channel too much, resulting in a loose window. The only cure for that is removing the channel strips and repositioning them.

Fig. 21. Widen the channels to give the window sash more room in which to move. Then apply lubricant.

After you've relieved the pressure in the channels, rub or spray a lubricant into the channels again.

Awning and casement windows aren't immune to binding because of humidity. The cure is the same: Treat the frames with lubricant.

Freeing Painted Windows

Paint can make a window stick so tight that it can't be opened. Getting it open so you can remove the dried paint is the first task:

Work from outside the house if you can reach the window without a ladder. Otherwise, work from inside, but be careful not to mar the finish.

1. Insert a putty knife in the joint where the sash and frame meet. Tap the end of the putty knife with a hammer to break the paint bond **(Figure 22)**.

2. Move the putty knife to another spot on the window and repeat the procedure. After each treatment, try to open the window.

3. When the window finally breaks free, scrape the dried paint out of the channels with a chisel **(Figure 23)**. Hold the chisel flat so its sharp edge doesn't cut into the wood.

4. Rub sandpaper up and down the channels two or three times to remove any paint the chisel may have missed.

5. Test the movement of the window. If it still binds, sandpaper the channels again.

Fig. 22. Use a putty knife and hammer to break the paint seal.

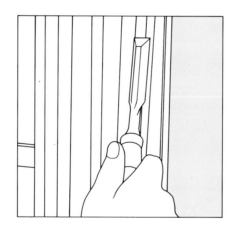

Fig. 23. Holding the chisel so the sharp edge doesn't gouge the wood, scrape away the dried paint.

CLEANING WINDOWS

Tools and Materials:
Soft, clean cloth rags; squeegee; commercial window-washing liquid; rubbing alcohol; mild soap or dishwashing detergent; sharp safety razor or glass-cleaning tool.

SAFETY FIRST

❏ Benzene, naphtha, and other volatile chemicals may be recommended by manufacturers for cleaning windows, but they can cause respiratory problems, cancer, and skin irritation. Use less-harmful glass cleaners, or rubbing alcohol diluted with water, as described in the text.

❏ If you use a ladder to wash windows, follow the ladder manufacturer's instructions. Don't stand on rungs higher than those recommended. The most common cause of ladder falls is improper use of equipment.

AVOID THESE PITFALLS

❏ Don't use scouring powder or pads to wash windows; they'll scratch the glass.

❏ Don't spray a cleaner directly onto the glass. Spray into a clean cloth.

❏ Don't use old or dirty rags to wash windows. Trapped grit may scratch the glass.

❏ Avoid using ammonia, strong solvents, or alkalis; they can destroy glazing compound.

"I don't do windows" has become a classic comic line. But unfortunately, windows have to be cleaned periodically. The more regularly they're cleaned, the less likely they are to become scratched by dirt and grit particles.

While dirt comes from many sources, often it's the runoff from your home's construction material—especially brick and concrete—that stains and dirties the glass. Rainstorms, snowstorms, and high winds help deposit loose soil, soot, and other airborne dirt on your windows.

Clean—Don't Scour

Although window glass is well-tempered at the factory, you can scratch or otherwise mar its surface by using gritty scouring powders, or by using rags or sponges that contain particles of old dirt. Use clean cloths and sponges, and finish with a squeegee.

1. If your windows aren't badly soiled, first give them a light rinsing with plain water to remove powdery surface dirt. If you're using a garden hose, adjust the nozzle to produce a broad mist.

A concentrated blast of water could allow particles to scratch the glass.

2. Next, use a commercial window-washing liquid. Instead of spraying the cleaner directly on the window, spray it into a soft clean cloth or paper towel. If you use a mild dishwashing liquid instead, dilute it according to the manufacturers' instructions, using warm water.

3. Thoroughly rinse or change the cleaning cloths frequently; trapped dirt can scratch the glass. With old wood-frame windows, keep cleansers away from caulking or you may discolor or even loosen it. Too much water could cause mold or mildew to form.

Cleaning Grease

To clean grease—anything from fingerprints to splattered cooking grease—from windows, you needn't use dangerous chemicals such as toluene or naphtha (which are carcinogens and environmental pollutants). Simply dilute 1½ cups (375 ml) of rubbing alcohol, or isopropyl alcohol (available at pharmacies and supermarkets), with 1 gallon (4 liters) of warm water, and wipe generously with a clean sponge or cloth. Clean the sponge or change rags often.

Removing Paint

If, while painting, you get drops of paint on your windows, wait for the paint to dry. Then scrape the spots off carefully with a sharp safety razor or special glass-cleaning tool. Keep the scraping edge at an angle of 45 degrees or less to avoid scratching the glass. Use a can of compressed air or a gentle spray of water to remove loose paint particles, and then wash the windows.

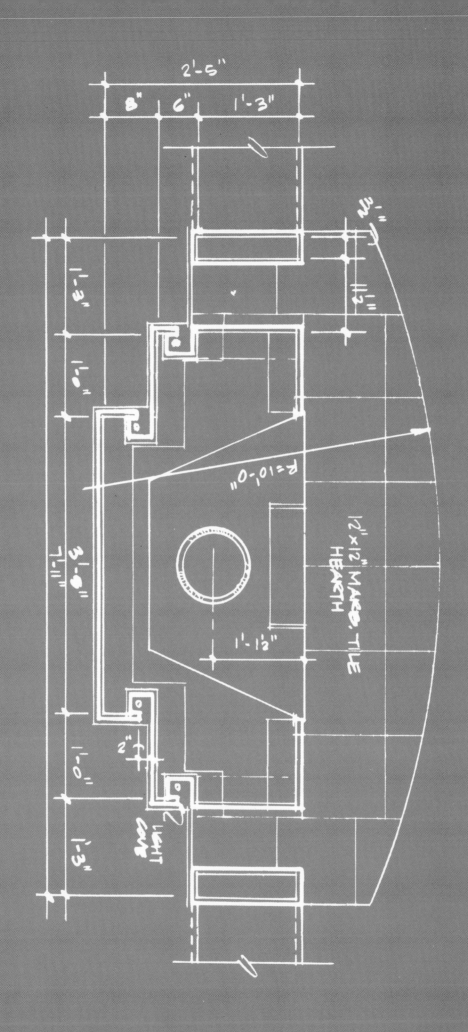

FLOORS AND FLOOR COVERINGS

Floors receive more wear and tear than any other surface in a home—which is why they must be replaced or refinished periodically. However, if the subfloor under the current floor is stable, you can lengthen the time between replacement or refinishing by doing some fairly simple maintenance and repairing minor problems before they become major headaches.

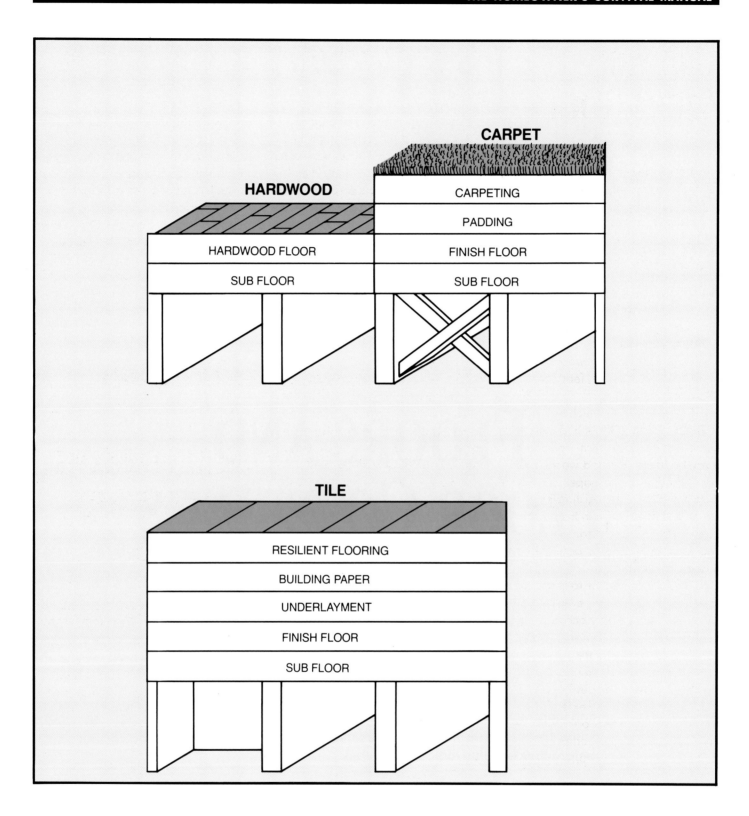

Fig. 1. These illustrations show the various components of hardwood, tile, and carpeted floors.

USE THE RIGHT TOOLS

With floors and floor coverings, as with most do-it-yourself jobs, you need the right tools to get professional results.

Carpeting is a good example. Don't try to lay carpeting unless you have a stretching tool called a knee kicker. After a carpet is in place for a while it "relaxes," or stretches. If it's laid loosely, it'll stretch even more and develop wrinkles. It not only looks unsightly, but it wears more quickly because passing feet scuff the edges of the wrinkles.

Using special aids—such as 3-foot- (1 meter) wide builder's paper to make a cutting pattern—also cuts down on frustration and waste. Position the edge of the paper on vinyl floor covering or on existing carpeting and cut it to fit. Then transfer the pattern to the new floor covering. That way, any mistakes occur in the paper, not the flooring.

As a rule, it's cheaper to buy hand tools than to rent them, even though you may use them only occasionally. Renting power tools makes sense, however, for one-time use.

You can rent knee kickers for installing carpet as well. The device consists of a head with teeth and extensions of pipe. You add extensions until the stretcher end is against one wall and the head is gripping the opposite end of the carpet.

With one end of the carpet secured by a hook-strip (a wood strip with tacks), you work the lever at the head until the carpet is stretched taut. Then hook the stretched edge over the hook-strip to secure the carpet in place. (You can also rent power-actuated guns that drive nails into concrete to secure a carpet hook-strip to a concrete floor.)

Carpet seams are joined using a seam iron and heat-activated carpet tape. Position the carpet tape under the seam, check that the edges make a good, well-concealed joint, then run the hot iron under the carpet edges to activate the adhesive and join the edges. The seam iron and carpet tape are available from most rental supply stores.

For cleaning and repair needs, don't overlook janitorial supply stores. Consumer liability laws restrict the strength of cleaners and other chemicals you can buy at the supermarket, but janitorial supply stores offer concentrated chemicals such as stain and wax removers. (Such chemicals may be hazardous. Follow the manufacturer's instructions precisely.) Also, check with a janitorial store when buying a floor buffer and even a vacuum sweeper. Often, such stores sell vacuum cleaners that offer more cleaning power than homeowner models, and for less money.

The key to easy maintenance is good-quality floor coverings and carpet. Economy grades can be much more expensive in the long run. For example, cheap vinyl floor covering may have a thin layer of color that quickly wears through to reveal a black background. Cheap carpeting may wear faster, show traffic patterns, and stain easily.

To be sure of carpet quality, check the label on the back. Look for brand names and check the warranties offered. Top manufacturers offer 10-year warranties for crush resistance and 5-year warranties for stain resistance. Ask whether the warranties are transferable if you sell the house.

Be sure you understand any warranty limitations. Carpet used on stairs, for example, isn't covered by many manufacturers because of wear from high traffic and premature edge-wear where the carpet wraps the edge of the tread.

Installation without proper padding may also void some warranties. Good padding cushions the carpet from impact damage. In fact, many installers feel it's better to economize on carpeting than padding.

Save leftover carpet and tile or floor covering scraps for repairs. If you have no scraps, consider cutting a repair piece from behind an appliance, a door, or a closet floor where it won't be noticed.

FINISHING AND MAINTAINING HARDWOOD FLOORS

Tools and Materials:
Latex wood patch; wood cleaner; restorer; cloth; putty knife; fine sandpaper; 0000 (fine) steel wool; rubber gloves; dust mask; goggles; paste wax; vinegar; oxalic acid, or bleach. (A good hardwood floor-repair kit includes most of those items.)

Badly scratched or gouged hardwood floors require sanding and refinishing. Sanding an entire floor, however, is a job for a professional, since removing too much wood in the sanding process can cause loss of stiffness and squeaks. If possible, strip off the old finish only around the damaged area, repair minor nicks or scratches locally, and apply a new coat of finish instead of refinishing the entire floor.

Latex wood-patching compounds are available already mixed at paint and home centers. They're easy to apply **(Figure 2)** and sand **(Figure 3)**; and they accept stain well. Those qualities make latex wood patch an excellent product for repairing hardwood floors.

To clean and restore wood floors, ask for a floor-repair kit at your paint store. The kit should contain a cleaner, a restorer, and a cloth for applying and buffing the repair. Use a solvent-type cleaner, not a water or water-based cleaner, on hardwood floors. Water can enter the cracks between flooring strips and cause a black stain in the hardwood. Oak is particularly subject to water stains if unprotected.

SAFETY FIRST

- Wear a dust mask and goggles when sanding.
- Provide plenty of ventilation when finishing floors; maintain the ventilation until the finish is completely dry. Turn off the forced-air furnace or air-conditioning to avoid spreading varnish fumes through the house.

AVOID THESE PITFALLS

- Polyurethane finishes may not be compatible with older floor finishes such as varnish. Test your product in an inconspicuous spot—a corner or a closet.

Checklist

- Remove wax buildup and grime from hardwood floors with odorless mineral spirits.
- Coat hardwood floors once or twice a year with a paste wax and buff the surface.
- Rearrange furniture periodically to change traffic patterns and reduce wear on floors and carpets.
- Place mats at entryways.
- When you install new flooring, save scraps of floor covering or carpet for future repairs.
- When moving appliances or furniture, use a dolly to avoid scratching vinyl flooring.
- Secure throw rugs placed on slippery vinyl surfaces with double-faced carpet tape.
- Wax standard vinyl floors regularly; strip off the old wax when polishing no longer produces a satisfactory sheen.
- Vacuum no-wax flooring frequently so dirt particles don't mar the finish.
- Vacuum glazed tile floors frequently so dirt particles don't scratch the tile.
- Give carpeting a light vacuuming daily; vacuum thoroughly once a week.
- Invest in a vacuum with a revolving brush or beater bar, if you don't already have one.
- Replace worn brushes on vacuum attachments when necessary.
- Change vacuum-cleaner discharge bags when they are three-quarters full.
- Clean carpets and carpeting once a year; do the job yourself or have a professional do it.

Stains from water or pet urine can be bleached and the area refinished. Buy oxalic acid, a wood-bleaching agent, and mix it with water according to the directions. Wear rubber gloves and goggles when using acid. Sand the stain. Then pour the oxalic acid mix on the stain and let the solution stand for at least one hour or until the stain is bleached away **(Figure 4)**. Deep stains may require several treatments. Rinse the area with vinegar and smooth with 0000 steel wool **(Figure 5)**. Finally, refinish the area with the wood-restorer product **(Figure 6)**, applying as many coats as necessary to match the existing finish.

Some prefinished flooring products boast of having no-wax finishes, but most hardwood floors look better if coated once or twice yearly with a paste wax. Wax not only enhances the wood finish but protects it from spills, stains, and scratches.

Odorless mineral spirits will loosen carpet padding that is stuck to a hardwood floor. They can also remove built-up wax and grime to restore the original luster of the wood.

Fig. 2. Use a putty knife to apply latex wood patch to scratches and gouges in the floor, and let it dry.

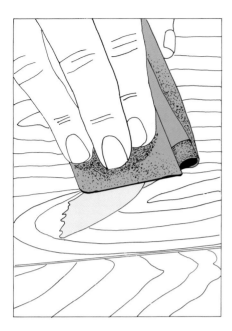

Fig. 3. Sand in the direction of the grain, using fine sandpaper. Then apply one or more coats of wood restorer to the patch, feathering the edges into the old finish.

Fig. 4. After sanding the stained area down to bare wood, apply oxalic acid bleach and cover with a cloth. Check in 1 hour; if necessary repeat the procedure.

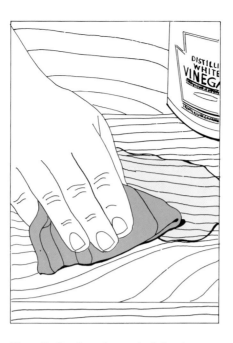

Fig. 5. Soak a clean cloth in vinegar and rinse the stained area. Let the wood dry, then smooth with extra fine, 0000 steel wool.

Fig. 6. Apply one or more coats of wood restorer until the repair blends into the old finish.

CARPET REPAIR

Tools and Materials:
Fingernail clippers; double-faced carpet tape; carpet cutter; seam adhesive.

Remove carpet spills immediately: If the spill is liquid, place a towel over the area and step on the towel to force liquid from the carpet. When you have blotted up as much liquid as possible, wipe the area with a towel soaked in club soda to reduce stains.

For damage such as superficial burns, remove the damaged fiber ends carefully with fingernail clippers. If the burn or other damage is deep, cut away the damaged area with a circular carpet cutter, or "cookie cutter" **(Figure 7)**. Cookie cutters are available at carpet stores, or you may be able to borrow one from a carpet dealer.

1. Place the cutter over the damage and turn the cutter while pressing down to cut away the damaged area.

2. Use the cutter to cut a new repair plug from a carpet scrap.

3. Place double-faced carpet tape in the hole, working it under the cut edges so it extends from one side to the other **(Figure 8)**.

4. Place the repair plug in the hole and press it in place.

5. Apply carpet-seam adhesive around the perimeter of the repair **(Figure 9)**.

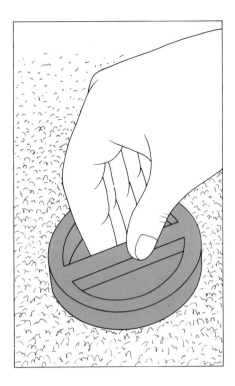

Fig. 7. Use a circular carpet cutter, called a cookie cutter, to cut a hole around the damaged area.

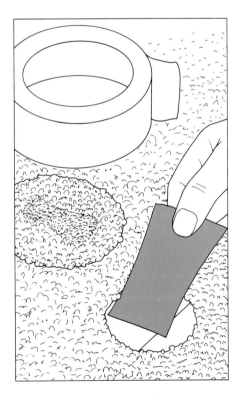

Fig. 8. From a scrap of matching carpet, cut a repair plug. Position double-faced carpet tape in the hole, then press the repair plug into the hole.

Fig. 9. When the repair plug is in place, spread the fibers between the carpet and the patch and apply a thin bead of seam adhesive to prevent the patch fibers from unraveling.

INSTALLING STAIRWAY CARPET

Tools and Materials:
Electric staple gun with 7/8-inch staples; knee kicker; razor knife.

Replacing a worn stair carpet on a closed stairway—one with walls on both sides—is relatively easy. If the stairway is open on one or both sides, the job is slightly more complicated. The easiest approach is to run the carpet between the railing spindles, leaving an equal space at each side that clears the spindles. To secure the carpet, fold it under the edge of the tread and staple it in place. If you prefer to fit the carpet around the railing spindles, you may be wise to hire a professional installer. A good fit requires exacting cutting.

Choose a quality carpeting for stairs, and use a 7-pound-per-square-yard polypropylene pad for best wear. You'll need to rent a knee kicker to stretch the carpet into the corners formed by the risers and treads. You'll also need to rent or buy an electric stapler that accepts 7/8-inch staples.

1. Warm the carpet in the sun to make it flexible.

2. As you shape the carpet, dampen the backing, spraying water from a spray bottle to make the carpet more pliable.

3. Check the width of the stairway between the finish stringers and/ or walls. If the carpet width is uniform, install the carpet in one continuous run. If the width of the stairs varies, cut the carpet into several 3-foot or 4-foot (1 meter) lengths and lap the carpet at the end joints.

4. Soften the carpet backing and use the knee kicker to force the fold under the tread, into the corner ("crotch") where the riser and tread meet **(Figure 10)**.

5. Staple the crotch only, using ⁷/₈-inch staples. Stapling along the edges where the carpet meets the treads can cause dimples or puckers.

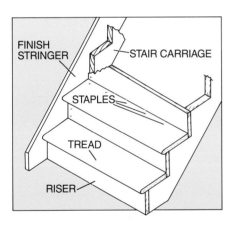

Fig. 10. Force the carpet fold into the corners (crotch) where the tread and riser meet. Use ⁷/₈-inch staples to secure the carpet at the crotch only.

REPAIRING VINYL FLOORS

Tools and Materials:
Carpenter's square; razor knife; rolling pin or bottle; pencil; masking tape; hair dryer; cloth or sponge; putty knife; paste wax.

SAFETY FIRST

❏ Use double-faced carpet tape to secure throw rugs on slippery vinyl surfaces.

AVOID THESE PITFALLS

❏ Don't move appliances or furniture over vinyl flooring without a dolly. Sliding heavy loads across the floor can damage it.

❏ If the old floor covering is hard to remove, don't bother; simply install a layer of ¼-inch plywood over the old flooring to provide a fresh base.

You can patch a damaged vinyl floor with a process known as double-cutting:

1. Place a piece of scrap floor covering over the damaged area. Align the scrap material with the existing floor to match patterns **(Figure 11)**.

2. Tape the scrap in place with masking tape.

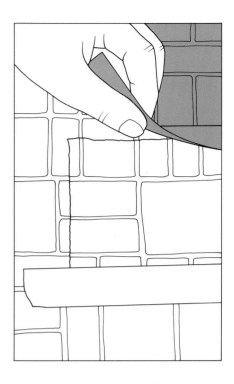

Fig. 11. Place a scrap of vinyl over the damaged area, aligning the patterns. Secure the scrap to the old vinyl with masking tape.

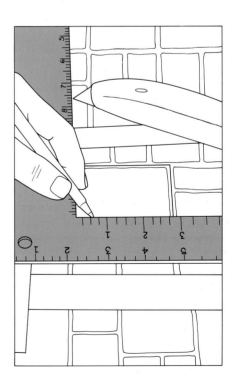

Fig. 12. Cut along the pattern, using a carpenter's square as a guide. If there's no pattern, make a wavy cut to conceal the joint. Cut through both layers of vinyl.

3. Cut through both the scrap material and the old floor covering with a razor knife **(Figure 12)**. That method ensures that the patch fits perfectly. If the floor covering has a pattern such as brick or stone, cut along the mortar or grout lines so the patch is less noticeable. If the floor covering has no pattern, cut lines that are wavy show up less than straight lines. When you've cut through both layers, set the patch aside.

4. Heat the damaged area with a hair dryer to soften the old adhesive, and then lift the damaged area by prying gently with a putty knife.

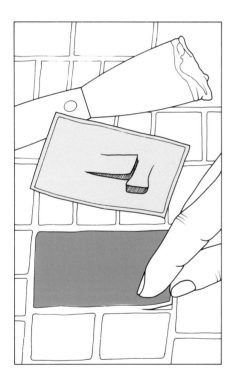

Fig. 13. Remove the old vinyl and check the fit of the patch. Apply vinyl adhesive to the patch, place the patch in the hole, and smooth the area with a rolling pin or a bottle. Wipe away excess adhesive with a clean cloth and a solvent. (Check the directions on the adhesive for the proper solvent to use.)

5. Scrape away the old adhesive and test-fit the patch **(Figure 13)**.
6. Apply adhesive to the patch and place it in the hole.
7. Use a rolling pin or a bottle to press down the patch, then wipe away excess adhesive.
8. After the patch has set, apply paste wax to the joints around the patch to conceal them.

CLEANING FLOORS, CARPET, AND CERAMIC TILE

Most modern flooring today requires little maintenance. Simply using the right cleaning product will help keep the flooring attractive for years.

SAFETY FIRST

❑ Cleaning compounds may contain dangerous chemicals; keep the area well ventilated.
❑ With any cleaner, read the manufacturer's recommendations and warnings.
❑ If you use a heater to speed-dry damp carpeting, don't let the heating element touch the carpet, or a fire could result. Don't leave the heater on unattended.

AVOID THESE PITFALLS

❑ Don't vacuum vinyl floors with the beater-bar attachment used for carpeting; you can damage the floor surface.
❑ Don't wax or buff no-wax flooring; you can yellow or mar the protective coating.
❑ Rinse away all wax removers or strippers completely to prevent yellowing or other damage.
❑ Dry shampooed carpeting quickly to prevent mildew.
❑ When washing small carpet mats and area rugs in your washing machine, use a mild detergent; don't use high washing or drying temperatures.

Standard Vinyl Flooring

Tools and Materials:
No-rinse vinyl floor cleaner; nonyellowing floor wax; wax remover; sponge mop; vacuum cleaner.

Older, standard vinyl flooring requires more maintenance than does the new generation of urethane-coated and vinyl no-wax flooring. Nevertheless, regular cleaning and waxing can keep the older flooring looking as good as its more modern and expensive counterparts.

Since standard vinyl doesn't come with a protective finish, you have to supply it. On new flooring, apply three or more coats of a long-lasting, nonyellowing floor polish, allowing each coat to dry before applying the next. The polish helps protect the vinyl against wear and stains.

To maintain the shine and prevent abrasion from dirt particles, wash the floor regularly with a no-rinse floor cleaner, and apply a coat of wax immediately afterwards.

When polishing no longer produces the shine it once did, remove the wax build-up with a wax stripper or remover. (Wax remover effectively cleans very dirty floors as well as removes wax deposits.) Rinse the floor thoroughly after applying wax remover.

No-Wax Vinyl Flooring

Such flooring comes from the factory with a coating of transparent urethane that makes the flooring much more durable, stain-resistant, and easier to maintain than standard vinyl flooring.

Vacuum no-wax flooring regularly to keep particles of food and dirt from marring the finish. Use the wand attachments—not the ''beater bar'' normally used on carpeting, which can visibly damage the urethane coating.

Wash no-wax vinyl with a no-rinse floor cleaner. Don't wax or buff, or you may yellow or damage the protective urethane wear surface.

Cleaning Ceramic Tile

Tools and Materials:
Sponge, window-cleaning solution; general-purpose household cleaner; mop; vacuum cleaner; household bleach; scouring powder; hard scrub brush.

Ceramic tile, often used in high-traffic areas such as the kitchen and bathroom, is easy to maintain. To clean the tile, wipe it with a damp sponge; use either a commercial window cleaner full-strength or one of the general-purpose household cleaners diluted with water.

Regularly sweep or vacuum tile floors—particularly glazed tile—to remove gritty particles that can scratch the surface. For high-traffic areas, use a household scouring powder; mix it with water to form a pasty consistency, and mop the paste over the floor. Let the paste stand for about five minutes, then scrub vigorously with a scrub brush. Don't use a scouring pad or steel wool because of the risk of rust-staining.

Cleaning Carpeting

Tools and Materials:
Vacuum cleaner; aerosol foam cleaner; dry rug shampoo; electric carpet cleaner; dishwashing liquid; plastic sheeting or aluminum foil; carpet steam cleaner; scrub brush; broom; bucket; garden hose (for outdoor carpeting); soft carpet brush or carpet rake; small space heater or fan.

You can keep carpets and rugs new-looking by cleaning them regularly. Most carpet manufacturers recommend a light vacuuming daily and a thorough cleaning weekly. (Light vacuuming means passing the vacuum head over an area three times, while thorough cleaning may require seven or eight passes to clean deep down.)

Move the vacuum slowly to let the suction remove deeply embedded soil. While standard suction-type vacuum cleaners are adequate for removing surface dirt, a vacuum with a revolving brush, or beater bar, allows more vigorous cleaning. A beater bar is available in some upright models and in vacuums with separate power attachments.

Make sure that the vacuum cleaner is in top working condition. Replace worn brushes. Change discharge bags when they are three-quarters full, or suction may be decreased. Adjust the cleaning attachment to the recommended height for the kind of rug you're cleaning. For a long-pile or shag rug, use the proper attachments.

When Carpeting Needs More Than Vacuuming

After a few years, your carpeting may look a little dull or dingy even if you've vacuumed regularly. Light colors may appear darker and drab. The problem is an accumulation of fine soil particles that vacuuming can't remove.

Extremely soiled or stained carpeting may require professional help. But generally, you can improve the appearance of carpeting yourself, thanks to a variety of commercially available cleaning aids and the convenience of rental equipment. Several methods are available:

Aerosol foam cleaning. You apply a thin layer of aerosol foam spray to the carpeting with a wet sponge or electric carpet cleaner and let the foam dry. Then, vacuum thoroughly. Follow the recommendations (which may suggest testing for color-fastness) and don't apply too much foam or add water.

Dry extraction method. Instead of foam, this method uses an absorbent compound that's saturated with detergents and solvents. The compound acts like a wick to lift embedded soil, which is then vacuumed away. The compound is particularly effective when used with professional-quality electric carpet-cleaning machinery, available at many local tool-rental centers. Keep the cleaning area well ventilated; many absorbent cleaning compounds can irritate the eyes and can be harmful if inhaled.

Rotary shampooing. This method requires an electric rotary carpet cleaner. Use a mild detergent especially formulated for shampooing carpet. Avoid harsh agents such as ammonia, soap, and strong household cleaners intended for hard surfaces; they may leave a sticky residue that attracts dirt. Also avoid overwetting the carpet; that can cause shrinkage, discoloration, and mildew. Before you start, remove furniture from the room to prevent staining. If that isn't practical, wrap thick plastic film or aluminum foil around the furniture legs.

Steam cleaning. This method is also known as water extraction. A special machine injects a detergent solution under pressure into the carpet pile and then extracts the loosened soil. Steam cleaning equipment is available in tool-rental centers, but this process is best left to professional carpet cleaners.

Cleaning Outdoor Carpeting

If you use outdoor carpeting indoors, treat it like any other carpeting inside your home.

If the carpeting is outdoors, sweep up surface litter with a broom or brush. For more thorough cleaning, wash the carpeting with a good carpet shampoo, diluted according to manufacturer's recommendations. Sprinkle the solution onto the carpet with a watering can, and then work it into the pile with a scrub brush. Rinse thoroughly with a garden hose, and wait until the carpeting is fully dry before you vacuum it.

Dry the carpeting as quickly as possible to prevent mildew. Use a space heater, fan, or air conditioner to speed drying. When using a heater, make sure the carpet doesn't touch the heating element, which could cause a fire.

After cleaning, brush the damp pile in one direction with a soft brush or carpet rake.

Cleaning Small Rugs

Clean small area rugs or carpet doormats in your washing machine, using a mild detergent. White and light-colored mats may be washed together, but wash dark-colored rugs separately. The washing temperature shouldn't exceed 90°F (32°C) for dark colors, and 105°F (41°C) for lighter colors, or the colors may bleed.

Set the dryer at the lowest temperature. If you don't have a dryer, hang the carpet outdoors in the shade; brush it lightly when it's dry.

Removing Spots and Stains

The following chart is adapted from the *Du Pont Complete Book of Carpeting* (courtesy of E.I. du Pont de Nemours & Company). Although written for Du Pont carpeting, the following procedures should be effective for treating carpets composed of a combination of synthetic fibers including nylon, olefin, and polyester. If you have any questions, it is recommended that you consult the manufacturer of your carpeting or a professional before attempting any of these procedures.

These "Basic Cleaning Steps" (BCS) are recommended for carpets made of Du Pont fibers including nylon, olefin, and polyester.

1. Immediately scoop up as much of the spill as possible. Then **blot, do not rub,** with clean, white absorbent cloth or paper towels to remove excess moisture. Use a wet/dry vacuum if spill is large.

2. Douse stain with warm, **not hot**, water and **blot** with clean white cloth or paper towels. Press down firmly to remove as much moisture as possible. Repeat until no stain is evident on cloth or towels.

3. If stain remains on carpet, make a solution of warm water and mild non-bleach liquid laundry, not dishwashing, detergent (1 tsp. to 1 qt. [5 ml to 1 l]) water. Apply enough solution to cover stain and let soak for about 5 minutes.

4. Rinse with warm water and **blot thoroughly** to extract water. Repeat until all detergent is removed.

5. Absorb remaining moisture with layers of white paper towels, weighted down overnight with

non-staining glass or ceramic object.

6. When completely dry, vacuum or brush the pile to restore texture.

Ghost Stain: After drying, if the stain reappears, it may be because some stain remained deep in the pile and wicked up to the surface. If so, repeat steps 3 to 6.

These guidelines refer to stains from substances other than foods and beverages. Regardless of source, any spill should be cleaned up immediately. The longer it sits, the longer it takes to remove.

The substances below can clean up with prompt, proper steps. Even then, some stains may require professional cleaning. Check below for the type of *Stain* and cleaning *Key*. Then check the Cleaning Procedure which will refer you to specific Basic Cleaning Steps (BCS).

A. Follow BCS No. 1. Then apply dry cleaning solvent (follow instructions and precautions on container). Then follow BCS No. 2 through 6.

B. Follow BCS No. 1, 2, 3. Then apply solution to clear, white non-suds ammonia (2 tbs. to 1 qt. [30 ml to 1 l] water). Blot with clean white cloth or paper towels. Repeat BCS No. 3. Then BCS No. 4, 5, 6.
Note: For blood stains, all ingredients must be cold.

C. Follow BCS No. 1, 2, 3, 4. Then apply solution of white vinegar (2 tbs. vinegar to 1 qt. [30 ml to 1 l] water). Blot with clean white cloth or paper towels. Repeat BCS No. 3. Then BCS No. 4, 5, 6.

D. Follow BCS No. 1, 2, 3. Then apply solution of white vinegar (2 tbs. to 1 qt. [30 ml to 1 l] water) and blot. Next apply solution of clear, white non-suds ammonia (2 tbs. to 1 qt. [30 ml

to 1 l] water) and blot. Repeat BCS No. 3. Then BCS No. 4, 5, 6.

E. Freeze area with ice cubes. Shatter gum with blunt instrument. Vacuum up pieces. Follow BCS No. 3, 4, 5, 6.

F. Test nail polish remover on an obscure nonvisible section of carpet to see if it removes color.

If not, apply remover and blot. Repeat if necessary.

G. Follow BCS No. 1, 2, 3, 4. If stain remains, apply dry cleaning solvent (follow instructions and precautions on container). Repeat BCS No. 3, 4. Then BCS No. 5, 6.

H. Vacuum thoroughly. If needed, follow BCS No. 1 through 6.

Types of Stains and Removal Key

Stain	Key	Stain	Key
Acne Medicine†	G	Lacquer	A
Asphalt	A	Latex Paint	A
Bleach†	G	Lipstick	A
Blood	B	Linseed Oil	A
Carbon Black	G	Machine Oil	A
Chalk	H	Makeup	A
Charcoal	H	Mascara	A
Crayon	A	Merthiolate	D
Chewing Gum	E	Nail Polish	F
Cough Syrup	D	Paste Wax	A
Dirt	H	Plant Food†	G
Drain Cleaner†	G	Rubber Cement	A
Dye†	G	Rust	C
Flea/Tick Powder or Spray†	G	Shellac	A
Fungicide††	G	Shoe Polish	A
Furniture Polish	A	Solder†	G
Furniture Stain	A	Soot†	G
Graphite	H	Tar	A
Grease	A	Toilet Cleaner†	G
Hair Oil	A	Toothpaste	B
Hair Spray	A	Urine/Feces*	C
Hand Lotion	A	Varnish	A
Ink†	A	Vaseline	A
Insecticide††	G	Vomit†	G
Iodine†	G	White Glue	B

*Pets often have repeat "accidents" because they're drawn by the odor. This can be discouraged by the professional application of a deodorizer approved for use on your carpet.

†These substances can affect or damage the actual color of the carpet. While you may try to remove the stain as described here, it is recommended to consult a professional carpet cleaner.

††Some fungicides, insecticides and pesticides may harm carpet stain resistance. Consult your manufacturer prior to use.

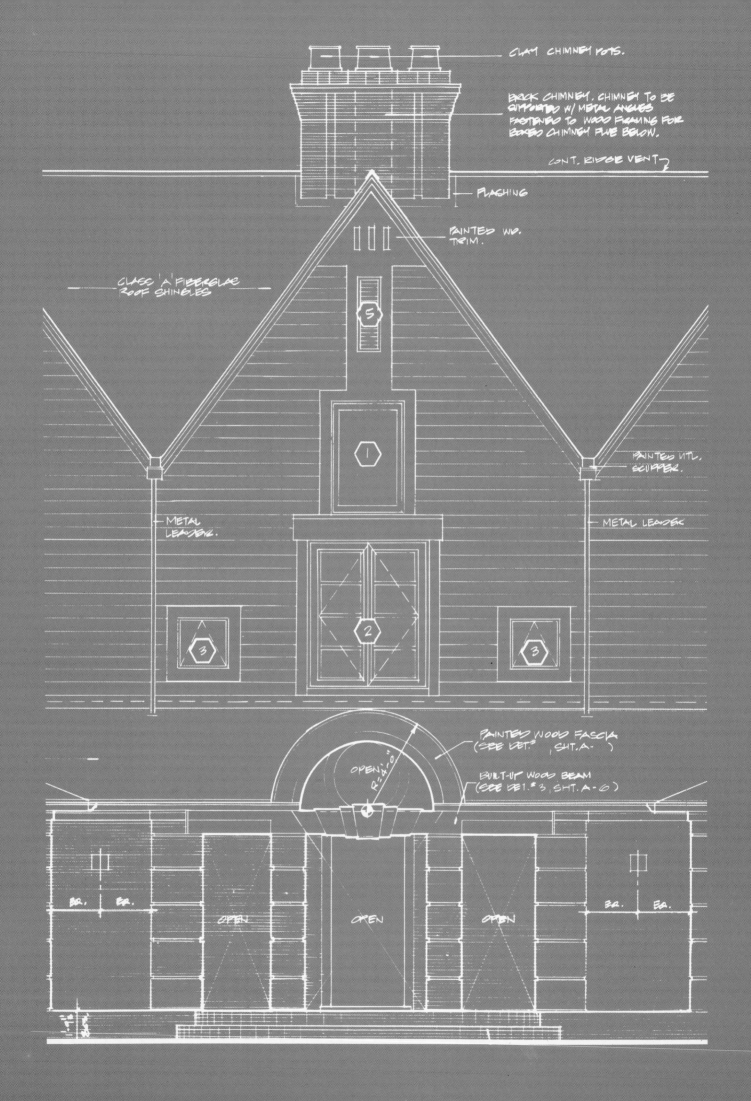

CLAY CHIMNEY POTS.

BRICK CHIMNEY. CHIMNEY TO BE
SUPPORTED W/ METAL ANGLES
FASTENED TO WOOD FRAMING FOR
BOXED CHIMNEY FLUE BELOW.

CONT. RIDGE VENT

FLASHING

PAINTED WD.
TRIM.

CLASS 'A' FIBERGLAS
ROOF SHINGLES

PAINTED MTL.
SCUPPER.

METAL
LEADER.

METAL LEADER

PAINTED WOOD FASCIA
(SEE DET.# , SHT. A-)

BUILT-UP WOOD BEAM
(SEE DET. # 3, SHT. A-6)

OPEN-R=4'-0"

BR.   BR.   BR.   BR.

OPEN   OPEN   OPEN

EXTERIOR MAINTENANCE

If so many interior components of a house require the do-it-your-selfer's frequent attention, it's not surprising that the outside of the house should require periodic care as well. The elements can be harsh: Constant exposure to sun, wind, rain, snow, and temperature extremes exacts a heavy toll on the roof and siding. Shingles turn brittle and crack, allowing rain water in. Caulking shrinks, opening gaps for drafts. Blacktop driveways crack and pit. Siding and concrete become soiled and mildewed.

The maintenance that your house requires starts at the foundation and ends at the roof. These tasks become more manageable if you follow an inspection and repair checklist.

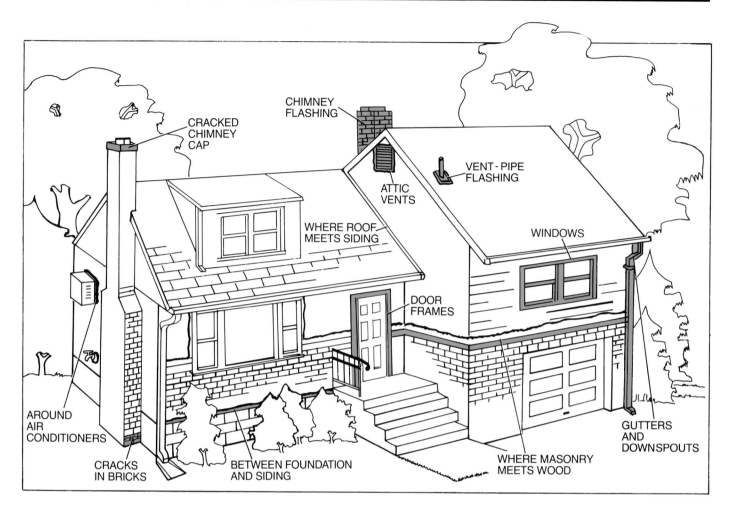

Fig. 1. Some areas on the outside of a house are more likely than others to cause problems. Begin your periodic inspections with these trouble spots.

LADDER SAFETY

While most of the tools used for exterior maintenance work are the same ones you use indoors, extension ladders are more commonly encountered outdoors than indoors.

Using the proper ladder—and using the ladder properly—is critical for safety as well as convenience. Aluminum ladders are handy to move because they're lightweight. They have one severe drawback, however: They conduct electricity. Keep an aluminum ladder clear of any electric power lines, and make sure the ladder can't cut any extension cords while you're working.

Also make sure the ladder has a secure footing, especially if you're working on muddy or uneven ground. A ladder should form an angle of approximately 30 degrees from the vertical **(Figure 2)**. A much greater or smaller angle will make the ladder unstable. If your ladder lacks nonslip feet, buy add-on feet at a hardware outlet. Your ladder also should have a secure resting place at the top. Many kinds of brackets and stand-offs are available **(Figure 3)**.

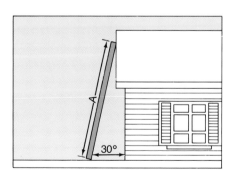

Fig. 2. For safety, position a ladder so it forms an angle about 30 degrees from the vertical.

Checklist

❑ Inspect and clean gutters and downspouts at least twice a year. Repair any leaks.

❑ Check the pitch of the gutter, and adjust it if necessary.

❑ Paint wood or galvanized-steel gutters if their finish is worn.

❑ Check downspouts to make sure they discharge water away from the house; install a diverter or splash block if necessary (see "How to Solve Wet Basement Problems" in Chapter 5, page 86).

❑ Inspect the attic for leaks during a heavy rain, and replace any wet insulation.

❑ When the rain has stopped, inspect the roof exterior for the source of the leak. Do that from the ground, using a pair of binoculars.

❑ Clear off any twigs and leaves that accumulate in roof valleys. If possible, do that from the ground, using a broom or bamboo rake tied to a long handle.

❑ Inspect the outside of the house for cracks and gaps; fill where necessary, using the appropriate caulk.

❑ Check the driveway for cracks. Make repairs before freezing temperatures arrive.

❑ Check the outside of the house for mold and mildew, and treat it if necessary.

❑ Inspect concrete surfaces and clean them where necessary. If mildew recurs, apply a concrete sealer.

❑ Check outside brickwork for efflorescence; clean with water from a garden hose.

❑ Clean vinyl siding with water from a garden hose; follow with a wipe-down with a sponge.

For a painting or remodeling job involving a large area, consider renting a portable scaffold. The added security is well worth the modest rental fee.

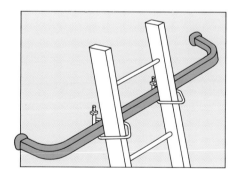

Fig. 3. This ladder stand-off improves stability. It also keeps the ladder away from the house, protecting the siding.

EXTENSION CORDS

Extension cords for outdoor work should be heavy-duty, three-wire cords with rugged insulation **(Figure 4)**. Most extensions made for indoors use fairly fine wire, which can't adequately handle the longer distances required for many exterior jobs. And the insulation on most interior extension cords won't stand up to the rough treatment that outdoor work involves.

If possible, plug extension cords used for outside work into an outlet protected with a ground fault circuit interrupter. It can protect you from a dangerous shock even if the insulation is damaged.

Put away extension cords at the end of each working day. Sunlight and weathering can quickly destroy even a good-quality cord.

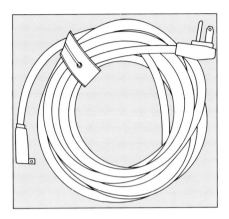

Fig. 4. Heavy-duty extension cords should accept a three-prong grounding plug and be 14-gauge. For safety's sake, plug them into an outlet protected with a ground fault circuit interrupter.

MEASURING DEVICES

Tape measure. Long tapes—particularly those that measure 25 feet (8 meters) or more—are useful for exterior jobs. Some tapes have a small hole at the free end so you can slip the tape over a nail. That's handy if you're working single-handed. Don't forget to add the length of the measuring tape's body to the reading if it's part of the length you're measuring. The housing on a long tape can be 3 or 4 inches (75 to 100mm) long.

If your tape isn't long enough, stretch sturdy twine between the points you're measuring. Mark the ends, and measure the twine in a more convenient location. Cotton or dacron twine works well; nylon stretches too much.

Spirit level. Attached to a length of twine, a level allows you to make sure that two widely separated measurements are on the level. Position the device at the center of the length of string, since the string unavoidably sags no matter how tight you pull it.

Chalk line. This device lets you connect two points with a dead straight line, an important consideration in many jobs **(Figure 5)**. Chalk lines usually come in enclosed reels; you unwind enough line to stretch between the two points, pull the string slightly away from the surface you want to mark, and let it snap back. The chalk on the string will leave a clear, straight line.

Most chalk lines are set up to double as plumb bobs: If you hang the loose end of the string (which is equipped with a ring for the purpose) over a nail and allow the reel to hang down, the unwound portion of line will be perfectly vertical. Snap the line against the wall, and you have a handy reference line for laying out construction work.

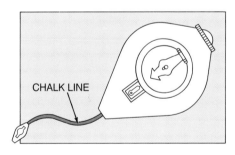

CHALK LINE

Fig. 5. A chalk line connects two points with a dead straight line, marking it with chalk. It also doubles as a plumb bob.

GARDEN HOSES

These lowly products perform many jobs around the house. Think of a garden hose as an extension cord for your faucet.

Like an electric extension cord, a garden hose lasts longer and performs better if you give it some basic care. Don't leave it out when you're not using it. Sunlight is one of a hose's worst enemies. Another potential enemy is your lawnmower; a hose can be hard to see in tall grass.

Don't shut off the water at the nozzle when you're through using the hose. That leaves the hose full of water at full line pressure, which weakens the hose as the sun's rays heat it. Instead, open the nozzle and shut off the water at the faucet.

If your hose leaks, you can try several simple fixes. Most leaks occur at the fittings and can be eliminated by replacing the soft gasket ring that makes the seal. You should be able to get a good seal by hand-tightening the fitting; if you can't, change the gasket rather than resorting to tightening the fitting with pliers or wrenches.

If the leak occurs between the hose itself and the fitting, buy replacement fittings, available at most hardware stores. Cut off the old fitting and bring it with you when you buy the replacement. Hoses come in several sizes; the wrong fitting won't work.

REPAIRING CRACKS IN DRIVEWAYS

Tools and Materials:

Wire brush for patching concrete; caulking gun; patching compound (or dry premixed sand mix, driveway crack filler, or cold-mix asphalt); putty knife; long nail or piece of stiff wire; container of water; cold chisel; ball-peen hammer; trowel; damp rags; oakum; weed killer; tamper; shovel.

AVOID THESE PITFALLS

❏ Don't put off patching cracks and holes. Small, easy-to-fix cracks can become major projects in surprisingly little time.

❏ When cleaning out cracks and holes, be thorough. You can't make a firm patch in a poorly cleaned site.

❏ Keep blacktop compounds out of the house; they're easier to remove from your shoes than from carpets and furniture.

It's fair to say that all cracks in concrete or asphalt (blacktop) driveways result from moisture, freeze-and-thaw cycles, temperature changes, and settling. It's also fair to say that large cracks in concrete or asphalt are caused by small cracks that weren't dealt with promptly.

Patching Concrete

Any crack provides an entry for damaging water. Fortunately, small cracks in concrete aren't difficult to deal with.

Hairline cracks are most easily repaired with a premixed masonry paste patching compound. It comes in cartridges and is applied with a caulking gun.

1. Clean out the crack thoroughly, using a stiff bristle or wire brush; you can dig out loose debris or dirt with a scraper or putty knife.
2. Cut the nozzle of the cartridge of patching compound at a 45-degree angle with a utility knife; the narrower the crack to be filled, the closer to the tip of the nozzle you should cut.
3. Poke a long nail or piece of stiff wire through the nozzle until you break the cartridge seal.
4. Rest the nozzle tip on the crack and squeeze the trigger. As the patching compound flows out in a smooth bead, move the tip along the crack. Force the compound deep into the crack.
5. When you've finished, use a putty knife to smooth out the

patch. If you dip the putty knife into a container of water from time to time, the compound won't stick to the blade, and you'll get a smoother line.

Fixing Large Cracks in Concrete

1. Remove any weak, crumbling concrete, in addition to any dirt, dust, and debris. With a cold chisel and a ball-peen or small sledge hammer, widen the crack to about 2 inches (50mm), chipping away any ragged portions of the concrete **(Figure 6)**.
2. If you haven't waited too long to repair the crack, the concrete on both sides of the crack will be at the same level. But if you've put off the repair until water seepage has washed away some of the fill under the concrete, you'll

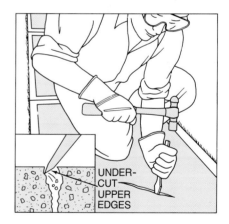

Fig. 6. A good concrete patch depends on good preparation. With a cold chisel and ball-peen hammer, chip away loose or crumbling concrete from the crack. Undercut the upper edges of the crack so the patch can bond firmly. Remove dust and debris with a wire brush.

have to pry up the low section and fill it with gravel or crushed stone until it's at the same height as the other section.

3. Before applying the patching compound, wet the repair site thoroughly with water.

4. For larger cracks, use a dry pre-mixed sand mix; mix with water to a fairly stiff consistency.

5. Use a trowel to force the mix into the crack **(Figure 7)**. Make sure that the crack is filled all the way to the bottom.

6. Smooth the patch with the trowel until it's level with the concrete.

7. Cover the patch with rags and keep them damp for two or three days; concrete must be kept moist for proper curing. Don't attempt concrete work if there's a chance of freezing temperatures during the first few days after the concrete is applied.

Holes or chips in concrete pavement are dealt with in much the same way as large cracks. To make the patch stick well to the old concrete, use a hammer and chisel to square the shallow sloping edges of the hole or chip, giving the patching com-

Fig. 7. Using a trowel with a pointed end, force the patching compound into the crack in the concrete as deep as possible. Working from the center of the crack outward, smooth the compound onto the surface of the surrounding concrete.

pound a surface to grip. Again, wet the site thoroughly before patching with a sand mix, and keep the patch damp for two to three days afterwards.

Patching Blacktop

Different types of damage require different repair methods. Driveway crack filler in cartridges is a simple and convenient material for filling cracks up to 1/4 inch (6mm) across. If the crack isn't more than 1/2 inch (13mm) deep, simply fill it with compound, smoothing the surface afterward with a moistened putty knife. If the crack is deeper, pack it to within 1/2 inch (13mm) of the surface with oakum—a material resembling rope that's available at hardware outlets.

Patching Wide Cracks in Blacktop

For wider cracks, or for patching holes in blacktop, "cold-mix" asphalt is most effective. It's available premixed in 66-pound (30 kg) bags, sufficient to patch approximately 1 1/3 square feet (about 1/8 square meter) of blacktop to a depth of four inches (100mm). It comes in two forms: emulsion mix and cut-back mix; either generally works well. But if moisture is present, use the emulsion mix.

Don't try to patch blacktop if the air temperature is less than 40°F (4°C). (If you've stored the cold-mix in an unheated garage or shed, place it in a heated room for a few hours before you use it.) Put several sheets of news-

paper under the bag to prevent staining of the floor.

1. Remove loose material and debris from the void to be filled. If grass or other vegetation is growing through the crack, dig it out completely and apply a weed and vegetation killer to make sure the weed doesn't regrow. (Weed killers are extremely toxic: Use them with care, following the instructions on the label.)

2. Use a cold chisel and ball-peen hammer to cut back the edges of the hole until you reach sound blacktop. Make the edges vertical to help secure the patch.

3. If you have a deep hole to fill, you can save a bit on cold-mix material by placing a few large stones in the hole. Then fill in the space around the large stones with smaller stones, cinders, or crushed rock. Make sure no vegetable matter or seeds are in the fill, and leave at least 1 inch (25mm) of depth to fill with cold-mix. Tamp down the fill as firmly as possible, using a tamping tool made of two door pulls attached to a 4- or 5-foot (1 1/2 meter) piece of 4x4 **(Figure 8)**.

4. Fill the hole half-full of cold-mix compound **(Figure 9)** and compact it thoroughly with the tamping tool. Work out air pockets and force the compound into any cracks and crevices. Don't rush this part of the job.

5. Add successive 1/2-inch (13mm) thick layers of cold-mix, tamping each layer thoroughly, until the top of the patch is flush with the rest of the blacktop. If the patch is in a place where car wheels will roll over it, add one extra layer to form a raised plateau. Automobile traffic will flatten it in short order.

If you're filling a large crack, follow the same procedure. You may have to improvise a tamping tool that fits into the crack, but that's the only difference.

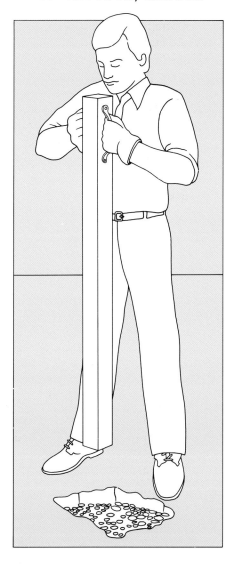

Fig. 8. A pair of door handles mounted on a length of 4x4 lumber makes a useful tool for packing down cold-mix patching compound. After removing loose or damaged material from the hole to be patched, tamp the earth at the bottom of the hole to provide a solid foundation for the patch. If the hole is deep, fill it partially with crushed stones before tamping.

6. When you're done, fence off the patch temporarily to keep people from tracking asphalt into the house. Alternatively, keep sand spread over the patch for three days to keep the compound from sticking to shoes.

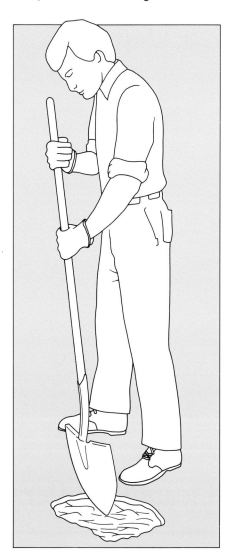

Fig. 9. Fill the hole to half its depth with cold-mix, slicing through its surface in several places to open any air pockets. Then pack the patching compound with a tamping tool. Add a 1/2-inch- (13mm) thick layer of compound, and tamp it again. Repeat until the patch is even with or a bit higher than the surrounding blacktop.

Sealing Blacktop

The asphalt compound used as a binder in blacktop paving is attacked by weather, frost, ice-melting salt, and car drippings. To protect the blacktop, give it a coat of sealer every five years or so. The sealer is available from most hardware stores and lumberyards. Simply pour it onto the blacktop, and spread it with a long-handled squeegee or push broom. The sealer will also fill hairline cracks and hide any patches you've applied. Plan to seal the blacktop a week or so after you've completed your patching chores.

INSTALLING AND MAINTAINING GUTTERS AND DOWNSPOUTS

Tools and Materials:
Ladder that extends above the gutter; ladder stand-off; rag; heavy work gloves; bucket; wire brush; garden hose; plumber's snake; silicone caulk; roofing cement; aluminum flashing; tin snips; hanger nails; locking-grip pliers; gutter fasteners; chalk line; nails; spirit level; wire or twine.

SAFETY FIRST

- ❏ Protect your hands with heavy work gloves when you clean leaves and debris from gutters. Many gutters and gutter guards have sharp edges.
- ❏ Keep metal ladders clear of electric power lines.

AVOID THESE PITFALLS

- ❏ It's easy to damage a gutter by resting the ladder against it. Use a ladder stand-off.
- ❏ Direct the downspout away from the house so water doesn't collect against the foundation.

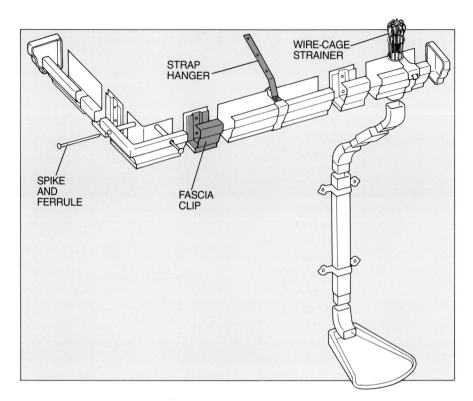

Fig. 10. This illustration shows the components of a typical gutter-downspout system. Modern metal or vinyl gutters and downspouts are available in a modular form. They let you assemble a roof drainage system that fits virtually any house, without custom fabrication.

Gutters and downspouts perform a simple but important function: They move rainwater and melted snow from a place where they can do damage to a place away from the house, where they can't. The amount of water involved can be considerable; a 1-inch (25mm) rainfall dumps almost 75 gallons (300 liters) of water on a 30x40-foot (9x12 meter) roof. If allowed to run off directly, that water would run down the side of the house, staining the siding, washing away nearby flower beds, and eroding the soil. In many cases, it would also flood the basement and damage the foundation walls.

To do their job, gutters and downspouts must be large enough to handle a heavy rain. Also, the gutters must be pitched so water will run down to the downspouts. Small roofs, of 750 square feet (70 square meters) or less, can get by with 4-inch-(100mm) wide gutters and 3-inch (75mm) down-

spouts. Roofs up to 1,500 square feet (140 square meters) should have 5-inch (125mm) gutters, while roofs larger than that should be equipped with 6-inch (150mm) gutters. Four-inch (100mm) downspouts should handle even larger roofs adequately.

Cleaning Gutters and Downspouts

The most common problem with gutters and downspouts is blockage caused by leaves and other debris. Inspect and clean your gutters at least twice each year—in late autumn, after the trees have dropped their leaves, and in early spring, to see whether winter storms have caused damage.

1. Use a ladder that extends at

least a foot above the gutter, and be sure it rests securely against the house. Various ladder accessories are available to allow the ladder to rest against the wall or roof, rather than the gutter itself.

2. Plug the downspout outlet with a rag, and remove any strainers or gutter guards.

3. Remove debris from gutters, using a putty knife and a small garden trowel. Wear a pair of heavy work gloves; gutters and gutter guards often have sharp edges. Hang a bucket from the ladder to collect the junk you remove.

4. Sweep the gutter clean with a small stiff brush.

5. When you've finished cleaning a horizontal run of gutter, remove the rag and flush away any remaining debris with a forceful spray from a garden hose.

6. If a downspout is clogged, rout out the debris with a plumber's snake. Work from the bottom up to avoid compacting the clog. Then flush out the downspout with water from a hose.

7. Inspect the cleaned gutter for leaks; water from the hose should reveal any that may be present.

8. Reinstall the leaf strainers in the downspout openings. If there are no strainers, consider installing them. But keep in mind the tradeoffs: Leaf strainers or gutter guards help keep the system from becoming clogged, but they make cleaning considerably more difficult. Also, the more effective the gutter guard is in blocking leaves, the less effective the gutter usually becomes in dealing with heavy rains.

Repairing Leaks

Leaks in gutters are fairly easy to repair. If the leak is at a joint, separate the sections, apply silicone caulk liberally to the seam, and reassemble the sections. To repair small pinholes in the gutter itself, clean the inside of that section thoroughly with a wire brush and hose. After that section dries, apply a coat of roofing cement to the inside.

To repair larger holes, apply a coat of roofing cement, then a layer of heavy aluminum foil. Top off with a second layer of roofing cement, making sure you smooth the top coat so water will flow without obstruction. If the hole is especially big, use the same basic procedure—but instead of foil, substitute a piece of aluminum flashing or sheet steel that matches the material of the gutters **(Figure 11)**. Cut the piece to fit with tin snips, and sandwich it between two layers of roofing cement.

Fig. 11. To patch a large hole in a gutter, spread a layer of roofing cement over the area and extend it at least 2 inches (50mm) beyond the hole on all sides. Use tin snips to cut a patch from a piece of thin sheet metal; a piece of aluminum flashing is ideal, but a tin can will do in a pinch. Press the patch into the roofing cement, and cover the patch completely with a second layer of cement.

Realigning a Gutter's Pitch

If the gutter is sagging or the pitch needs adjustment, remove and replace hanger nails to achieve the proper positioning. Be careful not to damage the gutter when removing nails; use locking-grip pliers to grip the nails and twist them out. Don't forget to check the condition of the straps that fasten the downspout to the wall; if they're loose or missing, the downspout could fall off.

If your gutters and downspouts are vinyl or aluminum, they shouldn't require painting. Wood gutters, however, do require repainting every two or three years. That chore is best done during a dry spell. Clean out the gutter thoroughly, as described previously, and let the wood dry for several days. Then paint the inside of the gut-

ter with roofing cement thinned to paint consistency with mineral spirits. Let the gutter dry for another couple of days, and apply a second coat. To finish the job, scrape and sand the exterior of the gutter, and apply two coats of house paint.

Galvanized steel or iron gutters require painting whenever rust appears. Sand off rust, and brush on two coats of rust-resistant paint.

A properly designed system should have no more than 35 feet (10 meters) of gutter leading to a downspout, and the gutter should have a pitch of $1/4$ inch (6mm) per foot of horizontal run from the highest point of the gutter section to the downspout opening. Usually, the gutter's high point is in the center of a run, leading down to downspouts at either end, although other arrangements are possible.

The downspouts should empty into soil that provides good drainage, away from the foundation. A bottom elbow, for example, that directs water flow onto a concrete splash block should accomplish that goal. If drainage isn't adequate and water puddles in spots, you may need to install an underground drain or dry well.

Replacing Gutters

Wood and galvanized steel gutters were once the most popular types. These days, aluminum and vinyl systems dominate the replacement-gutter market because of their low maintenance requirements. Both are available in prefabricated sections that make installations relatively easy.

Measure carefully. If your old system was satisfactory before it needed replacing, you can simply duplicate it with a new one. If your old system was causing problems all along, a new installation provides an opportunity to eliminate those problems.

Three common types of supports are available for gutter systems: strap hangers, which fasten to the roof under the bottom row of shingles; fascia clips, which attach directly to the fascia (the board at the edge of the roof); and spike-and-ferrule fasteners, which pass through the gutter and fasten directly to a rafter. If your house permits a choice, use the spike-and-ferrule system; it's the easiest to work with.

1. Stretch a chalk line between nails to mark a line on the fascia **(Figure 12)**. Use a spirit level to make sure the line is perfectly horizontal.

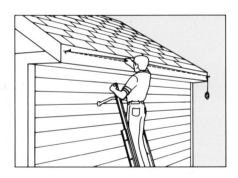

Fig. 12. When you replace a gutter, make sure it's pitched so that water flows to the downspout. Tap a nail into one end of the fascia, and attach one end of a chalk line to it. At the other end of the fascia, drive a second nail that's level with the first, using a spirit level to check. Measure down 1 inch (25mm) from that second nail for every 16 feet (5 meters) between it and the first nail. Snap the chalk line against the fascia to give you a visible guide for installing the gutter. Remove the two nails.

2. Allowing ¼-inch (6mm) pitch for every foot (⅓ meter) of horizontal run, mark off the proper incline for the gutter, with a sturdy nail at each end.
3. Hang one end of the gutter from one of the nails with wire or sturdy twine, and adjust the pitch to follow the line you've marked out **(Figure 13)**.
4. Starting from the opposite end, nail in the hangers, checking the pitch against the line.

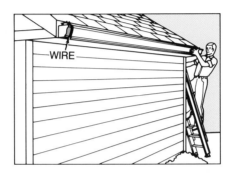

Fig. 13. Attach one end of the assembled gutter to the first nail, using a loop of wire. Nail the hangers to the house, following the chalk line. It's generally easier to start nailing from the end opposite to the wire loop, and finish by replacing the loop with a permanent hanger.

FIXING A LEAKY ROOF

Tools and Materials:

Felt-tip marker; binoculars; utility knife; wire brush; linoleum knife; putty knife; roofing cement; roofing nails; pail; roofing felt; pry bar; metal patch; ball-peen hammer; cold chisel; prefabricated vent flashing assembly; quick-setting shingle cement in a cartridge; caulking gun; shingles.

SAFETY FIRST

❏ Don't climb up on a wet roof. Wear shoes with treads that grip well.
❏ Don't lean out to one side on a ladder. Keep your belt buckle between the uprights.
❏ Don't tie up your hands with tools and supplies. A tool pouch, and an S-hook to hang cement from a ladder rung, will leave you a free hand.
❏ Keep metal ladders away from electric power lines.

AVOID THESE PITFALLS

❏ Don't ignore minor leaks; eventually, they can cause major damage.
❏ Treat shingles gently. They have some give, but they're brittle and easy to break.
❏ Don't leave low spots in a flat roof; build them up with roofing felt and roofing cement.

A leaky roof can cause stained and damaged interior walls and ceilings, insulation that's waterlogged and ineffective, and even structural damage to the house. But periodic inspections and prompt repairs can save the day.

Finding the leak is the hardest part of the job. Water may seep a long way from the area of the leak, always following the most direct downward route. Start your search in the attic—simply because it's easier and safer than getting out on the roof to inspect the entire exterior surface. An attic inspection can narrow the search to the general area of the leak; after that, finding the damaged area on the roof is usually easy.

The best time to inspect the attic is during a heavy rain. If you find water dripping inside the attic, mark the point where the drip appears. Then look for signs of discolored sheathing, an indication that the damage to the roof is upward of the point where you first saw water. Place a pail or other container under the drip to prevent further damage to the area beneath the drip. If you have insulation between the rafters, you'll have to remove it to find the leak. Plan on replacing any insulation that's damp. When the rain stops, inspect the roof's exterior for the source of the leak.

Don't climb up on the roof while it's raining; wet shingles are slippery. Examine the roof from the ground, or from the upper window of a neighbor's house, using binoculars. Look at those areas of the roof where you suspect the leak originates. The more diligent you've been with your indoor inspection, the less time you'll need for an outside examination. If you don't find the damage where you expected to, work your way up the roof's pitch.

Most roof leaks occur at a roof's flashing, where different roof slopes meet to form valleys, or where chimneys and vents penetrate the roofing surface. An accumulation of debris such as twigs and leaves where two roof surfaces join is a common source of leaks. When water can't run off from the roof, it seeps between the shingles instead. The remedy is easy: Clean up the debris from the ground, using a broom or bamboo rake tied to a long handle.

If more than a cleanup is required, wait for fair weather. For safety's sake, use the proper equipment—safety lines, roof scaffolds, and the like—particularly on steeply pitched roofs. Roof repairs are usually easy, but the specifics depend upon the type of roof you're dealing with.

Repairing a Flat Roof

Flat roofs are usually covered with multiple layers of roofing felt, alternating with layers of tar. If the roof is badly cracked, hire a professional; the job requires special equipment and experience. However, fixing an isolated tear or blister (which soon can become a tear) is well within the ability of most householders.

1. Cut open the damaged section with a linoleum knife or utility knife, working on the top layer first **(Figure 14)**.
2. Brush away any loose material, and inspect the layer of roofing you've just exposed. If it's damp, remove more layers, getting down to the bare sheathing if necessary. Allow damp sheathing to dry thoroughly before you start to patch.
3. Use a putty knife to spread asphalt roofing cement into the cutout area.
4. Cut a patch of roofing felt large enough to extend 3 or 4 inches (75 or 100mm) beyond the damaged area on each side.
5. Nail down the patch with roofing nails, and cover the nailheads and the edges of the patch with more roofing tar **(Figure 15)**.

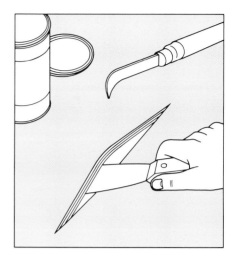

Fig. 14. To repair a blister or tear in a flat roof, first brush away loose granules from the surface with a stiff wire brush. Then cut the blister open with a linoleum or utility knife. Use a putty knife to force roofing cement under the edges of the cut, and nail down the edges with roofing nails long enough to reach the wood sheathing below.

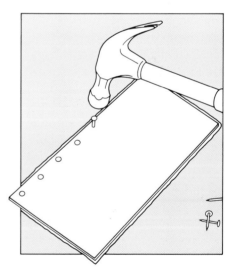

Fig. 15. Nail down a cover patch of roofing felt, and seal the edges and all exposed nailheads with roofing cement.

If the blister is only one or two layers deep, simply slit the blister open, clean out loose material, and work roofing cement in. Then patch as before. Flatten curled shingles with roofing cement **(Figure 16)**.

If the damage is extensive, cut a rectangular opening large enough so it's surrounded by sound roofing. Fill the void with layers of roofing felt and tar, and finish up with an overlapping patch of roofing felt, nailed down and covered with tar.

Fig. 16. If an asphalt shingle is curled or lifted, use roofing cement to hold it down flat. Apply quick-setting shingle cement from a cartridge, using a caulking gun to force the cement under the lifted edge. Press the edge down firmly into the cement. If a crack in a shingle doesn't extend under the adjoining shingles, force roofing cement under each side of the tear; then nail both sides of the tear with 1-inch (25mm) roofing nails. Cover nailheads and the surface of the repaired tear with roofing cement.

Repairing Flashing

Flashing (which consists of thin sheets of metal, or sometimes roofing felt) is used to seal the troughs formed where two roof sections meet, or the gaps where pipes and chimneys protrude through the roof's surface. Repair a damaged section as follows:

1. Cover the surrounding surface of the flashing with roofing cement.
2. Cut out a metal patch large enough to overlap the hole in the old flashing by 2 inches (50mm) and press it into the cement. The patch should be made of the same metal as the flashing, or severe corrosion could result.
3. Make sure the adjoining shingles are cemented firmly to the edges of the flashing. Secure loose shingles with roofing cement.

Replacing vent flashing, once a tricky job, is much simpler since the introduction of prefabricated metal or plastic moldings with rubber seals that fit over the vent pipe like a collar. Install it as follows:

1. Take off several old shingles to expose the old flashing.
2. Remove the flashing, and chip away the old asphalt cement with a chisel and hammer.
3. Slip the new flashing over the vent pipe and cement it in place **(Figure 17)**.
4. Replace the old shingles with new ones and cement them in place.

Replacing Asphalt Shingles

Most roof shingles are made of asphalt composition. If you shop around, you can usually find replacement shingles that are a good color match. Shingles are generally sold by the "square"—100 square feet (about 9 square meters) —but many home-repair centers will sell you smaller quantities. Here is how to replace a damaged asphalt shingle:

1. Pry out the nails that hold the shingle **(Figure 18)**. You'll find about eight nails, four in each of two courses, or rows, of shingles above the shingle you're replacing. The nailheads aren't exposed, so you'll have to lift the shingles in the two courses above the damaged one. Use a pry bar, and remove the lower row of nails first. Then gently lift the shingles two courses above the one you're working on to get at the remaining nails.
2. Slide out the broken shingle.

Fig. 17. To reflash a vent pipe, chip away the leaky seal around the pipe with a ball-peen hammer and cold chisel. Then remove the two shingles above the vent to get at the old flashing; remove and discard the flashing, pulling any nails and loosening any cement securing it to the roof. Follow the instructions for removing shingles in **Figure 18.** Repair any damaged roofing felt below the flashing with roofing cement and, if needed, a patch cut from new roofing felt. Seal any nail holes with roofing cement. Slip the new prefabricated flashing assembly over the vent. Replace the shingles, using roofing cement rather than nails to secure the metal flange.

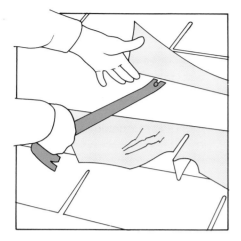

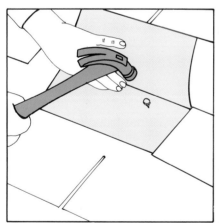

Fig. 18. To replace an asphalt shingle, remove the nails holding down the damaged shingle with a flat pry bar. You'll have to lift the two courses of shingles directly above the damaged one to remove both sets of nails. Remove and replace the damaged shingle, nailing down the new one through the existing nail holes in the two courses of shingles above it. Be careful not to bend or break the intact shingles.

3. Apply roofing cement to any holes or tears in the roofing felt.

4. Slip the new shingle into place, and nail it down, using the old nail holes in the existing shingles as guides. Start from the top. To avoid breaking the undamaged shingles by bending them back too far, slide the flat end of the pry bar under the shingle but over the nailhead, and hammer down directly on the edge of the bar, just clear of the covering shingle.

If the damage to the shingle doesn't extend underneath the overlapping shingles, you can probably just patch the shingle instead of replacing it. Raise the cracked or lifted shingle slightly, work roofing cement under it with a caulking gun or putty knife, and nail it down. Apply roofing cement to exposed nailheads.

While you're on the roof, take the time to check for potential trouble spots. Raised, cracked, or missing shingles or loose or missing flashing, if ignored, can cost you hundreds of dollars in water damage. It's wise to check your roof twice each year: in the spring, when the weather tends to be mild, and in the fall, possibly when you clean the gutters.

Exterior Caulking

Tools and Materials:

Caulking gun; caulking compound; rag; putty knife; wire brush; solvent; utility knife; long nail or piece of stiff wire; plastic spoon; container of water; thin plastic gloves; razor-blade scraper.

AVOID THESE PITFALLS

❑ Don't caulk in warm weather; cracks swell too much to permit effective filling.
❑ Don't caulk in extremely cold weather; compounds become too stiff to apply properly.
❑ Before applying new caulk, thoroughly remove old caulk.
❑ Don't use silicone caulks if you have to paint the caulk or a nearby surface; the paint may not stick.

Caulking compound is a putty-like material designed to seal cracks in the exterior surface of a house. The many different materials from which a house is built expand and contract at different rates with changes of temperature. As a result, a gap may open where two dissimilar materials meet. Weather, vibration, and settling can enlarge these gaps, allowing air and water leaks. Such gaps also provide an opening for insects. The small gaps around doors and windows, between the foundation and the exterior walls, and around pipe and cable entry points can easily account for as much loss of heat or cooling as an open window **(Figure 19)**.

When your house was built, any such gaps were probably caulked. But many caulks become rigid and crack over time. Once they can no longer flex and stretch enough to provide an effective seal, they separate from one or both surfaces, and a leak develops. That's when it's time to re-caulk.

Many types of caulking material are available, each with good and bad points. No one material is best for all caulking jobs. Caulks come in solid form, in strips or rolls; as a foam, in a pressurized can; and, most commonly, as a thick paste in a cartridge or tube.

Choosing a Caulk

Solid caulks are generally rubbery, ropelike materials suitable for filling wide cracks, 1/4 inch (6mm) or wider. Such cracks may appear at a house's sill plate—the area where the wooden walls join the concrete block or poured concrete foundation. To apply a solid caulking material, simply use a putty knife or screwdriver to force the strip into the crack. If the crack is deep, use a paste-type caulk.

Foams are most useful for filling large voids such as oversized holes cut in walls to permit pipes to pass through, or where chunks of foundation are missing. A foam caulk's combination of characteristics—extreme stickiness before curing, and expansion to fill a hole completely—make it useful for filling large cavities. Foams, though, aren't suited for applications that are visible; they're difficult to control accurately, and they leave a messy, unattractive finish. If you wish to use a foam for a problem area, plan on covering it with a more attractive material. Two tips on using foams: When possible, use masking tape to contain the foam to a specific area. And plan to do all your foam caulking at one time; once you start a can, its useful storage life is limited.

Fig. 19. Places to caulk.

Paste compounds in cartridges or tubes come in many different types, with wide variations in physical properties and price. It's important to use the right caulk for the job. The chart in this section advises you on which to use when.

Applying Caulk

The best time of year to apply caulk is in the fall, when temperatures are in the 50° to 60°F (10° to 16°C) range. In the summer, building materials tend to expand, making it difficult to work caulking material into the cracks. Avoid caulking in winter; cold temperatures make the caulk stiff and hard to apply.

Low-shrinkage caulks are best for cracks in flat surfaces or outside corners; caulks that shrink will do a neater job on inside corners. Many of the paste-type caulks are available in tubes, which work fine for small jobs. However, for larger undertakings, use a caulking gun.

1. Clean the area around the crack with a putty knife and a wire brush and then with a solvent such as mineral spirits.

2. To load a cartridge into a caulking gun, rotate the plunger rod until the teeth face away from the trigger, and pull the rod back as far as it will go. Snap in the cartridge and rotate the rod until the teeth engage the trigger mechanism **(Figure 20)**.

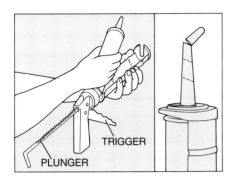

Fig. 20. For most caulking jobs, the most economical way to buy caulk is in cartridges. To load the caulking gun, rotate the plunger rod so the teeth face up, and pull the rod back all the way. Insert the cartridge and turn the rod's handle so that the teeth face down. Then snip off the cartridge's tip at about a 45-degree angle. The farther back you snip, the larger the bead. Poke a long nail down into the cut tip to break the seal at the base of the nozzle.

3. With a utility knife, snip off the end of the nozzle at a 45-degree angle. The more of the nozzle you cut off, the thicker the bead of caulk that you'll lay down. Poke a long nail or piece of stiff wire through the nozzle to break the seal at the base of the nozzle; if you don't use all the caulk in the cartridge, you can seal the tip with a larger nail to keep the remaining compound from hardening.

4. Hold the caulking gun at a 45-degree angle to the crack, and force compound into the gap with a steady trigger pressure **(Figure 21)**. Draw the gun along the crack slowly, leaving a bead that overlaps the edges of the crack. On a long crack, start at one end, and work your way along it slowly. Keep the gun moving steadily even when you need to use multiple trigger strokes; try to avoid interrupting and restarting the bead.

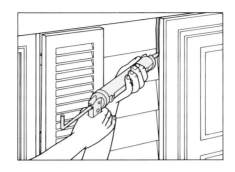

Fig. 21. When you pull the trigger, the plunger rod forces a bead of caulk out of the cartridge's tip. Keep the gun moving as you pull the trigger, to avoid a lumpy bead. Work with the gun at about a 45-degree angle to the surface, and draw the tip slowly so that the teeth face upward; pull it back a bit to stop the flow of caulk.

Fig. 22. To seal individual window-panes, apply a glazing compound—an oil-based caulk that comes in cans—to the joint between the window frame and the glass. The simplest way to apply that material is with a gloved fingertip. Then smooth it down with the moistened back of a plastic spoon. Remove excess glazing compound with a rag dipped in mineral spirits, and use a razor-blade scraper to clean excess material from the glass.

5. Use the bottom of a plastic spoon that's been dipped in water to smooth the bead. Keep a container of water nearby; keeping the spoon wet helps to prevent sticking. You can also use a gloved finger to tool down the bead, but don't lick your finger to moisten it; some caulks are toxic.

6. When you're done, clean up right away, following the instructions supplied with the caulk. Different caulks require different clean-up procedures, but all of them are easier to clean up if you do it promptly.

Fig. 23. Don't try to fill cracks wider than 1/4 inch (6mm) with a paste caulk; it's apt to pull away from the sides of the crack with time. First, fill the crack with a strip of solid rubber or rope caulk (oakum). Force the material into the crack with a putty knife or screwdriver until the crack is filled to a depth of 1/4 inch (6mm) below the surface. Then use a caulking gun to lay one or more beads of caulking compound to finish the job.

Paste Compounds in Caulking Guns or Tubes

Type	Price	Adhesion	Shrinkage	Durability (years)	Paint	Applications	Comments
Oil	Low	Fair	High	3–5	Should be painted	Noncritical, glazing	Easy to remove
Latex	Low	Very good, except for metals	High	3–10	Optional	Porous surfaces need primer	Works on damp surfaces
Acrylic	Moderate	Very good, except for metals	Moderate	3–10	Optional	Porous surfaces need primer	Works on damp surfaces
Butyl	Moderate	Excellent	Moderate	4–15	Optional	Good for water-resistance; good for use on metal	Difficult to make neat joint
Neoprene, nitrile	Moderate	Good	Moderate	15–20	Optional	Good for concrete	Toxic; requires good ventilation
Polysulfide	High	Good	Low	15–20	Optional	Use anywhere	Bad odor; skin irritant until cured
Polyurethane	High	Excellent	Very low	20–30	Optional	Use anywhere	Skin irritant until cured
Ethylene copolymer	High	Excellent	Very low	10–20	Optional	Best for use on asphalt	Can't be used on many plastics
Silicone	High	Fair	Very low	20–50	Most types can't be painted	Good for water-resistance	May interfere with future painting

CLEANING CONCRETE, BRICK, AND VINYL SIDING

Tools and Materials:

Sponges; vinyl brushes; paint scraper; small hammer; paper towels; household bleach; dry-cleaning fluid; portland cement; cat litter; commercial concrete sealer; sodium peroxide or hydrogen peroxide; phosphoric acid; hydrochloric acid; paint remover; kerosene; dry ice; ammonium or aluminum chloride; powdered talc; goggles; mason's gloves; particle mask.

Eventually, the exterior of a house becomes dirty. Pollution, fungus growth, and oxidation take their toll on stained and painted wood siding, brick, concrete, vinyl, and aluminum. If your house doesn't receive enough sunlight, mold and mildew may form in areas that receive constant moisture, such as the foundation—especially on the dark, northern side of the house.

Cleaning Concrete

You can clean concrete with either a dry or a wet method. The dry method consists of sandblasting and abrasive brushing and scouring. The wet method involves using chemicals to either dissolve the staining substance or bleach it to make it less visible. Whichever method you choose, be aware that removing stains from old concrete may leave the treated area lighter or different in color than its surroundings.

Before you start, protect all non-concrete architectural details (wood, glass, metal), since they can be damaged by contact with chemicals or abrasives. Note, also, that many cleaning chemicals are toxic. Carefully follow the manufacturer's recommendations, which may include using protective materials such as gloves, goggles, and particle masks.

The following are methods for removing specific stains from concrete:

Common food stains. If a stain is fresh, washing it with soap and warm water should remove it or lighten it substantially. Remove stains such as ice cream, soda, tomato sauce, cooking grease, or syrups by rubbing vigorously with a sponge and soap or powdered detergent. For more difficult stains, as from artificial coloring, for example, use a dry-cleaning fluid, available in hardware stores and supermarkets.

If all else fails, try scrubbing the stain with muriatic acid. Note, however, that muriatic acid is corrosive and its fumes are hazardous. Follow the manufacturer's safety instructions carefully.

SAFETY FIRST

- ❏ Many commercial cleaning fluids and powders can cause chemical burns or lung damage, and some are suspected carcinogens. All should be handled with respect. Follow the recommendations on the label.
- ❏ When you use alkalis or acids for cleaning, don't let the solution drip onto plants or into a pond or a swimming pool. Most of those compounds can kill plant life and injure people.
- ❏ Follow the manufacturer's recommendations for disposal. Some compounds can explode if exposed to fire or flame or if mixed with certain other chemicals.
- ❏ Wear gloves and goggles when handling acids and alkalis. Even the relatively safe acetic acid (vinegar) can irritate hands and eyes.

AVOID THESE PITFALLS

- ❏ If you can't identify a stain, test by treating a small section that isn't prominently visible. If plain soap and water don't work, ask your hardware dealer for advice.
- ❏ Thoroughly wash brick, concrete, or vinyl siding after treating it with anything stronger than soap and water. Failure to remove acids and alkalis completely may cause staining later.
- ❏ If cleaning calls for a stiff brush, use one with vinyl bristles. Metal brushes may flake and the particles may adhere to the brick or concrete and eventually cause rust stains.
- ❏ Don't use abrasives such as steel wool and scouring powders on vinyl siding. They produce a high-gloss shine that won't match the duller surrounding vinyl.

Oil or grease from a car leak.

1. While the oil spill is fresh, quickly blot up the surface oil with a rag or paper towel. Don't wipe; that would only spread the stain and drive the oil deeper into the concrete.
2. Cover the spot with a dry absorbent material (cat litter or portland cement works well) and leave it on for 24 hours.
3. Remove and replace the absorbent material; repeat the process until no more oil is absorbed.
4. Scrub the area with a strong soap or abrasive scouring powder.

Moss, mildew, algae.
Although various commercial algicides and fungicides are available, liquid laundry bleach works just as well.

1. Mix 1 quart (1 liter) of laundry bleach with 3 quarts (3 liters) of water, and apply the solution to the discolored area with a soft paintbrush.
2. After about 15 minutes, rinse the area with a hose to remove all traces of bleach.
3. To prevent the problem from recurring, apply a commercial concrete sealer. Look for a sealer that contains 33 percent sodium silicate in water and 1 percent ammonium chloride. While the sealer doesn't entirely prevent regrowth, it does make the concrete easier to clean.

Blood stains.

1. Wet the stain with water.
2. Cover the stain with a thin layer of sodium peroxide powder, available at pharmacies. CAUTION: The powder is extremely caustic; don't breathe it in or get it on your skin.
3. Sprinkle the powder with water, or lay a water-soaked rag or paper towel over it.
4. Rinse the area with clear water.
5. Apply white vinegar to the surface to neutralize the sodium peroxide, which is alkaline.
6. Rinse again.

A less toxic (but less effective) substitute for powdered sodium peroxide is hydrogen peroxide. If you use it, you needn't apply the vinegar.

Airborne dirt and pollution.

Dirt from the air can form dark or oily stains on concrete, particularly on old buildings. Depending on the size and condition of the area to be cleaned, you can do the job yourself or call in a company that specializes in steam cleaning or sandblasting. If you decide to do it yourself, be careful: Some of the materials you'll have to use are highly toxic.

A solution of one part phosphoric acid to three parts water will remove light to moderate staining. Rub vigorously with a stiff brush.

For dirtier surfaces, the Portland Cement Association, a trade group, recommends scrubbing vigorously with a solution of one part hydrochloric acid to 20 parts water. Use a stiff brush and rinse thoroughly.

Hydrochloric acid is extremely caustic, and handling the acid full-strength is dangerous. You may prefer to use a commercial concrete cleaner instead, following the manufacturer's recommendations.

Paint stains.

1. Soak up the spill with a paper towel. Don't scrub, or you'll spread the stain outward and force it deeper into the concrete.
2. After the bulk of the paint is absorbed, scour vigorously with an abrasive scouring powder and water. Keep working until you see no further improvement.
3. Wait at least three days, until the paint has hardened, and scrape off as much paint as possible from the area.
4. Apply a rag impregnated with commercial paint remover to the area, and allow it to stand 20 to 30 minutes.
5. Scrub the stain gently to loosen the paint film.
6. Rinse with water.

For other stains, contact the Portland Cement Association, 5420 Old Orchard Road, Skokie, Illinois 60007–1083. The association publishes a range of publications on concrete construction and maintenance to help homeowners and professionals.

Cleaning Brick

Mineral salts. One of the major problems affecting the appearance of exterior brickwork is ''efflorescence,'' a crystalline deposit of mineral salts that forms green, yellow, or brown stains. Often, it's the chemical composition of the mortar used to cement the bricks that causes the unsightly staining. Sometimes, the pigment within the brick is responsible. Mineral salts are easily cleaned with water from a hose.

Oil and tar. To clean oil from brick, use the procedure recommended for cleaning oil from concrete (previous page).

Tar stains are only slightly more difficult. Simply apply kerosene. After you've removed the tar, rinse the area thoroughly, using a hose or a stiff brush and a pail of water. Another way to remove tar is to apply dry ice or compressed carbon dioxide gas to cool the tar and make it brittle. Tap the tar lightly with a small hammer and pry off the residue with a putty knife.

Copper or bronze stains. Old homes with copper leaders and gutters or bronze architectural details are especially vulnerable to such stains. Usually, the stain spreads from its source, which is easy to trace.

1. Mix one part ammonium chloride (or aluminum chloride) to four parts powdered talc.
2. Add ammonia water until you get a thick paste.

3. Smear the paste over the stain and let it dry.
4. Wash thoroughly with water and a stiff nylon brush.

Commercial Cleaning

If the outside of your home is badly stained, or if you'd rather avoid handling dangerous chemicals, consider professional dry sandblasting or steam cleaning. While those methods are more expensive than doing it yourself, neither causes damaging chemical reactions, which sometimes occur when you clean with acids or alkaloids.

Cleaning Vinyl Siding

Vinyl siding became popular in the 1970s, when homeowners discovered that it was even easier to maintain than aluminum siding. For ordinary airborne dirt, hose down the siding and wipe it vigorously with a sponge.

If the dirt is tough, dilute 1/3 cup of laundry detergent in 1 gallon (4 liters) of water. Avoid vigorous rubbing, or you may buff the finish and make it glossy. For the same reason, don't use abrasive cleaners on vinyl siding. For stains such as oil, mildew, or paint, follow the preceding instructions for cleaning brick and concrete.

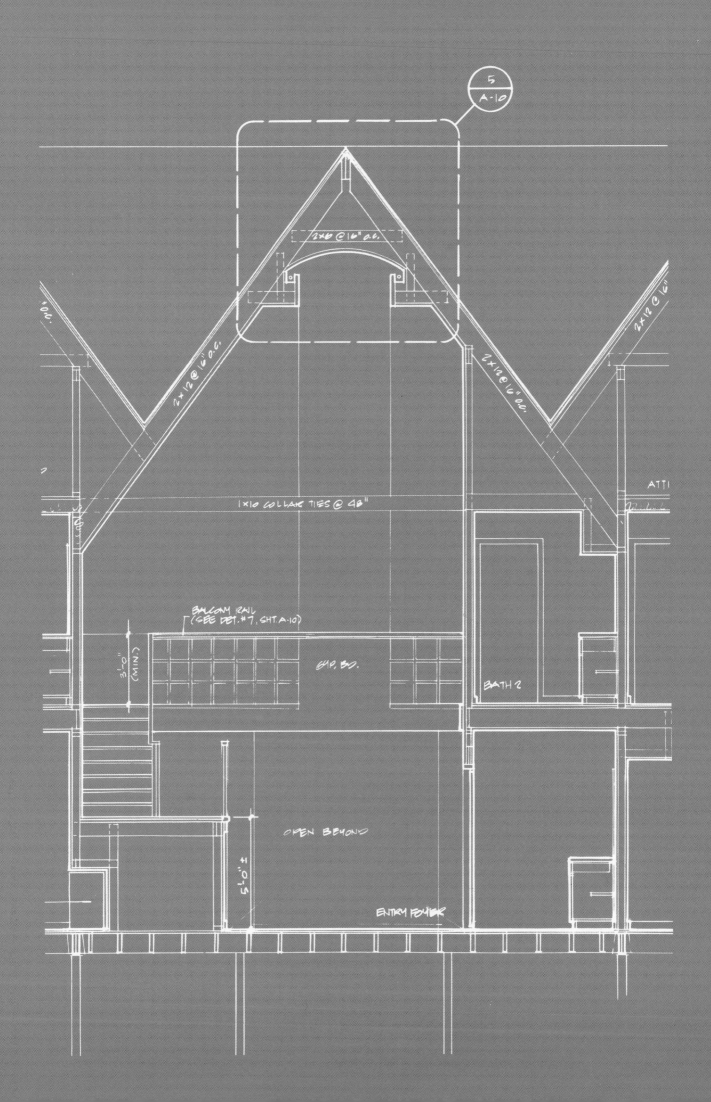

5
A-10

2×8 @ 16" o.c.

2×12 @ 16" o.c.

2×12 @ 16" o.c.

2×12 @ 16" o.c.

2×12 @ 16"

ATTI

1×10 COLLAR TIES @ 48"

BALCONY RAIL
(SEE DET. #7, SHT. A-10)

3'-0"
(MIN.)

GYP. BD.

BATH 2

OPEN BEYOND

5'-0" ±

ENTRY FOYER

Chapter Eleven

PROTECTION FROM FIRE AND LIGHTNING

Although this is the last chapter of *The Homeowner's Survival Manual*, its subject should be at the top of your list of home-related priorities.

Recent advances in fire detection equipment, lightning protection systems, and voltage surge arresters and protectors now provide more effective ways of coping with the threats of fire and lightning.

PROTECTING YOUR HOME FROM FIRE

Smoke alarms, escape ladders, and fire extinguishers are the basic tools for combating the dangers of fire. Equipment, though, isn't the whole answer. Ultimately, the safety of your family will depend on prompt, appropriate action by all family members if a fire should occur.

Planning Ahead

Every household should prepare a disaster plan for dealing with a fire. Don't wait until there's a fire to read the instructions on a fire extinguisher or decide on the best exit route from the house.

The most critical part of any effective fire plan is an early warning system. Fire spreads with frightening speed, and a few minutes' delay can mean the difference between a small, localized fire and a full-scale blaze.

Smoke Detectors

A smoke detector is the basic warning device, and there's no question that it saves lives. Safety experts estimate that a fire is twice as likely to kill in a home that's not equipped with a smoke detector.

But good as they are, smoke detectors aren't perfect. For one thing, their batteries don't last forever. Different smoke detectors provide different means of testing the batteries, but a good method for testing any detector is to hold a lit candle about 6 inches (150 mm) underneath. Test your smoke detectors at least monthly, and replace the batteries as

soon as they begin to weaken. Some detectors beep or otherwise warn you when the battery is weak, but don't rely on such a feature as a substitute for monthly checks. When you test the detector, you are checking the entire device, not just its batteries.

Besides checking the batteries, follow the manufacturer's cleaning instructions. Dust or grease may affect the operation—which is why some manufacturers recommend periodic vacuuming.

How Many Detectors, and Where?

Locate at least one smoke detector on every floor of your house, in addition to one in each bedroom. Mount them on the ceiling, at least 6 inches (150 mm) from the nearest wall, or high on a wall, at

Checklist for Fire Prevention

- ❏ Make sure your home has at least one smoke detector on every floor, in addition to one in each bedroom.
- ❏ Check that detectors are mounted either on the ceiling (the preferable location) or 6 to 12 inches (150mm to 300 mm) below the ceiling on the wall.
- ❏ Check that detectors aren't mounted near air conditioners, fans, air vents, or registers.
- ❏ If anyone in the household is hearing-impaired or a deep sleeper, install detectors with loud alarms and flashing lights.
- ❏ Test smoke detectors monthly; replace the batteries (or the detector) if necessary.

- ❏ Periodically vacuum the grillwork of your detectors and clean them according to the manufacturer's instructions.
- ❏ Make sure fire extinguishers are mounted near the exits.
- ❏ Replace fire extinguishers every six years.
- ❏ Review the ratings on existing fire extinguishers to make sure they are the right type for the job. Also make sure they have sufficient capacity for the area they're intended to protect.
- ❏ Check the pressure gauge on fire extinguishers every few months. Replace the extinguisher if necessary.

- ❏ If you have expensive electronic equipment, mount a halon extinguisher at the exit nearest the equipment.
- ❏ Plan two exit routes from each room of the house. Consider escape ladders for second-story rooms with only one exit route.
- ❏ Conduct periodic fire drills to practice the plan. Make sure all family members participate.
- ❏ Make sure that safety bars on windows have a quick-opening feature.
- ❏ Make sure that keys for doors with deadbolt locks are located near the door, in plain view.

least six inches from the ceiling or any other wall **(Figure 1)**. Don't mount a smoke detector in the kitchen; false alarms from cooking fumes can become extremely annoying. And don't mount a detector near an air conditioner or fan, which could blow smoke away from the detector.

The latest smoke detectors have special features for special needs: loud alarms and flashing light alarms for people with impaired hearing, AC-powered alarms that need no batteries, and alarms with smoke-penetrating lights to illuminate escape routes.

SAFETY FIRST

❏ Locate fire extinguishers near exits so you don't expose your-self needlessly to a fire.

❏ Buy the right type of extin-guisher for the job.

❏ Check the pressure gauge on fire extinguishers every few months and replace the extinguishers, if necessary.

AVOID THESE PITFALLS

❏ Don't rely on a smoke detec-tor's automatic warning feature that signals weak batteries. Check the detector at least once a month to make sure it's work-ing.

❏ Don't mount detectors near fans or air ducts.

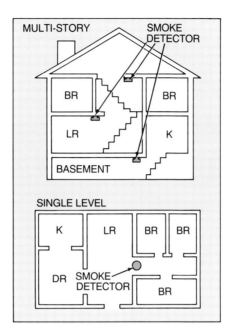

Fig. 1. Place at least one detector on every floor. Install detectors either on the ceiling or 6 to 12 inches (150mm to 300mm) below the ceiling on the wall, keeping them away from air vents and registers. At the mini-mum, detectors should be located between bedrooms and the rest of the house.

Extinguishers

Fire extinguishers carry letter codes that identify the types of fires they are designed to extin-guish: A, ordinary materials such as wood and paper; B, flammable liq-uids such as oil and gasoline; and C, electrical fires. Along with the letters you'll find numbers (for example, 2–A 40–B:C) to present a rough esti-mate of how big a fire the extinguisher can handle. An extin-guisher with a 2–A rating, for exam-ple, can put out a 100-square-foot (9 square meter) panel of burning wood; one with a 4–A rating can handle a fire twice that size. Similarly, a 10–B rating means that the extin-guisher can handle an oil fire cover-ing 25 square feet (2 1/3 square

meters), while a 40–B extinguisher can deal with a fire four times that size. An extinguisher with an ABC rat-ing—effective against all three types of fires—is the most versatile kind for the home.

The latest innovation in fire extin-guishers is the halon extinguisher, which uses compounds of bromine, fluorine, chlorine, carbon, and hydrogen. Halon compounds have some important advantages: They are suitable for all three classes of fire; they leave no messy residue (which could ruin delicate, expensive equipment such as stereo systems and computers); and, unlike water, they are safe to use on electrical fires and flammable liquids.

Halon has its disadvantages, too. Typically, it costs about five times as much as a dry-chemical extinguisher of comparable capacity. And the halon vapor dissipates quickly, so it's quite ineffective against reflashing.

Extinguishers don't need much attention. Every few months, check the pressure gauge to make sure the extinguisher is fully charged. Read the instructions on the extinguisher's ID plate.

Mount extinguishers near exits so you don't expose yourself unneces-sarily to the fire. Don't try to put out a large fire with a household extin-guisher; let the fire fighters handle the blaze.

Planning Escape Routes

Smoke alarms can give you time to deal with a small fire or to escape from a large one. That time can be a lifesaver if you use it wisely.

Plan your exit routes in advance, and practice using them during peri-odic home fire drills. You should have two exit routes from each room of the house **(Figure 2)**. An escape ladder can make any window a fire escape.

Some householders, to secure their homes against burglaries, install security bars across ground-floor windows and use exterior doors with deadbolt locks that require a key to open them from both inside and out. Security bars should have a quick-opening feature as required by many local building codes. Keys for dead-bolt locks should be located near the door.

A smoky fire can reduce visibility to practically zero, so mark escape routes with night lights. Keep the lights near the floor; smoke and fumes tend to rise.

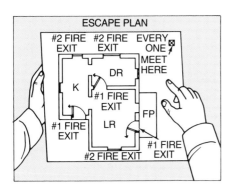

Fig. 2. Planning ahead is key to surviving a fire. Plan primary and alternative escape routes, and rehearse them periodically with the entire family. Your plans should include at least two exits from each part of the house, as well as a predetermined meeting place outside the house where the family can gather to be sure everyone is safe.

SURGE ARRESTERS AND PROTECTORS

You may have seen house lights flicker or brighten during an electrical storm. What you were seeing was a high-voltage surge of electricity caused by tiny transient voltages from distant lightning flashes or induced charges from lightning that hit nearby. Those surges, or spikes, on an electric line can damage electric tools and appliances.

Damage from voltage surges has become even more of a concern as homeowners acquire costly electronic equipment such as computers, sound systems, microprocessors, and color TVs. Such equipment is also vulnerable to lightning damage; direct strikes or lightning-induced currents can cause fire or internal damage in the equipment.

The electrical wiring system in your house probably already provides some protection from high-voltage surges. For example, the National Electrical Code states in Article 280: "Protection of premises wiring systems against accidental high voltage is one advantage of circuit and system grounding. If a system is grounded, lightning surges will be drained off to ground through the ground wire."

But while the system ground of your wiring helps protect the wiring itself, you may need added protection—surge arresters at the electric service panel and surge protectors at individual outlets—to prevent damage to electric appliances and delicate electronic gear.

Installing surge arresters to protect the entire wiring system in a home is a complicated job that should be left to an electrician.

Checklist for Protection Against Voltage Surges

❑ To protect expensive electronic equipment from voltage surges and lightning strikes, have a licensed electrician install a surge arrester at your home's electric service panel. For additional protection, buy surge protectors, which plug into the electrical outlet used to power the electronic equipment. If your home has a lightning-protection system, a surge arrester should already be in place at the electric service panel.

AVOID THESE PITFALLS

❏ Don't let price be your guide when choosing surge arresters to protect expensive electronic equipment. Ask the salesperson to help you select the right surge protection for your equipment.

❏ Don't try to install service-entrance arresters yourself; call an electrician.

How Surge Arresters Work

You've probably noticed how sparks jump from your fingers to a nearby ground object when you are charged with static electricity. The electricity cannot jump the gap from your body to the ground until the gap is quite small. Surge arresters for electric service entrances are installed with an air gap large enough so that normal 120–240 volt currents can't jump. But large voltage surges caused by lightning can. The benefit of that arrangement is that the voltage surge arcs across the air gap and flows to ground, instead of going into the house wiring. The conductor from the surge arrester to the ground should be as short and direct as possible, with no unnecessary bends, so the current flows to ground unimpeded.

Surge Protectors

In addition to the surge arrester at the electric service entrance, you may want to install individual surge arresters (or surge protectors) at outlets that serve your equipment **(Figure 3)**. Computer and electronic stores offer a variety of single- or multiple-outlet surge arresters. One model we checked provides six outlets, with two warning lights. One light (red) indicates that the surge arrester is working and another (green) indicates a continuous ground. A multioutlet model is a good choice for a home office where you might want to provide protection for a computer, a microprocessor, and other office equipment. A single- or double-outlet model is satisfactory for a TV, stereo, or any single piece of electronic equipment.

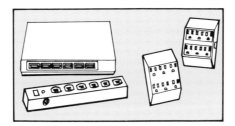

Fig. 3. Surge arresters, also called surge protectors, are available in various sizes and capacities. Simply plug these units into the electrical outlet used to power electronic equipment, then plug the equipment into the unit.

LIGHTNING PROTECTION SYSTEMS

More deaths and property loss are caused by lightning than by floods, hurricanes, and tornadoes combined. Despite those statistics, only one home in twenty has a lightning protection system.

At any given time, 1,800 thunderstorms are raging around the world. If your home is in a high-frequency area or in a rural area—and especially if it's on a hill or mountaintop—consider adding lightning protection. Contact your fire department, your insurance agent, and a lightning protection contractor for advice on how much protection you need.

Adding lightning protection to your home is not a do-it-yourself job. Choose a contractor who is a member of the Lightning Protection Institute. You can find such contractors in the classified telephone directory—generally, under Lightning Protection Equipment.

Lightning rods don't prevent lightning strikes; rather, they provide a path for discharge of the lightning energy to the ground. Each building requires its own special design; failing to protect a sector properly can result in poor protection or none at all.

In the United States, when contractors install lightning protection, they affix a "Master Label" that is numbered and that carries the Underwriters Laboratories (UL) approval. That label signifies that the materials have been approved and that the installer is accredited. Give the number on the label to your insurance agent; having lightning protection may qualify you for lower insurance rates.

SAFETY FIRST

During an electrical storm:

- Stay away from windows, doors, and fireplace openings.
- Avoid using small hand-held appliances such as hair dryers.
- Stay away from metal pipes, tubs, and sinks.
- Stay near the middle of a large room, not near the walls.
- Don't talk on the telephone or use electronic equipment. A direct lightning hit can be a danger even in protected buildings. Should you be caught outdoors during an electrical storm, follow these safety precautions:
- Go indoors into a protected building, or a car, if possible.
- Stay away from golf courses, lakes, and seashores.
- When camping, set up in a low, dry spot, but not under trees.
- At recreation areas, avoid rain shelters that are not equipped with lightning protection; they can increase your risk of being struck.
- If you are driving, slow down to avoid tree limbs or other debris that may fall onto the roadway.

How a Lightning Protection System Works

Air terminals, which resemble small antennae, are installed at 20-foot (6 meter) intervals along the ridge of the roof **(Figure 4)**. Dormers require their own pro-

tective terminals. The terminals are connected by a conductor cable that makes a continuous ground to downlead conductors, which provide a path for lightning to travel to the ground.

The downleads are connected to grounding rods buried at least 10 feet (3 meters) deep. (Grounds buried less than that distance can discharge lightning into the foundation and damage it.) The system should have at least two of those downlead/ground rod combinations, placed at corners diagonally, opposite to each other. More may be needed, depending on the shape and size of the house.

That's only the basic system. In addition, terminals should connect any objects projecting from the roof—chimneys, weathervanes, TV antennae, metal rain gutters, and other grounded metals—to that system **(Figure 4)**. Finally, a secondary

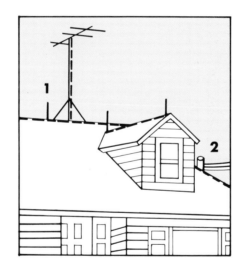

Fig. 4. The TV or radio antenna mast is connected to a roof lightning conductor, and an arrester is installed in the lead-in cable (1). A secondary surge arrester is installed on the service wires (2) to protect appliances and electronic devices.

surge arrester should be installed on electric service lines or at the service panel to protect appliances and electronic gear (see ''Guide to Surge Arresters and Protectors,'' page 174).

It's also important to ground any trees that are near the house or that overhang it. This prevents lightning sparks or current from jumping from the tree to the house. And consider protecting valuable trees even if they don't pose a danger to the house. The biggest threat to trees, after disease, is from lightning.

Checklist for Lightning Prevention

- Consider installing a lightning protection system if lightning storms strike your area frequently or if the location of your house dictates the need for such a system.
- Ask your insurance agent whether the addition of lightning protection will lower your homeowner insurance rates.
- Consider lightning protection for any trees near the house or overhanging the roof.
- Once a year, have a technician inspect the lightning-protection system.
- Teach your family what precautions to take during a lightning storm.

AVOID THESE PITFALLS

- ❏ Don't take chances; have your lightning protection system inspected each year to be sure all connections are intact.
- ❏ If you reroof or remodel your house, have the installer inspect the lightning system to be sure it still affords proper protection.
- ❏ Since the conductor cable must be large enough to handle high-voltage lightning charges, don't rely on the small cables attached to some TV antennae to do the job. They may vaporize if they are struck by a lightning bolt powerful enough to cause structural or fire damage to the house.

Fig. 5. Air terminals (1) are spaced no more than 20 feet (6 meters) apart. Downlead conductors (2) tie these terminals together and connect to at least two grounds (3), buried 10 feet (3 meters) deep. Weather vane (4) and chimney (5) are also tied into the system, as are dormers (6). TV or radio antennae (7) are connected to the downlead cable by connectors. Metal gutters (8) should also be included in the system. Surge arrester (9) on the service line or service panel protects electronic gear and appliances and is bonded to the TV antenna on the roof.

GUIDE TO SCREWS AND BOLTS

SCREWS & BOLTS	USES
STANDARD WOOD SCREWS	For attaching wood materials, these screws have threads along three-fourths of the shaft and come with a variety of heads—flat, oval and round. Round-head screws are best used for fastening thin woods with washers. Oval and flat-head are best for countersinking or for attaching hardware such as hinges.
DRYWALL SCREWS	For fastening drywall to metal or wood.
SHEET METAL SCREWS	For attaching thin metal to thin metal. They also have strong holding power when used with wood.
MACHINE SCREWS	For fastening metal to metal. They also hold well in wood because of their deep threads and their ability to cut their own thread as they're driven (called self-tapping). They may have a flat, oval, or buttonlike top.
LAG BOLTS (SCREWS)	For fastening items that require more strength than a standard wood screw.
STOVE BOLTS	For attaching thin metal to thin metal. They also have strong holding power when used with wood.
CARRIAGE BOLTS	For fastening wood that requires strong holding power in places where you wouldn't be able to reach the head with a wrench or where you don't want an exposed turnable head.
TOGGLE BOLTS	For hanging objects on hollow-wall construction.
MOLLY BOLTS	For hanging objects on hollow-wall construction.

REMARKS

TOOLS REQUIRED

REMARKS	TOOLS REQUIRED
If you are countersinking a screw for decorative purposes, use an oval wood screw. It's generally easier to remove, and slightly more attractive than a flat-head screw.	**STANDARD SLOTTED SCREWDRIVER** **PHILLIPS-HEAD SCREWDRIVER**
Two types of drywall screws are available—one for metal, the other for wood. However, the screws intended for metal work equally well on wood.	**STANDARD SLOTTED SCREWDRIVER** **PHILLIPS-HEAD SCREWDRIVER**
	STANDARD SLOTTED SCREWDRIVER **PHILLIPS-HEAD SCREWDRIVER**
Actually, these screws are really bolts, but they're driven with a screwdriver. Two thread sizes of machine screws are available: 24 per-inch and a finer 32 per-inch.	**STANDARD SLOTTED SCREWDRIVER** **PHILLIPS-HEAD SCREWDRIVER**
These are among the largest screws available. They're driven by a wrench.	**WRENCH**
These bolts are very similar to machine screws except that they're intended for use with nuts.	**STANDARD SLOTTED SCREWDRIVER** **PHILLIPS-HEAD SCREWDRIVER**
Since carriage bolts have a round head, you can't use a wrench or screwdriver to turn them. Instead, you tighten the bolt turning the unit.	**WRENCH PLIERS**
Toggle bolts are available with decorative heads. One disadvantage is that you must drill a large hole to insert a toggle bolt.	**DRILL AND SCREWDRIVER**
Molly bolts must be driven into previously installed anchors.	**DRILL AND SCREWDRIVER**

GUIDE TO NAILS

Nails come in many types and sizes. Some, like the common nail, are multipurpose; others, like the sheetrock nail, are made for a specific job. Generally, nails range in length from 1 to 6 inches (25 to 150mm). The longer the nail, the larger its diameter. Nails may also have intentional deformities, such as ridges or notches, or coatings for added strength.

While nails don't grip as well as screws, you can increase their grip in several ways. Since the holding power of a nail increases with length, you can get more holding power by using as long a nail as the wood will accept. If you need added grip, use a nail with a resin coating. Such nails are referred to as ''sinkers'' or ''cement coated.'' Nails that are uncoated are referred to as ''bright.'' Threading, ringing, and other deformities will increase holding power. But if it's maximum grip you need, you'd better use screws instead.

Nail length is measured using the **D system**—a way of coding actual length in inches. For example 2d indicates that the nail is 1 inch (25mm) long; 6d indicates that the nail is 2 inches (50mm). The D system is complicated to remember; it's much easier simply to ask for the length you need in inches.

Nails are sold in many different ways—in brown paper bags, in boxes, and on cards. Cards are the most expensive way to buy nails: Buy them in bulk instead and save.

The chart on this page shows some basic nails and their uses. Use the right nail for the job, or your work may not hold or may look shoddy.

NAILS	USES
COMMON NAIL	For many purposes, mostly for general construction.
DOUBLE-HEADED DUPLEX HEAD NAIL	For temporary work. Double head allows nail to be hammered in only up to the first head; you can then remove it by pulling on the second head, which extends out from the surface.
FINISHING NAIL	For surfaces on which you don't want the nail head to show.
BRADS	A small finishing nail for fine work.
SHEETROCK NAIL	For attaching sheetrock to a frame.
MASONRY NAIL	For fastening items to masonry (concrete).
SCREW, COMMON WIRE, AND SPIRAL NAILS	For projects requiring excellent holding power.
FLOORING NAILS	For attaching or repairing floor boards. Can also be used in rough carpentry.
SIDING NAILS	For fastening siding to sheating.
GYPSUM-BOARD NAILS	For fastening gypsum board to wood frames.

REMARKS | TOOLS REQUIRED

REMARKS	TOOLS REQUIRED
Available in many sizes.	HAMMER
	HAMMER
With a hammer and a nail set, this nail can easily be countersunk. If you fill the depression above the nail with wood putty and sand the area, the nail and the hole are virtually invisible.	HAMMER AND NAIL SET
	HAMMER AND NAIL SET
	HAMMER
Be sure to hammer the nail into the mortar and not the brick. Use as few hammer strokes as possible. Wear goggles to avoid getting masonry chips in your eyes.	BALL-PEEN HAMMER
Because of their strong holding capacity, these nails tend to damage the wood when they're removed. Use these nails only on projects that won't require disassembly.	HAMMER
	HAMMER
	HAMMER
	HAMMER

How Lumber Is Classified

When you buy lumber, you should know the five classifications that lumber manufacturers use:

- ❏ By type
- ❏ By group
- ❏ By grade
- ❏ By size
- ❏ By length

Types: The two basic kinds are hardwood and softwood. Hardwood comes from trees with leaves; softwood, from trees with cones. Unless you're a professional cabinetmaker, you probably won't want to use hardwood (oak, ash, maple, mahogany, poplar, birch, walnut, teak) for a home project. That leaves softwood. Pine, spruce, and fur are the best choices for most home projects.

Groups: The term "lumber" refers to sawed wood more than 2 inches (50mm) thick. Strips (or furring), boards, dimension lumber, and timber are the groups you'll need to know about.

Grades: The number and types of defects in wood determine its grade. Clear, or select, wood has few or no imperfections and is graded by letter. "A" denotes the highest quality, followed by "B," "C," and so on. Common wood has defects of various types and is described by number, starting with 1. "No. 1 Common" is the best quality; "No. 2 Common" is worse. The lower the grade, the less strong the wood.

Size: The thickness and width, in inches, of a piece of wood determines its size. A 2 x 4, for example, is nominally 2 inches (50mm) thick and 4 inches (100mm) wide. There's a difference between actual sizes and nominal sizes. For example, a 2 x 4 is actually 1 1/2 x 3 1/2 inches (38 x 90 mm).

Length: This refers not to how long a piece is, but to a board foot (1 inch thick x 1 inch square). That's one universal measurement dealers use to price lumber.

Picking the Best Wood For a Project

This is your most important choice, because the right wood can make or break a project. In general, choose dimension lumber for construction such as studs, joists, and beams, and boards for shelves, cabinets, boxes, furniture, and other, more finished work. Strips, also called furring, are used for edging, trimming, and crating. Timber is used to frame structures.

Consider the purpose of the project before choosing a species of wood. For instance, redwood and cedar are excellent for outdoor projects such as decks, furniture, and landscaping because they resist decay naturally and look better as they weather. Another option for outdoor projects is pressure-treated lumber—lumber that has been injected with chemicals to protect it against rot and decay. If your tools are sharp and you're experienced with wood, hardwood is your best choice for furniture. Not only is it more attractive, but it has a longer life than softwood, moves less, and produces a better fit when jointed.

Shopping

For the biggest and best selection, buy wood from a lumberyard rather than a home center or other outlet. Find a salesperson, explain your project, and ask questions. Grading systems can be complicated; pine alone has 25 different grades. Don't expect to understand everything fully. Just remember the basics.

When you find wood that looks usable, pick up a piece and ask yourself these questions:

- ❏ Is it straight? Tip the board up and look down it. If it's warped, you may still be able to use it, but you'll have to fix it first.
- ❏ Does it have knots? If they're live, they may not interfere with your project. If they're dead (surrounded by a black ring), cut them out and patch the wood, or avoid that piece entirely.
- ❏ Does it have pitch or sap pockets? If so, don't buy it.
- ❏ Is it split? Don't buy it.
- ❏ Does it have the shakes—distorted areas caused by uneven drying? Discard the affected areas.
- ❏ Is it damp? If so, it may shrink, warp, or reject glue as it dries out. To test for dampness, have the salesperson saw off a piece at least 10 inches (1/4 meter) from the end. If the exposed end feels damp, the wood needs further drying. If you buy damp wood, store it for three or four weeks in the room where it will be used. Or also ask for kiln-dried wood, which is ready to use.

Tip #1: If your project requires a clear wood that will be painted, you may still be able to use common wood. Buy up to three times as much as you need and cut away the dead knots, and you'll still pay less than you would for clear wood. First paint live knots with shellac or they'll show through the paint.

Tip #2: Lumber and plywood are graded by their quality, and you pay accordingly. Don't stint on grade, but don't buy a higher quality than you need.

Tip #3: Some home centers sell the best pieces of common wood as clear; they may also sell wood that lumberyards reject.

Tip #4: Use pressure-treated lumber when the wood will be placed underground.

Tip #5: Use common redwood for decks and heartwood redwood for posts and structures near to the ground.

Tip #6: Pressure-treated lumber is treated with chemicals that can be toxic. Follow the safety precautions on the label.

HOW TO ASK FOR LUMBER AT THE YARD

Before you go, write down the following information:

NO. OF PIECES	GRADE	SPECIES	THICKNESS, WIDTH, LENGTH
5	Common 1	Pine	2 × 4 × 10″

HOW TO PICK THE RIGHT SOFTWOOD

TYPE	CHARACTERISTICS	USES
Fir, spruce, and pine	Strong, finishes well, easy to work on with hand or power tools	Framing houses, trim, paneling, decks, fences, millwork, furniture
Cedar	Easy to work with. Resists rotting, shrinking, swelling, and warping	Trim, paneling, decks, walkways, fences
Redwood	Easy to work with. Finishes well and weathers beautifully	Decks, walkways, furniture, trim, paneling, fences

POINTS TO WATCH WHEN BUYING LUMBER

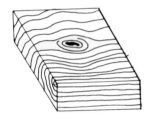

Dead knot: A knot with a black ring surrounding it. Avoid that wood, or cut out and patch the knot.

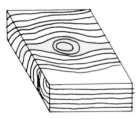

Live knot: Such a knot is acceptable unless it's large. Cover it with shellac.

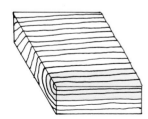

Falling shakes: A distorted area of grain. Do not use.

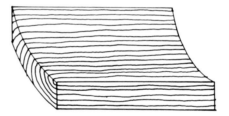

Warping: Wood that has curled. If the curl is lengthwise, cut the piece into short lengths. If the curl is across the width, rip the piece into narrow strips, plane the edges to 90 degrees, and rub-joint together.

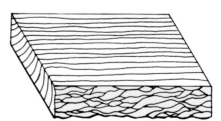

Waney edge: Consists of sapwood and bark and is often left on hardwoods. Both must be removed. The sapwood appears as a paler band of timber and is approximately 2 inches (5cm) wide.

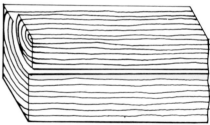

Cup shakes: The heart area of the wood has dried more quickly than the other areas. Cut out and discard the damaged area.

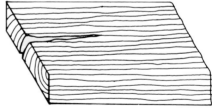

End shakes: This common type of shake is caused when the end of a board dries more quickly than the other areas. Discard the affected part or cut along the grain, plane, and rejoin the wood.

JANUARY

- ❏ Replace or clean filter on forced-air furnace.
- ❏ If your home heating system has a boiler, inspect the water-level gauge and add water to the boiler if necessary.
- ❏ Add salt or recharge water softener, as indicated. If you aren't getting sufficient soft water between regenerations, make timer adjustments, following the manufacturer's instructions. If you experience this problem and your unit uses a hardness sensor instead of a timer, call for service.
- ❏ Review home maintenance and improvement plans for the spring.
- ❏ Obtain bids and contract for work to be done before the schedules of capable remodelers and other housing professionals are booked solid.
- ❏ Review your homeowner insurance policy and update it if necessary.
- ❏ Test smoke detectors; replace dead or weak batteries. If you have never done so, test for radon gas now, since levels tend to be higher during the heating season. Use an approved test kit.
- ❏ If ice and snow have built up in your gutters, the drain openings may be plugged. Clear the openings and consider installing electric, thermostatically controlled ice melters in the gutters.
- ❏ Vacuum refrigerator condenser coils. Remove and wash the drain pan.
- ❏ Inspect refrigerator door gasket to make sure it is airtight.
- ❏ Inspect the door seal on microwave oven.

FEBRUARY

- ❏ Replace or clean filter in forced-air furnace.
- ❏ Add salt or recharge water softener if indicated.
- ❏ Keep foraging deer from damaging shrubbery, bushes, and trees by spraying shrubs with a solution of one egg to 1 quart (1 liter) of water.
- ❏ Inspect plugs on lamp or appliance power cords for damage; if necessary, replace with the appropriate type plug.

MARCH

- ❏ Add salt or recharge water softener if indicated. Vacuum refrigerator coils.
- ❏ Spin the spray arm on the dishwasher to make sure it rotates freely. If it binds, check for caked detergent and food.
- ❏ Clean the ports in the dishwasher spray tube.
- ❏ Clean the electric range to remove grease from surface elements, bowls, and terminals.
- ❏ In a gas range, periodically remove burners and use toothpicks to remove grease from the ports, then wash and dry the burners. Remove dust and debris from air vents and from around the pilot light.
- ❏ Remove and clean pop-up drains in bathrooms and clean debris from floor drain strainers.
- ❏ Pour a kettle of boiling water down sink and tub drains to dissolve grease.
- ❏ Scour the grouting between bathroom tiles with a small stiff brush and a scouring cleanser. At the same time, inspect the grouting and replace where necessary.
- ❏ Soak and remove hard-water mineral scale from tile with an all-purpose cleaner and nylon scrub pad. Use a razor blade (preferably, in a razor-blade tool) to remove hardened soap and mineral deposits from ceramic tile.
- ❏ Keep detailed records of any home improvement you make, and save receipts, building permits, and contracts. You may need them to substantiate deductions for capital gains when you sell your home.
- ❏ Inspect door frames and window sashes for drafts, so you don't waste energy and money on air-conditioning. Replace caulking and weatherstripping where necessary.
- ❏ Check that the weep holes in sliding aluminum storm windows are clear, so water won't get trapped on the windowsills.
- ❏ Conduct a roof inspection. First inspect the attic for leaks, preferably during a rainstorm. Then check the roof from the ground outside, using binoculars to spot missing or loose shingles and damaged valley flashing.
- ❏ Lubricate attic fan bearings; adjust tension of belts on belt-driven fans.

APRIL

- ❏ Add salt or recharge water softener if indicated. Inspect window screens for holes; patch the holes. If the screening is badly damaged, replace it.
- ❏ Seal wood decks and fences with a water repellent to protect the wood from weathering. Check manufacturer's recommendations for the amount of time to allow between treatments.
- ❏ Inspect gutters for leaks, and repair if necessary. Make sure the gutters are connected to the downspouts. Clean out debris that has accumulated over the winter. Install a rain diverter at each

downspout to direct water away from the house foundation. That's especially important in the spring, when the runoff from heavy rains can seep into your basement. Prepare for the possibility of spring flooding by pouring water into the pump to make sure that it is functioning properly.

❏ Check for water seepage on basement walls. Locate the problem and take corrective action.

❏ Caulk areas where the house structure meets the foundation.

MAY

❏ Add salt or recharge water softener if indicated. Set out garden furniture and clean it if necessary. Wipe vinyl coverings with a vinegar-soaked cloth. Remove rust from metal furniture with turpentine. Seal wooden furniture with a water-repellent.

❏ Vacuum registers in floors, walls, or ceiling to prevent dust from blowing into the house when the air-conditioning is turned on. Once every year, vacuum the ducts.

❏ Vacuum refrigerator condensor coils; remove and wash drain pan.

❏ Flush out sediment from water heaters. Also check the temperature-and-pressure valve and replace it if necessary.

❏ Check the draft diverter on gas-fired water heaters to make sure it's aligned squarely over the heater's vent outlet and is drawing properly. Check the color of the burner flame and pilot flame. Call a technician to adjust the flame if the color is yellow, orange, or blue.

❏ Listen to an electric water heater as it heats. If you hear a boiling sound, the temperature setting may be too high, or hard-water scale may have built up around one or both heating elements. Call for service.

❏ Check the ground around the water-heater tank for signs of water. If you notice any dripping from the tank, turn off its gas or electricity and its water supply, and call a technician.

❏ Check overhead garage doors for balance; adjust the springs if necessary. Check automatic openers and have any defects repaired by a technician.

❏ Schedule exterior house painting if your house hasn't been painted in the last five to seven years.

JUNE

❏ Add salt or recharge water softener if indicated.

❏ Move lamps and TVs away from air-conditioning thermostats; the heat those appliances give off could cause the air conditioner to switch on before room temperatures require it to.

❏ Make sure furniture does't block the registers.

❏ When reinstalling room air conditioners, check the support brackets to make sure they are secure. Install the air conditioner, and use a spirit level to ensure a slight tilt downward toward the outside to prevent condensate water from dripping into the room. If the air conditioner has been in the window all winter, remove the inside and outside covers.

❏ Insulate air-conditioner installations by slipping a strip of foam insulation between the lower sash and the top of the air conditioner before you lower the sash. Also, fill any large gaps around the air conditioner with insulation.

❏ Replace or clean the filters in room air conditioners.

❏ Replace or clean filter in forced-air air-conditioning unit.

❏ Open the condenser of a forced-air air-conditioning system and clean the coils. (Be sure the power to the unit is switched off first.) Also clean the evaporator coil inside the furnace plenum.

❏ When starting up a forced-air air-conditioning system for the season, turn on the power to the unit at least 24 hours before startup.

❏ Check your attic's gable or soffit vents to make sure they are open and unobstructed by paint residue or bird, bee, or wasp nests. Check inside the attic to make sure stored items aren't blocking the vents.

❏ Open basement windows; install window fans to increase ventilation if dampness is a problem.

❏ Remove and clean pop-up drains in bathrooms.

❏ Periodically pour a kettle of boiling water down sink and tub drains to dissolve grease.

❏ Test toilet to make sure it doesn't run and waste water.

JULY

❏ Add salt or recharge water softener if indicated.

❏ Replace or clean the filter in forced-air air-conditioning unit.

❏ Replace or clean the filter in room air conditioners.

❏ Check that forced-air air-conditioner vents aren't blocked by grass, weeds, and leaves. Make sure nothing blocks the top grille.

❏ Lubricate the window channels of double-hung windows that stick. If the windows still don't slide easily, widen the channels using the technique described in the section on freeing windows (page 135).

❏ Get bids for any heating or insulating work that needs to be done. Schedule the work before the fall when everyone else tries to get such work done.

❑ Test and adjust pool water for pH, total alkalinity, hardness, and chlorination. Buy a test kit that measures for all four factors, and plan to replace the test chemicals yearly.

❑ Clean the filter in the swimming pool filtration system when the pressure gauge indicates it's time to do so.

❑ Make sure all electrical equipment used in or near a pool (as well as all power equipment you use outdoors) is protected by a ground-fault circuit interrupter (GFCI). If your home's outdoor outlets aren't equipped with that device, have an electrician install it.

AUGUST

❑ Add salt or recharge water softener if indicated.

❑ Replace or clean the filter in forced-air air-conditioning unit.

❑ Have your family review safety precautions for lightning storms. Assess how much of a threat lightning may be to your home. Have a lightning-protection system installed if lightning is a special concern in your area.

❑ Take a vacation from home maintenance.

SEPTEMBER

❑ Add salt or recharge water softener if indicated.

❑ Change filter in forced-air air-conditioning unit.

❑ Schedule a professional furnace tune-up.

❑ Vacuum refrigerator condenser coils.

❑ Scour the grouting between tiles in the tub area with a small stiff brush

and a scouring cleanser. Inspect the grouting and replace it where necessary.

❑ Replace any cracked or loose ceramic tiles.

❑ Soak and remove hard-water mineral scale from ceramic tile with an all-purpose cleaner and nylon scrub pad. Use a razor blade (preferably in a razor-blade tool) to remove hardened soap and mineral deposits from ceramic tile.

❑ Inspect the caulking at the joints between walls and fixtures and replace it if it's loose or cracked.

❑ Remove worn decals in tub or shower area and replace with new ones.

❑ Remove mildew from bath/shower area with a 50/50 solution of household bleach and water.

❑ Remove and clean pop-up drains in bathrooms.

❑ Clean debris from floor drain strainers frequently.

❑ Pour boiling water down sink and tub drains to dissolve grease.

❑ Check the attic for condensation or leaks in the roof. Lubricate attic vents with moveable louvers.

OCTOBER

❑ Add salt or recharge water softener if indicated.

❑ Cover the condensing unit in forced-air air-conditioning systems to keep out dirt, ice, and vermin during the winter.

❑ Before turning on the furnace for the season, have a technician tune up the furnace and make precise combustion adjustments. *Don't* try to do that job yourself.

❑ Vacuum both the hot-air and cold-air return registers, using a brush attachment. Make sure registers aren't blocked by rugs or furniture.

❑ Remove the cover on bimetallic-coil thermostats and vacuum the interior with a brush attachment. If the thermostat stops working, clean the contacts with a piece of emery paper—but first, turn off the power.

❑ If you have a mercury-switch thermostat, check that it is mounted straight, using a spirit level.

❑ If your home has a hot-water heating system, vacuum the convectors to remove dust before starting the system.

❑ If your system has a boiler, draw water from the boiler's draincock at the beginning of the season and check for unusual amounts of rust in the water; flush the boiler if necessary.

❑ Inspect the boiler floor beneath the pressure-relief valve for signs of water. If water is present, drain the expansion tank.

❑ Periodically inspect the water-level gauge and add water to the boiler if necessary.

❑ Inspect the chimney serving a wood-burning stove for creosote buildup. Have the chimney cleaned by a professional if the buildup is 1/4 inch (6mm) thick or thicker.

❑ To save energy, check the temperature of the hot-water faucet in the kitchen with a thermometer to make sure your water heater isn't set too high; if it registers over 160°F (71°C), readjust the water heater.

❑ Spin the spray arm on the dishwasher to make sure it rotates freely. If it binds, check for caked detergent and food. Periodically clean the ports in the dishwasher spray tube.

❑ Remove room air conditioners from windows at the end of the cooling season. If that isn't feasible, cover the outdoor portion of the air conditioner with a snug-fitting cover. Also cover the inside panel to prevent cold drafts.

❏ Replace or clean the filter in forced-air furnace.

❏ Clean gutters and downspouts.

❏ Inspect windows and doors for drafts by moving your hand along the edges between the window or door and its frame. Make that check on a cold day. Install weatherstripping where necessary.

❏ Check for drafts at the threshold of exterior doors. Install weatherstripping where necessary.

❏ Remove screens from windows; they block heat gain from the sun —a source of free heat in winter. Wrap them in newspaper and store them in a dry place.

❏ Review R-value recommendations for attics and add insulation, if necessary.

❏ Seal the base of the chimney where it enters the attic; use a nonflammable caulking material. Also seal around the base of the plumbing vent stack.

❏ Weatherstrip the attic door.

❏ Keep attic fans connected year-round.

❏ Disconnect whole-house fans before the weather turns cold.

❏ Inspect whole-house fans for air leaks; make or buy a cover to eliminate winter drafts.

❏ Check attic vents to make sure screens are intact and vents are free of grime and debris that could block airflow.

❏ Make sure vents aren't blocked by insulation or stored objects.

❏ Inspect hot-air supply and return ducts for leaks; repair them with duct tape if necessary.

❏ Before you turn on the heat for the season, check the chimney for blockage with binoculars.

❏ Check the joints for gaps where the flue pipes from the furnace or water heater join the chimney.

Caulk any gaps with furnace cement.

❏ Inspect brick chimneys for loose mortar and repoint, if necessary.

NOVEMBER

❏ Add salt or recharge water softener if indicated.

❏ Replace or clean filter in forced-air furnace.

❏ If your home has a forced-air heating system, notice whether heat is distributed evenly from room to room. If one room is consistently colder, balance the system by adjusting the dampers in the ducts.

❏ If your home is heated by a hot-water system, and the radiators or convectors heat unevenly, release trapped air in them by loosening the air-bleed valve.

❏ If your home is heated by a steam system and the radiators don't become uniformly hot, remove the vent and listen for escaping air. If you don't hear a hiss, check the inlet valve to make sure it's open. Also check that radiators are pitched down toward the supply pipe; if not, slip shims under the vent end of the radiator.

❏ Flush out sediment from water heaters. Also check the temperature-and-pressure valve and replace if necessary.

❏ If you have a gas-fired water heater, check the draft diverter to make sure it's aligned squarely over the heater's vent outlet and drawing properly. Also check the colors of the burner and pilot flames. Call a technician to adjust the flames if they are yellow, orange, or blue.

❏ Listen to an electric water heater as it heats. If you hear a boiling sound, the temperature setting may be too high or hard-water scale may have built up around

one or both heating elements. In either case, call for service.

❏ Check the ground around the water-heater tank for signs of leaking water. If you notice dripping from the tank, turn off its gas or electricity and water supply, and call a technician.

❏ Apply caulk to cracks and joints in your home's exterior when the temperature is about 40°F (4°C) —cold enough to cause the joints to spread, but not cold enough to prevent the caulk from setting.

❏ Check overhead garage doors for balance and adjust the springs if necessary.

❏ Make a cover for the whole-house attic fan to prevent a major source of heat loss. Before you cover the fan, unplug it or shut off its power.

❏ Check the gasket around the doors of a wood stove; if it's frayed or broken, replace it with a non-asbestos gasket.

❏ Clean the electric range to remove grease from surface elements, bowls, and terminals.

❏ If you have a gas range, remove the burners and use toothpicks to remove grease from the ports. Then wash and dry the burners. Also remove dust and debris from air vents and from around the pilot light.

DECEMBER

❏ Add salt or recharge water softener if indicated.

❏ If you have a forced-air furnace, replace or clean the filter.

❏ Check duct-mounted humidifiers for scale buildup; clean if necessary.

❏ Remove and clean pop-up drains in bathrooms.

❏ Pour a kettle of boiling water down sink and tub drains to dissolve grease.

INDEX